Family Histories of Adults with Developmental
Disabilities as Told by Families and Caregivers

Susan Kessler Barnard

October 12, 2017

SUSAN KESSLER BARNARD

outskirts
press

Dreams Die Hard
Family Histories of Adults with Developmental Disabilities as Told by Families and Caregivers
All Rights Reserved.
Copyright © 2017 Susan Kessler Barnard
v4.0

The opinions expressed in this manuscript are solely the opinions of the author and do not represent the opinions or thoughts of the publisher. The author has represented and warranted full ownership and/or legal right to publish all the materials in this book.

This book may not be reproduced, transmitted, or stored in whole or in part by any means, including graphic, electronic, or mechanical without the express written consent of the publisher except in the case of brief quotations embodied in critical articles and reviews.

Outskirts Press, Inc.
http://www.outskirtspress.com

Paperback ISBN: 978-1-4787-8442-5

Cover Photo © 2017 thinkstockphotos.com. All rights reserved - used with permission.

Outskirts Press and the "OP" logo are trademarks belonging to Outskirts Press, Inc.

PRINTED IN THE UNITED STATES OF AMERICA

I dedicate this book to the three people who helped me survive the difficulties of life. Dr. Ray Craddick entered our lives when my son, Christopher, was seven. He diagnosed him correctly, and gave him a future that had previously been denied to him by earlier doctors. Over the years he shored up my whole family when we began to crumble, and all it took to reach him was my message on his answering machine: **"HELP!** This is Susan Barnard, 237..."

My mother, Cecilia T. Kessler, was a tough and elegant woman who fought with me every step of the way to make me strong and independent. No matter how difficult our relationship was, she was always loving and understanding with Christopher. In the end, with the help of Dr. Craddick, we bridged a huge gap and were each able to say, "I love you."

And to Nancy Kessler Tilchin, thanks for being my favorite sister.

Acknowledgements

Words cannot express my deep appreciation to the parents and siblings who shared their stories in honest and compelling ways. Because they spoke to me anonymously, their names do not appear in the book. They talked candidly about their doctors, families, marriages, their feelings about their special needs siblings and their personal feelings. Many shed tears when they remembered how hard the journey had been. Without their help this book would not exist. Many parents said they were glad that I was writing this book. One summed it up best when she said, "I appreciate you doing what you're doing. The more people know, the more people read, the more people are made aware, the more opportunities our population is going to have for a better life, and have a positive impact on society." Another said, "I'm thrilled that you asked [to interview me]. It brings back these thoughts and memories. I used to boo hoo every five minutes. I can handle it now. You become stronger...I hope it helps. This is something for us. It's our book."

My thanks to the special education teachers and those people who manage programs for special needs adults. You are extraordinary because you choose to spend hours each day helping our children achieve their potential. My thanks to Harmon L. Barnard III, Susan Feinberg, Dr. Linda McCuen, Jessica Kasten, Heather Lubeck, Miriam Smith and Rebecca Wilkie.

These programs for people with developmental disabilities provide services such as housing, job coaches and jobs for their clients. They also are a wonderful source of activities where our adult children socialize with one another, and participate in dances and trips.

My son, Christopher, lives in the Little Friends, Inc. Community

Living Program in Naperville, Illinois, and works in the Spectrum workshop in Downers Grove. The staffs from these programs graciously talked about their part, and recommended parents for me to interview. So, thank you Janette Antink, house manager at Christopher's group home; Erika Detrick, Spectrum Vocational Services Floor Supervisor; Tammy Niemeyer, Little Friends, Inc.; Thomas Pendziszewski, Vice-President Adult Day Services, Spectrum; and Kathleen A. Schildback, Community Integrated Living Arrangement, Little Friends, Inc.

Becky Dowling, the director of "Just" People in Atlanta and Kelli Salyer talked with me and helped me find "Just" people and their parents for me to interview.

Webb Spraetz, Developmental Disabilities Director of Atlanta Federation's Jewish Family and Career Services, and Ginny Riley, Administrator of the Georgia Evaluation and Satisfaction Team, Inc. in Atlanta also gave interviews. Both also offered names of parents to be interviewed.

Arbor Academy, Inc., *Havanah* Sunday school and the Atlanta Group Home, Inc. were established by dedicated people. The first two wanted the finest school and Sunday school for their special needs children, and the latter wanted a home for their adults. I wish to acknowledge the original founders of the programs.

Arbor Academy, Inc. founders: Kenny Koblitz, John Wheeler of the Northside Jaycees; parents: Susan and Harmon Barnard, Dr. Joseph and Jane Girardeau, Charles and Margaret Rudd, Robert and Patricia Ott, Josiah and Bertie Benator, Leo and Bella Neuhaus, Dr. Leroy and Kitty Antrobus, Mrs. Ethel Reinsmith; and teachers Patricia Jenkins and Patricia Viskil.

Havanah Sunday school founders: Susan K. Barnard, Dr. Leon Spotts, Sidney Kaplan, Shirley Michaelov, Sadell Sloan, Annette Lashner, Jackie Metzel, Maxine Marcus, Sue Hollander, Soyna Rabinowitz, Ed Krick, Murray Kudroff, Sharon Draluck, and Leonard Cohen.

The Atlanta Group Home, Inc.: Susan K. Barnard, Sonia Kuniansky and Stan Lefco, Mac and Minette Meyer, Royce Bemis, Frances Kuniansky, Dr. Perry Schwartz, Patti Cotts, Paul Muldawer, Herbert Cohen, and Max Kleinman.

Table of Contents

Dedication iii
Acknowledgements v
Preface ix
Chapter 1. Children with Major Speech Problems 1
Chapter 2. Children with Down Syndrome 28
Chapter 3. Children with Epilepsy, Seizures and Strokes 38
Chapter 4. Children with various forms of Palsy 69
Chapter 5. Children with Encephalitis and Meningitis 81
Chapter 6. Children with Marfan Syndrome 87
Chapter 7. Kazmier Syndrome 96
Chapter 8. Fragile X Syndrome 100
Chapter 9. Children Who Don't Fall Into a Specific Category ... 112
Chapter 10. Parents With Two Special Needs Children 166
Chapter 11. Siblings 190
Chapter 12. The "Kids" Speak 206
Chapter 13. Special Education Teachers 220
Chapter 14. People Who Provide Services
            for Special Needs People 237
Epilogue 256
Footnotes 259
References 262
Glossary 264
Resources for the Handicapped 272
A Letter to Christopher 273

Preface

The Centers for Disease Control and Prevention, and the Health Resources and Services Administration, published a new study on their pediatrics research: *Trends in the Prevalence of Developmental Disabilities in U.S. Children, 1997-2008*. The study notes that there are "about 1 in 6 children in the U.S. who had DD in 2006-2008. These data also showed that prevalence of parent-reported DDs has increased 17.1% from 1997 to 2008." (1) The 17.1% "is about 1.8 million more children with Developmental Disabilities in 2006-2008 compared to a decade earlier." (2)

The authors of *The Special Child* described developmental disabilities: "... [as] any physical or mental condition that can impair or limit a child's skills or causes a child to develop language, thinking, personal, social, and movement skills more slowly than other children." (3)

The public in general has a hard time being around and dealing with people who are different. Not long ago I was at a bookstore with a very intelligent woman who became hysterical. She ran up to me in another aisle, and as her eyes darted around fearfully, and her arms flailed, she said that a strange man kept looking at her in a funny way. It turned out that the man was developmentally disabled, and he just happened to like looking at pretty women.

"When specific terms are heard, uninformed people may imagine the worst and then, out of fear, avoid meeting, associating with, and learning about handicapped persons and their families," the authors of *The Special Child* stated. Some people think they will catch a disability just by association. This is particularly hurtful for parents of young children whose neighbors and friends are afraid to let their children play together. (4)

Words for describing the disabled have changed over the years. "Retarded", "moron" and "imbecile" are being replaced by developmentally disabled, Mildly Intellectually Developed (MID), or special needs. *"Mongoloids"* are now being referred to as children with Down syndrome.

Years ago I was a guest on a television show discussing Arbor Academy, Inc., a special education school that I had helped to establish. When the interviewer used the word "retarded," I forgot where I was and challenged her to use better words to explain special needs children. I explained how hurtful words can be by feeding into stereotypes and creating even more problems for these children and their parents.

Of the 63 families that I interviewed for this book 12 were told that their child should either be put immediately into an institution, or that he or she would eventually end up in one. Every one of these children has attended school, church or synagogue, works in the community, or is in a sheltered workshop. A few are still living at home, but most are in group homes or apartments. Some are married, and some have become parents. They have far surpassed their doctors' original diagnoses and are leading moderately productive lives.

The author Pearl S. Buck had a mentally disabled daughter. She said, "The Chinese believed that since heaven ordains, it was a person's fate to be whatever he was, and it was neither his fault nor his family's. They believed, too...that if a person were handicapped in one way, there were compensations, also provided by heaven." (4)

All of the parents and siblings I interviewed for this book have children or brothers and sisters who are 20 years old or older. Young children are just starting on their long and arduous journey through the maze of doctors, schools, relationships with family and friends, and coping with public scrutiny. Their stories are still evolving.

I began this odyssey in 2001, but because life often gets in the way, it got pushed to the back burner. With the urging of my son, Christopher, who keeps asking when I'm going finish "his" book, I promised to make it a priority.

Consequently, the present situations of all the people I interviewed have not been brought up to date. If I did that, the book would probably not be ready until the 22nd century.

It is my hope that *Dreams Die Hard* will inspire young parents who are learning to deal with their problems. They can see that with the proper help and resources there is a bright light at the end of their tunnel. And to the doctors who treat the types of patients such as are described in this book...**listen** to the parents and don't be so quick to dismiss them. Please help them find the proper resources then read my book several more times.

Chapter 1
Children with Major Speech Problems

"Einstein didn't speak until he was five," said by many Pediatricians

"Language is the most complex skill that people acquire... (1) Speech disorders affect the ability to produce speech but not the ability to express or to understand language." (2)

Glenn Doman explains in his book, *What To Do About Your Brain-Injured Child,* that those people who suffer from aphasia have "...an inability to communicate due to an injury in the cortex... (3) and that they suffer a loss in the whole area of communication and not simply in the area of speech itself." (4)

Unlike the child aphasic, the adult who acquires aphasia as a result of a stroke has a "loss of communication (that) occurred after the acquisition of education, so that they did not become shut out by the intellectual curtain before life had begun for them. They had material for recall in related fields when therapy was instituted." (5) For the child aphasic who has no base for language, learning to speak is like swimming upstream through mud.

Christopher

My mother and I sat in the doctor's office at St. Christopher's Hospital for Children in Philadelphia, and heard him say, "Christopher will probably be in an institution by the time he is seven." In that instant my world fell apart. I had just been told that my four-year-old son had no future.

When we returned to Atlanta, I told my husband what had happened. Then I fell apart...

Christopher Wilson Barnard was born on July 17, 1961. His brother, Harmon III (Tracy), was three years older. Our infant was scrawny and pitiful looking with a shock of brown hair combed up to a point on top of his little head.

One evening while visiting me in the hospital, our friends asked who Christopher looked like. My husband, Harmon, and I said he wasn't a pretty baby but we loved him and knew he would improve. We didn't want them to see him then say, with a gulp, what a cute baby we had. We were chastised for being insensitive.

The photographer came into the room and handed me the nursery picture. While our friends cooed over a rather good picture of Chris, Harmon insisted emphatically, "That's not our child."

"Of course it's our child, it's just a good view of him. Doesn't every mother recognize her own child?" I responded. Disgusted, Harmon left the room.

A few minutes later he returned, snatched the picture out of my hand, and said, "I told you that isn't our child." He handed me another picture and said, "That's our child!" It was a picture of the ugliest baby I'd ever seen. When I asked how he knew who had our picture, he said he heard a woman across the hall cry out, "That's not our baby!"

Within a few days Chris began spitting up after each feeding. Our pediatrician believed he was allergic to the milk, so we began changing formulas. Each new try ended up all over me. Then, during his first month's checkup he threw up all over the doctor. I said to him, "Now, do you see what I mean?" Well, a picture **was** worth a thousand words.

The doctor said that Chris might be suffering from pyloric stenosis, which is a "Narrowing (stenosis) of the outlet of the stomach so that food cannot pass easily from it into the duodenum." (6) Consequently, little or no milk was passing through into his intestines. He was placed on a muscle relaxer, and when the problem persisted we were sent to a surgeon.

Christopher was admitted to the hospital for observation. Because he was spitting up rather than projectile vomiting, a key component of the diagnosis, the surgeon felt he couldn't make a proper finding, and Chris was discharged after a week. A few days later he was readmitted to the hospital and after another week, he was again discharged. A week later we returned to the hospital where it was decided to discontinue the muscle relaxer. During his next bottle, Chris projectile vomited across the room, and was in surgery the next morning to correct the pyloric stenosis. I thought, "thank goodness everything would be all right."

The weeks in the hospital were awful. I stayed with Chris around the clock while Harmon and Tracy lived with my in-laws. The only time I saw a nurse was when she came by to take his vital signs (blood pressure, temperature), or when she brought me a bottle for the baby. I fed, bathed, and dressed him multiple times during the day. Sometimes we shared a room with a child whose mother was absent, so I tended to two sick children.

The only real kindness I received at the hospital came about 2:00 one morning while I sat on my cot feeding Chris and crying. An aide came in to put linens in the closet. Seeing my distress, she took the baby and relieved me for awhile.

During our next pediatric office visit a mother told me that her son had had the same surgery many years before. She told me not to be alarmed if Chris progressed slower than my other child, eventually he would catch up. I was grateful to hear that, it kept me from panicking when he was unable to match each of Tracy's milestones.

Tracy was in nursery school that fall and was exposed to every illness. He brought home measles, chickenpox, strep throat, the flu, colds, and he even came down with scarlet fever. These spread quickly to Chris and Harmon. It got so bad at our house that I began answering the phone, "Barnard's Infirmary, head nurse speaking". Fortunately, I didn't get sick because I didn't have the time.

Chris finally walked, and was potty trained, but by the time he was three and not talking, we were very concerned; his pediatrician wasn't. He only said "Da Da" and "No". His third word was "Sears" because Harmon worked at Sears and Roebuck. He finally said "Ma Ma" when he was seven years old, and I cried.

Chris (3) and I went to the grocery store one day. Ready to move to another area, I put my hand on his shoulder and said, "Let's go." He flung around to face me, and screamed, "Don't touch me!" (Ah, three more words!) Quietly, I repeated, "Let's go." And again he yelled, "Don't touch me!" By this time everyone within hearing distance thought I was beating my child. We quickly left the store.

When Chris was four and was still not talking, his doctor agreed it was time for a speech evaluation. In October of 1965 he was tested at a speech school in Atlanta. Afterwards, Harmon and I sat in their office anticipating good news, and expecting that they would enroll him for speech therapy. All we remember being told was that he had some problems and needed to be placed in a nursery school program. We didn't understand why he wasn't a candidate for that school since he had major speech problems.

I called nursery schools in the community and explained Chris' problems; no one would take him because he wasn't talking. Then I called a private nursery school and the owner/director said she was interested, and asked for Chris' speech school records. After reading the material she called me and said she would be glad to take Chris. Then she added, "Of course, you know that he is **mentally retarded**."

Stunned, I put the phone down, picked up my keys, and drove over to my mother's home. I sat down and said, "Chris is..."

"Chris is what?" she asked.

"I don't know," I answered in a stupor.

Then she began feeding me words such as sick, hurt, happy, sad. To each I answered with a shake of the head. I finally blurted out that he was mentally retarded, and collapsed into her arms and sobbed. I was shattered. In my mind, the word retarded equated to imbecile, no hope, no future, no dreams. Neither Harmon nor I remember getting that diagnosis from the speech school.

I called the director of the school back and explained why I had hung up on her. When Harmon and I took Chris to meet with her, teachers, dressed in Indian saris, continuously ran through her office chasing unruly students. Amidst the pandemonium, we left; that wasn't the place for him. He needed a quieter environment.

At the end of 1965, I was very pregnant and needed to get Chris into a kindergarten program. The head of another private school agreed to take him. It was very difficult for him, and he spent much of his time crying. Realizing that it wasn't working out, the director agreed to keep him until the baby was born. After David's birth in January 1966, I removed Chris from school.

I then looked in the phone book under Special Education and found The Northside School. I was told that they only took children from six to 16. We had to wait a year and a half.

Just after David's birth we found out that our pediatrician was dying of cancer. Our new doctor suggested that I take Chris to St. Christopher's Hospital in Philadelphia for a comprehensive evaluation.

In June, Mother, Chris and I headed to Philadelphia. The head of the Division of Endocrine and Metabolic Disorders Department oversaw the examination. For almost a week Chris was put through a battery of tests.

The days for Mother and me were filled with endless, agonizing waiting. Mother usually sat by Chris' bed and knitted, while I walked around, talked to other mothers, or stood staring out the window at a dirt playground situated between the hospital and some apartments; we each held our own thoughts. Often I would see tears streaming down Mother's face. Most of my crying came at night in the shower while hot water poured over my body. Back in our room I put on a better face. I found out later that she had done the same thing. We couldn't cry to each other because we needed each other's strength.

The day of reckoning came as Mother and I sat in the doctor's office hopeful that we would find out what was wrong with Christopher, how it had happened, and what could be done. Instead, we heard that not only was he brain damaged, the cause was unknown, and there was no cure. Then the doctor said, **"Chris will probably be in an institution by the time he is seven."**

I was devastated and heartsick. Back at home, I told Harmon of the diagnosis, and insisted that we put Christopher away immediately because I couldn't stand to love him anymore only to give him up. Then I fell into a terrible depression, I felt as if I had fallen into a deep black hole; I was inconsolable. Having been told that Chris was mentally retarded with an institution in his future was like a death warrant with no death.

"You were physically exhausted," Harmon said. "My greatest concern was not so much about what we were going do with Christopher. I was worried about you. I wondered, *how in the world am I going to get her out of this so she can get back to normal so we can find out what we're going to do?* I wasn't getting through to you...you were hearing but not listening." My breakdown only lasted for about a week.

I didn't know what to tell our friends. Mother offered me the best advice when she said, "Be honest. Today they talk about you, tomorrow they talk about someone else."

I felt so alone. Even though intellectually I knew there were other parents and children like us. One day Mother suggested that I call someone I knew who had a Downs syndrome child. She met me for lunch, and brought an armload of books on the handicapped; the news had gotten around fast. Her understanding, sympathy and empathy were a great comfort to me. I knew that I wasn't alone.

Shortly after my return from Philadelphia, Harmon and I dined with some friends. This turned into one of those serendipitous moments that seem to guide my life. I told them about what had happened. Ken asked if I had called The Northside School, and I said that I had but Chris had to be six to be enrolled. "I'm on the board of The Northside School," he said.

The following morning Ken called me from the principal's office and told me to bring Chris over immediately. We rushed over, were interviewed, and Chris was placed in a class on a month's probation; he passed and became a full-time student. He did well, made a good adjustment, and made friends with some of the students. I breathed a sigh of relief that we'd finally found the right school. I thought, *Thank goodness, now everything will be all right.*

Then one morning in January 1967 Chris' teacher called to say the school board was closing the school at the end of May; they were $6,000 in debt. Parents were invited to a meeting at our home. Several of us were chosen to meet with the board to see if we would reverse their decision. Our Plan B was to open our own school if the board turned us down, which it did.

Consequently, we founded Arbor Academy, Inc., a special education school for developmentally disabled children, and I became chairman of the board. Two Sunday school classrooms at Peachtree Presbyterian Church became our home. Arbor Academy was successful because of the commitment of the parents who were all in the same boat. For me it was the time when I grew up.

Harmon and I treated Christopher like we did the other boys; he fed the dog, got the mail, and took out the garbage. He kept his room neat, learned good manners, took swimming lessons, art lessons, and went away to camp.

One day I went into my bathroom and saw a small round object at the bottom of the toilet bowl. I reached in and found my wedding ring. I'd been doing housework and had put my wedding and engagement rings on my dressing table. For some unknown reason, Chris threw the rings into the toilet and flushed; only the small ring survived.

In a panic, I called our insurance agent who suggested that since we were on a septic tank, a plumber might be able to retrieve the ring.

Our backyard was torn up, and when the tank was opened, I pulled my lawn chair to the brink of the hole after the man said that many plumbers keep what they find. When the ring was found, I was waiting with a glass of ammonia.

In 1968, Christopher's teacher told us that she was having problems with him and that he needed to see a psychologist. He was seven and we were terrified that the Philadelphia doctor's prophecy was about to come true; was it now time to put him in an institution? That's when we discovered Dr. Ray Craddick at Georgia State University. After a battery of tests, Dr. Craddick explained that Chris was aphasic, he had brain damage in his speech area caused by a lack of oxygen. He said that Chris was in the right school, and he would never be in an institution. He had given Christopher a future.

That fall, I enrolled Chris in a special education Sunday school class that was sponsored by the Atlanta Bureau of Jewish Education. The class was run by a lovely grandmotherly woman who did her best to manage seven children whose IQs ranged from the educable (50-72) to the trainable (below 50), some of whom had physical disabilities. At best it was babysitting for three hours.

Several years later, I spoke with Dr. Leon H. Spotts at the Bureau about separating the program into three classes; educable, trainable and learning disabled, and hiring special education teachers. A Special Education Committee was formed, and I was named chairman. A call went out in the community for students and teachers. By the fall of 1971, the *Havanah* (Hebrew for understanding) program was up and running with 18 students.

Marital troubles that Harmon and I had been having came to a head in the fall of 1968 when he was transferred to Chicago. We felt it was an excellent opportunity for a trial separation, but in the end we decided to divorce. I remained in Atlanta with the children. Neither of us ever felt that Christopher in anyway affected our marriage.

While working in the Sears Tower, Harmon met and married Joann Krohn. From the beginning she and I hit it off, not surprising since we're very much alike. We joke about Harmon and his two wives. Our wonderful relationship has allowed the three of us to be parents, enabling us to share such milestones as graduations, weddings, holidays, and grandchildren.

Chris (11) went away to a YMCA camp for several summers beginning in 1972. I questioned whether I'd made the right decision, but when I received his letters I knew that I had. "I am making a belt in arts and crafts. I had a swimming test Friday. I like to swim. I went on a boat ride today. I went camping and ate and slept out doors." His counselor said there had been very little teasing from the other boys and they seemed quite understanding of his problems.

I'd been doing volunteer work at Grady Memorial Hospital, since I was 14 years old. During this period I was working in the surgical recovery room. One day I sneaked into the operating rooms, and knew instantly that that was where I belonged. The hospital trained me to be a surgical technician then offered me a job. A few years later, I moved to a private hospital, then struck out on my own and became the first free lance surgical assistant in Atlanta; my calling card read *Call Girl for the Operating Room*. Surgery became a 25-year career.

After talking with several anesthesiologists about administering anesthesia to infants, I believe that an anesthesia accident during Chris' surgery had probably resulted in his brain damage.

Chris' teacher wrote on his September 1969 report card, "Chris is doing great! Talking up a storm! I couldn't ask for a better, more willing student." Unfortunately, she retired at the end of the year.

The following fall his teacher said that Chris couldn't read. I said, "Of course he can read. Give him a TV Guide and ask him what's on TV on Tuesday night. He reads *TV Guide* and *People Magazine*." Otherwise, her reports were good: "Chris is enthusiastic and responsive...showing progress socially and academically. His speech shows some improvement...I'm so proud of him."

Dr. Craddick again evaluated Chris: "...Chris has shown improvement...His intellectual range is still wide, varying from the Mental Defective level to the average level. In particular, his verbal abilities are still very low...is handicapped in that he does not talk too well yet.

"I feel that Chris has a future head of him, that he can be further educated and further, I have fairly strong feelings that he may be underrated in terms of his intelligence...and may be a more perceptive boy than he has been credited with in the past."

One afternoon in May of 1974 my world again crumbled. During a meeting with Chris' teacher, she said, "Arbor was **no longer able to fill Chris' needs.**" While I sat dumfounded, she rolled off a list of problems that she had seen. She said his "lack of ability to communicate abstract thoughts may create a situation of intolerable stress...Chris is not progressing fast enough. I personally believe his academic & social progress is hindered by his emotional frustrations." She was afraid he would harm himself or others. When Chris gets frustrated, he directs his anger inwardly.

I was flabbergasted. After all the good reports, how could he have changed so abruptly without my noticing? I sat there trying to understand what she was saying. Slowly I computed that my child might harm himself or others, and that he was no longer welcome in the school I had founded.

She wanted me to see one of the psychologists on the board. Even though he already had a psychologist, she insisted that since the professional board members had reviewed Chris' records, we'd be better served seeing one of them. As I argued to go to Dr. Craddick, she argued to go to a different doctor.

Blindsided and beaten down, I saw her choice who took a history then tested Chris. A week later I returned for the results and was told that Chris had slipped backwards from his previous tests and could no longer attend Arbor. Period. When I asked where he should go, he shrugged, obviously uninterested. I told him, "If you take Arbor away from me you have to give me something else of value." Again he was unconcerned. When I explained that there was no other school like Arbor Academy in the Atlanta area, he said, "With your record you can start a new one."

I stood up and declared, "I'm not a Johnny Appleseed going around scattering special ed schools all over the place!" As I ran out of his office, I told the secretary not to bill me. Somehow I managed to make it home in rush-hour traffic, while sobbing my heart out.

I called Dr. Craddick who did what he could to assuage my guilt, and then told me to have the test results sent to his office; I also had a copy sent to me. Dr. Craddick said that the history and many of the test results were incorrect. He said Chris' outbursts were nothing to worry about; it just showed that his frustration level was high. Because of the aphasia he was unable to express himself. He had once said that Chris experiences more frustration in one day than most people do in a year.

At the urging of my friend, Lyn, I called Harmon to see if there were any schools in the Chicago area that might take Chris. After checking, he called to say there were very good special education classes in the public school systems in Illinois. "If we can get Chris in, could he come live with us?" he asked. Of course, I agreed.

"That was Joann, basically," Harmon said recently. "Both of us talked about it ... and she said, 'Why don't we have Chris come here?'"

Joann is my heroine because she took my child and raised him the rest of the way. When asked why she stepped forward to take him, she said, "Because there were such good programs here...It seemed the right thing to do for him."

Christopher, David and I flew to Illinois the last of August 1974. We settled Chris into his new home in Wheaton where Joann and Harmon opened their home and their arms to him. They gave him a bicycle, and made a place in the basement for his collection of musical tapes. He was given a set of drums so he could play along with the likes of John Denver and Barbara Mandrell. Despite his speech problems, he sings along perfectly to his music.

Several days after David and I returned to Atlanta I again fell into a very deep depression. It was terribly hard letting Christopher go, even though I knew that sending him to Joann and Harmon was best for him. Once again Lyn stepped in, saw what a terrible mess I was, and made me call the doctor to get an anti-depressant. She said, "You need a vacation from yourself." I finally rallied, and was offered a job as a private surgical assistant to the chief surgeon of a local hospital.

Christopher adjusted well, and settled into school and into the neighborhood. But Joann's adaptation was harder. "I really didn't know what I was getting into...I didn't have any children of my own so it was a big adjustment to have a child, then to have a child that was 13 and handicapped. I would get frustrated sometimes trying to teach him simple things that everybody should know...Christopher was always easy to handle; he was not a behavioral problem in any way."

Because Joann was also working, they found a big brother for Chris to be with him after school. "He took Christopher around, and they did things together...He was really, really good for him," Harmon said.

Christopher loves Joanne. Once while visiting me he said, "My mother..." He stopped and looked at me to see if I was upset. I asked, "Do you call Joann mother? Sheepishly he said he did. Then I said, "I think that's wonderful, you have two moms." With that, his face lit up. He calls me his birth mother.

Chris went through public school in special education, and at times was mainstreamed. He was also put into a vocational program. After graduation, he went to work at the Little Friend's, Inc. Spectrum sheltered workshop where he is today.

When Christopher was about 19, Harmon, Joann and I felt that it was time for us to think about eventually moving him into an assisted living situation with people like himself. As much as we all love him we didn't want him living with us for the rest of his or our lives. He needed some independence. Joann began looking into programs and placed his name on several waiting lists, while she worked with him to do things such as make his bed and do his laundry.

Meanwhile, I attended a meeting sponsored by HUD about housing for handicapped adults. I joined the director of the DeKalb County Developmental Disabilities Council, for lunch. Since some of the local churches were establishing group homes for special needs adults, we felt the Jewish community should do the same thing. We decided to see what we could do.

We approached the director of the Atlanta Jewish Federation with our idea, and with his encouragement, we spent the next several years doing our homework. We attended workshops on HUD's 202/Section 8 funding, visited group homes in the area to understand how they worked, and met with professionals in various fields. We assembled a board of directors, that I chaired, and incorporated our project as The Atlanta Group Home, Inc. We compiled a list of possible residents and met with their parents. We found a house that could be easily renovated for our use, and worked to secure the sponsorship of the Atlanta Jewish Home. The City of Atlanta granted us a Special Use Permit, and we received HUD funding. By the fall of 1982, success was ours.

During the process, tensions had arisen between me and several of my board members. Upset over the anguish it was causing me, Mother said it was time for me to retire. She was right. I called my vice-president, resigned, and asked her to meet me for the pertinent papers. I'd accumulated reams of material over the years, but I gave her one small folder. When asked where the rest of the material was, I replied, "One day I'm going to write a book."

Unable to understand the antagonism, our Atlanta Association for Retarded Citizens' board representative, explained, "Success has many parents, failure is an orphan."

Now that the Atlanta Group Home wasn't an option for Chris, I implored Joann and Harmon to find a suitable place for him. A place opened at Little Friends, Inc.'s Community Living Facility, and Chris was accepted. He (22) moved into the dormitory and shared a suite with three roommates. Some years later he moved into his present group home with three roommates and a house manager.

On February 26, 1983 I proudly accepted the Atlanta Association for Retarded Citizens' Mary Lee Brookshire Award "for your outstanding service on behalf of mentally retarded citizens and their families." I wrote to Christopher and thanked him for my award.

At one time Chris talked about getting married, and driving a car. He's not particularly interested in dating even though he's had several girls who "love" him. One considered herself his girlfriend, but she was so bossy he said she got on his nerves.

Harmon and I were very good friends with a couple, but after our trip to Philadelphia, things changed. When I called to get together, they were always busy; after awhile, I stopped calling.

During a meeting in North Carolina, my sister, Nancy, ran into this woman. She asked Nancy, "How are Susan and Harmon? We don't see them anymore because of Chris. After all, we have two normal and healthy children."

When my friend, Linda, heard about what had happened, she said, "Susan, I don't understand all about Chris, but you and Harmon are our friends. I don't understand how anyone could do that to a friend."

I asked Harmon how Chris affected his marriage to Joann. "I think it brought us closer together. Christopher was like her son, she accepted him as if he was her own... I think it affected our marriage in a very positive way."

Did raising Chris make him different? "Once he got into the workshop, and once he was able to get into the living situation his whole personality changed. You could see a very positive change and it made me feel good because I knew that without us that wouldn't have happened. I think it changed my outlook as far as what I think about myself. I found out that I was much more compassionate than I thought I was. I really cared about him and other people."

When asked the same question, Joann replied, "I think I appreciate what people go through who have problems, whether it's mental or physical...and it's given me a better understanding of handicapped people. The worst thing to me was the frustration I felt from time to time. I had to learn how to deal with him and learn how to teach him so he could learn," Joann said.

Having a special needs child took a toll on me. When Chris was young I had problems and anxieties that most people didn't have or didn't understand. I worried about his future. Today, I fear that if Chris's present situation doesn't work out, where would he go, and what will we do? I finally learned **not** to say, "thank goodness, everything will be all right".

Dealing with him, doctors, professionals, and founding a school, a Sunday school program and a group home forced me to jump into unknown waters because I needed programs for my child. It developed strengths I never knew I had, and forced me to grow up.

How did I cope? I just did what I had to do to give him the best life he could have. I know I wouldn't have survived without humor and the wonderful people in my life. My therapy was writing with my dear friend Gracie. We wrote a new-age dictionary (unpublished), a romance novel (unpublished) and the great American novel (unpublished). What we did have published were two articles on the Muscogee (Creek) Indians in a university journal.

Unlike many of the parents I interviewed, I haven't learned patience. I often say that "if patience is a virtue I'm not a virtuous person." But having Christopher has made me more aware of and, I hope, kinder to those people with handicaps. And I'm so very proud of all that he's accomplished.

The following are some of my favorite Chrisisms: When he was about 18 years old, he asked me, "Did you know that I'm handicapped?" I said I did. Then he said that he was the only person in the world who had a handicap. When I said that his friends at Arbor Academy were also handicapped, he was shocked. He didn't see them as having any problems.

My aphasic child often comes out with amazing statements. I had been an occasional cigarette smoker. In the late 1970s when smoking was becoming an unacceptable, Chris saw me smoking one day and said, "Okay, die!" Shocked that he understood that smoking often caused deadly diseases, I quit.

During Jimmy Carter's presidency, he ordered that all males 18 and over sign up for the draft. Armed with a letter from Chris' doctor to the Draft Board to exempt him from service, we went to the post office. I tried to explain the situation to the postal clerk, but he rudely made loud comments then told Chris to fill out some papers. On the way home I looked over at him and saw tears streaming down his face. I said, "I'm so sorry that you had to go through that. It's all President Carter's fault."

While watching the 1984 National Democratic Convention, Chris asked me, "What do you think of Jimmy Carter?" I told him, and then asked, "What do you think of Jimmy Carter?" He looked thoughtful, but didn't answer.

"Well?" I asked.

"I'm thinking," he replied.

Christopher is very exact. If you say call, or say come see me sometimes, he asks, "What time?" It's now become the family joke.

At his nephew's Bar Mitzvah, he asked the rabbi why his service had lasted two hours and ten minutes. The rabbi said that he tried to keep the service short. Chris said,"The service was two hours and ten minutes." The rabbi again tried to explain. Chris replied, "When I go to church the service is only an hour, how come your service was two hours and ten minutes?"

One day he asked me, "Why is there a God?"

Christopher is now in his 50s. He's become more relaxed, talks more, and is more understandable. He calls when he wants to talk, and most of the time when I hang up the phone I laugh. He just tickles me. Since I can now see his personality and his sense of humor, I'm privy to the real Christopher. I keep wondering what he would have been like had he not been brain damaged.

While he was at Arbor Academy, Chris was asked to write about what love is. He wrote, "Love is my mother kissing me at bedtime."

Claire

When Claire was around two years old, she came down with the measles and lost her ability to speak. "At that point, she was talking similar to the way she talks now (at 40). They're not complete sentences, she gets the verbs and nouns, but she leaves out all the adjectives... and we noticed that something had happened to the left side of her body. She had to walk with her arms out, instead of down by her side. They think it was encephalitis," her mother, Jody, said.

"Several doctors told me that I needed to institutionalize her, get her away from the family, because she was going to be such a strain on the family system. I couldn't put my baby away. She was going to be raised to the best of our abilities."

When Claire was three and a half her parents had her tested at a local speech school in Atlanta. "That's the first time I heard the word 'retarded'. They said, 'bring her back at six. If she can function like a three year old we'll be able to work with her, otherwise we can't.' I looked at them with a blank face. I didn't know what it meant."

Her husband took the diagnosis, "the way he takes everything, quite blank; no emotional reaction. He treated her as normally as he treated anyone in the family...He's an extremely hostile, abusive, controlling human being. So it wasn't pleasant for anyone.

"I got books to find out something about it. I had never seen a brain-damaged or mentally handicapped person before. So I had no concept."

Claire was evaluated at a hospital, and the doctors could find nothing definite. It was a matter of waiting to see how she would develop. It became "obvious that her speech center was shut down. To this day that is her main handicap. She understands almost all of what's being said to her but she can't initiate many words. If someone else initiates the word, she will then tell you when you hit the right word... She can't think in the abstract, has no time or money concept, but does have an excellent memory."

Claire and her younger sister (13 months younger) went to a church kindergarten, and after two years Claire enrolled in Arbor Academy. When she transferred to an educationally handicapped class in a public school, she had a terrible teacher. "Claire was physically abused even to the point of having her front tooth knocked out by normal kids on the playground, or coming in from the playground."

She was placed in another private school for a year, then was enrolled in a trainable class in public school when the family moved to a county with good schools. She received speech therapy from Georgia State University students working on their master's degrees. "I decided it was more important for Claire to recognize words that led to her safety than to learn how to add two and two... she began to thrive again. She was very happy there. She began to have the sense that 'I can do, I'm good.' She wasn't the lowest guy on the totem pole, she was a higher guy on their totem pole."

When Claire was about 13, she attended a vocational training class in school. Students learned how to wash dishes, and do gardening work; Claire was taught how to work in a day care nursery. "I started a program where the students could work outside," Jody said. "I got the school for the first time to do vocational training outside of their box...I helped them see that what these young adults needed most was anything that aided self-care. Teach them to wash their own clothes, and teach them how to cook at whatever level they're capable of. Get them ready to **not** be institutionalized...Get them ready to be at a higher level of self-sufficiency."

Claire got a volunteer job at a county facility working with severely handicapped people where she worked for about 15 years. She changed diapers, fed, exercised the patients, and got them in and out of their wheelchairs. "This was the happiest time of her life. She's a care-giver anyway...She identified with the teachers...Herself image soared."

Today Claire lives at home and is part of the "Just" People program that offers an array of programs for the developmentally disabled adult. Her job is to answer the phone, and this forces her to develop her speech.

Claire did not embarrass her two sisters. Th[e ...] someone who needed to be cared for and protec[ted ...]

"She really has no interest in marriage," Jod[y ...] boyfriends. Her idea of a boyfriend is a friend [who will buy] her a Coke and will hold her hand, dance...may[be kiss her on the] cheek. She has no sexual interest. "

When Jody's husband was physically abusive to her, "Clai[re used] to be my protector and that gave me a problem because she would try to have him hit her instead of me." Jody finally divorced him under the family abuse law.

"He told me if I ever divorced him Claire is who he would do harm to. And I would never be able to prove it or stop him. And he did." With prodding, Claire finally told her mother that her father raped her in 1996. "She calls it 'Daddy's cuckoo crazy love for Claire.' She can't put it together beyond that. She has bad dreams to this day...she's on medication to help her with her anxiety and fear of him. He told her that if she told me he would kill me. She must stay in contact with me at least daily, hear my voice, and know I'm okay because she worries daily that he's gotten to me... I've had a death threat written on a board, and he poisoned our dog...Claire's fears are very well founded." Claire's sisters went to court in a civil action against him on behalf of her. "He pled guilty...he's a felon for four years."

Going to church was important to the family. At first, Claire attended regular Sunday school classes, but later her mother picked a church that had special education classes.

When asked how Jody feels about raising her special needs daughter she answered, "It's a mixed bag. It's difficult to know you have a permanent six or seven-year-old, and that the responsibility is yours till the day you die. It's emotional, it's physical, it's financial, and it's spiritual. It cuts right across the core of you as a parent. You find out what you're made of. I have grown, and so have some of her sisters, a great deal more than I think we would have because we have Claire in the family."

When asked about the toll it took, she said, "What was my price think you are asking? It directed me for the rest of my life to ping someone who needed help... I would have directed my life in different manner if I had not had her. I would have used my time differently, but this for me was the first primary calling, so I put aside wanting to achieve in other areas... I would have liked to have gone on to college...Would have wanted to go out in the working world early on in my late 20s...as a divorced woman I would have liked to have done more dating. It didn't work.

"I remember when Claire was born I had no concept of how selfish and self-seeking I really was. When I found out she was brain damaged and would need help all the rest of her life, I had to do a 180-degree turn. And that had to happen inside my character...You have to let go of that anger and look at what is positive about it...it's constant work."

Alan

Everything appeared to be normal when Alan was born. But when he seemed slow to develop his parents become concerned. "Being our first child we had nothing to compare him with," his mother, Jean, said. "He didn't turn over when the books said to turn over. He didn't crawl at a year, and the doctors said that was normal. They said he's a big boy and he will eventually do these things.

"I think the first red flag was his language development. He didn't speak in normal progression. He'd say one word, and maybe two words. Because he couldn't talk, he'd be frustrated. The pediatrician then said, 'He's just a boy, and he was late, don't worry about it.'"

On the advice of a friend who was a teacher, Jean had Alan tested at a hospital when he was two and a half, and it was discovered that he was a year behind in language development. He was referred to the local speech school in Atlanta for a thorough testing. "They confirmed that his language development was far below normal, but the performance was almost average…his IQ was charted between 70ish to 75."

The speech school had recently added a special education class to their program, and Adam was enrolled. "Now having a second child I realize they learn from the air, colors, etc. Alan had to learn his colors over and over again. He had to learn everything step by step."

After a period, the speech school told Jean that Alan had reached his level, and needed a more permanent place. "That was my first 'hung out to dry'. I was devastated. Here I thought they were going to make him better, I thought they were going to make him normal. I thought they were going to fix him up. I thought he was going to catch up. When they told me he wasn't going to catch up, at first I didn't believe them." She said that her husband was wonderful and very supportive.

Looking for a program, she visited schools for the Learning Disabled. She finally found a special education class in her county public school district for Alan, and he graduated with a special education diploma.

"I always had creative jobs for him. When he was 13 he played sports at a neighborhood park. I knew the director, and he was nice enough to let Alan be a 'camp counselor'. I would pay him $10, and then at the end of the day he would pay Alan $10; he thought he was working. When he got in high school a grocery store near us hired Alan, he's worked Saturdays since he was 15."

After school, he spent a year in Warm Springs at the Roosevelt Institute. "It was iffy...On paper, in concept it was just what we wanted. I wanted Alan to learn to live away from me, and away from home." Instead of watching their charges and providing activities on the weekend, they were left to their own devices. Some of the students were going into town and checking into hotels.

Alan returned home and his mother found him a job at Kroger. One day during his 15-minute break, he picked up a bag of potato chips and stood in line to pay for it. When his break time ran out, he took the snack to the employee's room to pay for it later. Someone reported him for stealing. When his mother showed up at the store, the assistant manager told her, "'We have to fire Alan because he stole food. He didn't pay for the potato chips'...and the person who reported it got $200. It was devastating. But it was a lesson." He went to work for another grocery store.

"We tried independent living a few years ago...and had a bad experience, he went into a real deep depression...He had a breakdown...It's taken two years to get back to square one." Today Alan is living in an apartment and participates in the "Just" People, and the Jewish Family & Career Services' programs that provides counseling, Independent living, job placement, and social events for the developmentally disabled.

A friend of Jean's asked Alan "'what are you going to do when your parents die? You're going to have to learn to live on your own.' All of a sudden he thought, well, when are you going to die? He kept asking us, 'When are you going to die?' It scared the daylights out of him. He's very attached to me...he feels safe with his family. Our one fear is what happens to him when we're gone. I feel a little bit like I'm going without a net."

Alan's brother, Carl, and his wife are guardians until he's 21. "I want to get Alan as independent as I can for Carl's sake and for Alan's sake."

Carl is seven years younger than his brother. "All of a sudden your younger brother knows more than you do," his mother said. Carl, whom his mother described as smart, sweet and sensitive, is good to Alan, but when he was a teenager his special brother embarrassed him.

Alan doesn't date but would like to get married. "He met a girl at Warm Springs, they were buddies but she has more emotional problems. He is dependent on her call every week." Jean tried to put some distance between them.

When asked how having Alan affected her marriage, she said, "I don't know what it would have been like without Alan, we've been married 30 years. I think it's made us stronger. God gave this special child to us. It always makes me feel better because maybe that's why we're here."

What are her feelings about raising a special child? "You just assumed that when you have a child, and they have 10 fingers and 10 toes, that was it. I didn't realize what you have to put into it. I think it's made me a better and more understanding person...It's made me understand kids more. We all have something; maybe not to the depth of your child or my child, but they all have some little disabilities. It's made me a less shallow person."

In explaining the toll it has taken, she said, "I definitely have no freedom. My husband and I haven't been away...Sometimes I want to say *let us have a week off. If I could just have some time off*...I haven't expanded my free life. On the other hand, I was late when I got married and I had a free life before I got married, I was 30. I'm going on 60, and now people are in their empty nest and we don't quite have an empty nest...Transportation is the big thing...I just call it baby steps like in Bill Murray's movie, *What About Bob*.

"There were times when you go to parties, people would be bragging about their kids. I thought, *how can they do that when know that Alan isn't like that?*"

Is she different having gone through the journey? "I don't know, what was I like before? He's enriched our life more than I can say. Taught me what real love is. It's made me a better person."

Kevin

Kevin seemed fine at birth in Philadelphia in 1966 but as he grew, his development was slow. "When I left him for a few hours with my mother at about nine months old, she got really upset when he wasn't sitting," his mother, Bonnie, said. "The doctor kept saying he was fine."

He would sit and continuously rock back and forth. He had a vocabulary of very few words. But because his brothers and sisters answered his commands, his parents were not concerned until he was four. Then they took him to a neurologist at Children's Hospital in Philadelphia. After doing a brain scan on him, "They said, 'Well, this child is retarded. He will never be more than probably a 13-year-old.' So I set out to prove them wrong.

"I was very upset. It was very hard to accept that he was retarded. My husband took longer to accept it. Maybe for lack of understanding, I was the one that was there dealing with the doctors, and trying to find programs for him."

Kevin attended a private school that took in children with learning disabilities. When he was ten years old the family moved to Long Island, New York. "They had a BOCS, Board of Cooperative Services program that covered all special handicaps. So he was bused out to the BOCS program. It worked. I was always active with the teachers, PTA. Then all of a sudden I noticed the higher functioning children in his class were no longer there. He was in with a bunch of children who were lower than he was." His parents convinced the school system to start a class for Kevin and other students with similar problems.

"Kevin always had a problem with his speech...clearly, he has aphasia. He knows what he wants to say, keeps saying the same word until he gets it out."

While living on Long Island, Kevin attended a baseball camp. He fell in love with the sport and became the team's 'manager'. "He reads the *New York Times* sports page, and now that he lives in Atlanta, he is the Braves (baseball team) biggest fan."

When the family moved back to Pennsylvania, Kevin spent three years in a school program that had vocational training. Afterward, he got a job in a nursing home washing dishes.

When the family moved to Atlanta, Kevin tried several jobs until he got a full time job in a hospital kitchen. He now lives in his own apartment, and works in a nearby Kroger grocery. He is also involved with the "Just" People program.

When he first moved out of his parent's house, "I got phone calls almost every night, he wanted to come home. It was a big step. He has a very good roommate; they complement each other. It's hard giving a child up that you've nurtured. When I put him in that apartment I suffered more than he did. But I knew that I had to cut those apron strings and give him the chance to be on his own because I knew he could do it."

One day Kevin was at an intersection waiting to cross the street. He pushed the button for the light to change. Even though it didn't change, he walked out into traffic and was hit by a car. He broke his knee and recuperated at home.

Bonnie is looking to the future when she and her husband will no longer be here. She feels that it is not fair to burden her other children with the responsibility of making major decisions for their brother.

Kevin has a girlfriend that he met at "Just" People. "The thing that is so wonderful about them is that they care about each other," his mother said. She sees marriage in his future.

How about her marriage? "I guess it was hard in some ways. It took my husband awhile to understand," Bonnie said. "He's proud of where our son is and what he's done...Over the years we worked our way through it and think it has strengthened us.

"There hasn't been a toll per se. It's been a challenge every step along the way. I guess I'm more understanding, more compassionate; I'm more of a fighter.

"I feel that God gave him to me because I could deal with him. I know I've become a stronger person. I'm proud of him and proud of where he is and what he's done. Back in those days I had hoped for more, you always do, but I am happy where he is," Bonnie said.

Russell

At the end of Doris' delivery in Chicago in 1959, she heard a doctor out in the hall say, "'Get the baby before you lose them both!' That was my beginning." After her son Russell's birth, she and her husband were told that he was fine and healthy. Looking back, they felt that their baby had probably been deprived of oxygen during the delivery.

When Russell was not speaking at the age of two and a half, his parents became concerned. Their doctor said, "'don't worry about it, Einstein didn't talk until he was five.' We wanted to believe him so we took Russell home and treated him like a normal child. But little by little we could tell there was something different, but we didn't know what it was. He just wasn't like our other two children." Finally, he was evaluated at Illinois State Pediatrics. "I was told that he would never tie a shoe, ride a tricycle, never, never, never many things. Most of which he has already done," his mother explained proudly.

When her husband heard the doctor's prognosis he felt, "Disbelief," Stan said. "I wasn't very happy about it. But the doctor told us that we should probably consider institutionalizing him and getting on with our life. We sat down with our two older children to discuss it, and it was quite obvious that it was not an option… We said we have him and we'll do the best we can, we are not putting him in an institution."

"My older boy was 12 at the time, and he shook the house with his sobs. I think that probably made me strong for the moment to try to explain to him that we can accept what God gives us. We can still hurt, and we did hurt, sometimes we hurt today. We see so much potential in him which he's not able to give back," Doris said.

"We're people of strong faith and so whatever God gives us we try to accept it from Him. It probably gave me more strength than I deserved even. (She didn't cry), nor did I say *why me,* or any of those things."

Russell attended regular kindergarten and the teacher recommended that he repeat the class. "Not too many fail kindergarten," Stan said. Then he was placed into a special education class in public school, "Which was a disaster." He felt the director of the program just had to put the disabled someplace.

When Russell was eight or nine his parents decided that he needed to be in a private school and that the school system should pay for it. They called in a specialist who went to bat for them, and the school district agreed. Russell was placed in a residential learning center for five years and went home on weekends.

When the family moved to Kansas, Russell was enrolled in another residential program. That school was only fair and the house parenting was not good. Russell was a "sociable, gregarious, outgoing person with a very serious speech defect." The parents were told there was a behavior problem; it seems that he had been pushing corn and peas onto his fork with his finger. Afterward, the family moved to Chicago, then to Indiana where Russell attended public school special education classes.

While in Indiana, Stan was president of a university. He and his wife organized a group of students called "Russell's Rangers" who were to help their son after school and on the weekends. It worked like a Big Brother program. While at the college, he and Doris also started a gym program, a special education Sunday school program, and a day camp. When the family returned to the Chicago area their son was placed in the Spectrum workshop in Downers Grove.

Russell's parents had planned to put him in a church group home, but at the time of the interview he was living at home. When they are no longer here, their daughter and son-in-law plan to take care of Russell. Their son will take care of him financially. They feel their other children know that they can put him in a group home if need be.

"Our daughter accepted Russell 110%. She wanted to stay home and play with him instead of playing with friends. We had to push her out of the house or pull her friends in. She became like a second mother. We didn't want that," Doris said. One day her daughter came to her and said, "I understand that I can love Russell and hate what he does."

Stan said that dealing with their child, "Made us stronger. I believe that when you have a child with a disability it does one of two things. It either splits the family or makes it stronger. We have lots of friends and acquaintances who can't handle it, the man usually leaves."

Chapter 2

Children with Down Syndrome

"He can hold my hand now and walk me down the street," a parent

Children with Down syndrome have 47 chromosomes in each cell instead of 46. Their eyes "slope upward at the outer corners, the face and features are small, and the tongue is large and tends to stick out. Other characteristics include a flat-backed head, sometimes, a little finger curved toward the third finger, and often double-jointedness... On the average Down syndrome affects about one or two out of every 100 babies born. But a woman is at greater than average risk of having a baby with this abnormality if she is over 35 or if she or her spouse has some rare chromosome abnormality." (1)

The Centers for Disease Control and Prevention stated in 2001 that, "Down syndrome is the most common form of retardation, affecting one of every 800 infants... and it causes a slate of problems from lower IQ to heart defects and greater vulnerability to infection." The CDC study discovered that the life span of people with Down syndrome has greatly improved over the years. Today, the average life expectancy of Caucasians is 50 years and half that for African-Americans. This is a far cry from the 1960s when the average age of death was no more than two years. (2)

Keith

Everything seemed normal until Keith was six months old (1961), and he was not performing like his two older brothers were at that age. His mother, Betty, questioned her pediatrician who "passed it off. When he was about nine months old, and wasn't even sitting up in the playpen, and was hardly holding his bottle, I got the doctor to confess to me that he did have developmental problems. We had him tested... for Down syndrome. He had three characteristics of Downs; the big neck, missing bones in his elbow and knees, and thick thumbs...We weren't sure what his future would be as far as his development."

When Keith was about three, he began saying words, not sentences. Through her husband's brother, who was a child psychiatrist at a major university, their child was tested and found that his IQ was below normal and he was developing behind his chronological age. "But he was making progress. " The doctor advised them to find a special education school for him.

"It devastated me because it made me feel that I was not on the same par with my friends. I had a hard time dealing with my friends who had children the same age, because we couldn't do things together, we couldn't keep up with them. It made me more or less (socially) isolated...I'm sure I felt inferior and embarrassed with Keith when my friends' children were having these great recognitions."

Her husband, Alexander, "accepted the fact that we had a special child, and that we needed to research resources to help develop the quality of life he would be able to maintain."

Finally her pediatrician admitted "that Keith would never be able to be independent or think independently, that he would always have to be under our wing."

Keith attended a private kindergarten for two years, and then spent three years in public school until they found The Northside School. When it closed, she and her husband helped found Arbor Academy, where he served as vice-chairman. Keith attended Arbor for six months until a program was found for him in the public school.

When Keith was in his early teens, he spent a year at the Georgia Mental Retardation Center in Athens, Georgia. "He was teaching reading to some of the students who couldn't read...It did give him the independence of living without us. He also learned to drive a car.

"Our church...is where he got his real socialization. Although he was functioning three years behind his chronological age, we put him in a class at his chronological age. He was quiet and introspective... That's where he got to know women and girls," Betty, explained.

Today Keith lives in an apartment with a roommate, has a girlfriend and drives a car. He's an office boy at an architectural firm where he has worked for over twenty years.

Betty said that she didn't know if her other two sons were embarrassed by Keith but they weren't ashamed of him. "They were very gentle with him, they would include him in things he could participate in, and they didn't work their lives away from him. The middle child, suffered the most...He now admits that he felt like a stepchild, so to speak."

"I don't think it bothered the marriage at all," Betty said. "It made us stronger...neither one of us felt responsible for it. It probably brought us closer together. Both my husband and I have deep faith, and we just felt like this was something that we were entrusted with. We did the best we could."

"I let him (Keith) develop at his own speed," Betty said. "I explored as many avenues as I could...and then I just had to depend on my intuition...Had he been the first child I probably would have reacted differently. I had enough responsibilities with the rest of my family; I couldn't concentrate the whole time on him.

"I had to stay at home, and I felt sorry for myself. I ended up with an alcohol problem because it was easy for me to drink during the day when I had to be home with him all the time...I am a recovering alcoholic.

"I've always been a very shy person...Have been in leadership roles all my life, I never felt adequate. I don't know if I would've been different if I hadn't had a special child...it's really made me more introspective than I would have been."

The doctor, who once said that Keith would still be dependent and need his parents to hold his hand when he was 16, would be astonished. "All that has changed entirely, he's totally independent. He can hold *my* hand now actually and walk *me* down the street. And I'm very grateful that his prediction was not true."

Adam

When Adam, the oldest of three children, was two weeks old in 1964, his parents were told that he had a mild heart defect. When he was six weeks old, they were told that he had Down syndrome.

"The first night was terrible. For 24 hours I cried and my husband cried, we both had a tough time. After 24 hours I was just fine. I felt like God had given him to us for a purpose. There had to be a reason for it because even the conception was almost a miracle, because we should not have conceived at that time and we did," his mother, Carolyn, explained.

"My husband is tremendously supportive; we both kind of feel the same way. It took him a little longer than it took me to adjust to it. It took him about a month before he figured out what was going on and, to get a hold of it, and feel comfortable with it."

Adam went through public school in special education classes. Afterwards, he got into the Little Friends' Community Living Facility (CLF) in Naperville, Illinois, (and roomed for awhile with my son, Christopher). After living there for seven years, his parents bought a condo with two other families. He presently works at the Spectrum sheltered workshop.

Carolyn helped start a special education Sunday school class in her church, but the minister was not very supportive. When they moved to nearby Naperville, "Someone called and said, 'What can we do for you?' It just blew my mind. I said, *you can help me start another class*. So she directed me to the right people and we started another special ed class."

Adam has been engaged twice. "The first time was when he was about 24 or 25 and that engagement lasted about five, six months. The young lady that he was engaged to was an absolute doll but had a string of broken hearts that she had left behind," his mother said. "He was really quite smitten with her...He always had girlfriends. Now he's engaged a second time. This is an engagement that will probably last forever...I don't think they'll ever get married. I think it's fine provided they don't have children."

Carolyn said that Adam strengthened their marriage. "It made it richer, our whole life has been richer…We are very much on the same page with it."

How does Carolyn feel about having a special needs child? "It's wonderful. It continues to be wonderful. We've had experiences we never would have had otherwise. We have opportunities to give to other people and do things that if we hadn't had Adam we wouldn't have done…He's an absolute treasure. He's a very easy person to be around and a very easy person to live with.

"I'm more accepting of retarded people…and of the handicapped, or of people who have problems."

Jay

Jay was born prematurely in 1956, and remained in the Army hospital until he weighed five pounds. When his parents, Leigh and Grant, went to bring him home, "The doctor said, 'Well, we think there may be some problems. We think he may be Mongoloid.'" Since the diagnosis was not conclusive, Grant suggested seeing another doctor because, he said, "'we need to know so we can get on with life.' We took him to a local pediatrician in Clarksville, Tennessee and he confirmed for us, yes, Jay had Down syndrome."

The family was shattered. "We knew it meant mental disability. Certainly the doctor didn't offer any additional information (or help). Prior to taking Jay to (the pediatrician), we had decided that Jay was ours, the Lord had given him to us, we already made the decision that he was going to be in our family, we were going to live as normal a life as possible. Jay's presence was not going to deter us from doing anything we wanted to do; he would just be a part of it.

"Grant didn't suffer any ego destruction in all of this at all. In fact, I really felt that during my most difficult times, he was my support, my strength, my backbone."

The doctor in Clarksville said, "'Mom and Dad, your ego has been crushed, you need to have more kids.' I was so grateful for that." They had two more children.

The doctor gave them some articles by "Dr. Bender in Children's Hospital in Boston who was experimenting with administering pituitary and thyroid extract. This was to enhance growth and would heighten the level of intelligence. So we said we have nothing to lose, it's not going to hurt him, so why don't we go ahead and give it a try and see what happens." Jay was on the therapy for five years. "It didn't help his IQ because we didn't know at the time that he had suffered brain damage. ... He's about five feet, five inches and doesn't have the short, fat, puffy appearance that many people with Down syndrome have...He does have the eyes of a person with DS, other than that you can't tell by looking at him."

The pediatrician also said, "'You need to do anything you possibly can for Jay to look physically acceptable to society because society will see him first before they ever get to know him.' We've always made sure that Jay was well dressed...We would say to him, *boy are you really handsome, you're really one neat looking young guy and I'm so glad you're a (Smith)*."

The pediatrician also linked the family up with another family who had a seven-year-old Down syndrome child. The child was undisciplined. "She taught me a lesson...Jay will be disciplined the same as any other child. I don't want him to grow up, be in society, and be in the public and acting like a spoiled brat."

By the time Jay was four, the family was living in Atlanta. Because there was nothing available in the public schools for him, he was enrolled in a private school. Then the family was on the move again, and in each city their goal was to find the right school program for their son.

When Jay completed school, he was placed in a sheltered workshop operated by the Florida Association for Retarded Citizens. While in Florida, Leigh observed the founding of a group home. At a meeting "I saw parents in their 70s, in their 80s still parenting. I thought to myself, *Lord, I love Jay, he is as precious to me as life itself, but please don't let me be parenting when I'm 70 or 80, I think I'll be worn out.*"

Jay was evaluated by a social worker who asked Leigh, "'What are your plans for Jay's future?' I said, *Gosh, I really hadn't made any, just that Jay will live with us for as long as possible.* She said, 'Uh, uh. You're doing a real disservice to your son if you continue with that kind of thinking. What would happen to him if you or your husband were killed today, where would he go? Who would he live with? Who would help him make that adjustment? It's not fair to him to put him in that kind of a position... You need to help him find some place else to live to establish his own form of independence while your whole family is well, where you can help him make his adjustment out of love and not out of a tragedy. The other side of that is when people become adults it's the normal sequence in life. They leave home, and Jay needs that opportunity also.'

"I did some mental arguing with her for quite some time and thought no way, there's no one who would love him and care for him as we do. My prayer was, *Lord, take him home before we ever have to consider that, that is just not an option*...(But) I was intregued by that group home movement where the people he would live with would become his substitute family, a family of friends...I thought this would work."

Jay's family is very religious. As they moved around the country, "If there wasn't already a Sunday school class, I started one," his mother said.

When the family moved back to Atlanta, Jay went into a county training center, and Leigh thought of putting his name on an Atlanta Association for Retarded People group home list. Then she decided to start one herself. She got together with other families struggling with the same problem, and they formed an association. They applied to HUD (Department of Housing and Urban Development) for funding for two homes, and were accepted; the homes opened in June 1982. Today there are 18 group homes that serve about 90 people. Leigh's organization provides sheltered employment and residential opportunities for the handicapped.

"We learned by mistake. We were really pioneering for the benefit of our sons." (When our group was working to establish the Atlanta Group Home, Inc., Leigh was a valuable resource in sharing her knowledge of applying for the HUD loan.)

Today Jay lives in one of Leigh's group homes, and works in a sheltered workshop. "He's just blossomed."

Leigh's son, Harry, told her, "'Growing up with Jay has taught me to care so much that it hurts.'"

Her son, Mike, said, "'I can remember wanting to bring friends over to the house, but I wasn't sure how they would accept Jay. When I brought them over to the house they all accepted Jay very easily.'" She told her son, "That is a tribute to you because they watched you to see how you interacted with Jay, so they would mimic that. Their acceptance of Jay is just proof of your own acceptance and love for your brother."

Jay has never dated. During his summers at Camp America he became enamoured with a girl who stayed with them and "he blew her a kiss."

How has this affected her marriage? "It has bonded us together more closely than I would ever have imagined. I have seen over the years that my husband's love and sensitivity to Jay continues to grow, and if I'm seeing it in him it's probably occurring in me as well. We feel blessed that the Lord chose us to parent Jay and our other sons," Leigh said. "We are so blessed. Jay has taught us, and shows the real meaning of love...he loves unconditionally, and he's taught us to do the same thing. He is such a treasure, he's so precious. He exudes love."

Did the parents pay a toll? "None whatsoever. We have lived absolutely completely normal lives. There've been challenges in finding the right services for Jay, finding the right doctor, starting the residential program, but no toll. To be here now, past retirement age, doing what I'm doing, I attribute it to Jay ...I feel energized and motivated and want to continue to help Jay and others like him."

My husband, Grant, said 'it's made him so sensitive to others he can hardly stand it.' It has certainly taught me to be sensitive to other people and particularly persons with challenges like Jay. Jay has certainly given me a purpose in life I never would have dreamed of when he was first born. Am I really different from other people because of Jay? I don't know."

Chapter 3

Children with Epilepsy, Seizures and Strokes

"Go home, take two aspirin, and call me in the morning," a pediatrician

"There are many forms of epilepsy, each with its own characteristic symptoms. Whatever its form, the disease is caused by a problem in communication between the brain's nerve cells. Normally, such cells communicate with one another by sending tiny electrical signals back and forth. In someone with epilepsy, the signals from one group of nerve cells occasionally become too strong; so strong that they overwhelm neighboring parts of the brain. It is this sudden, excessive electrical discharge that causes the basic symptoms of epilepsy, which is called an epileptic seizure, fit, or convulsion." (1)

"A stroke occurs when part of the brain is damaged because its blood supply is disturbed. As a result, the physical or mental functions controlled by the injured area deteriorate." (2)

Aaron

"I [now] suspect there may have been some damage during delivery (1967). I noticed that there was a portion on the right side of Aaron's head, right at the temple bed, where it looked like the hair had been damaged in some way," his father, Garrett, said describing the area that was shaped like a perfect half moon. He wonders if forceps were used during delivery.

At first Paula and Garrett "thought everything was normal. He was slow with the normal things of walking and talking, crawling, but everybody (including their pediatrician) said, 'don't worry, that will come along'.

"When Aaron was a year old, he came down with a cold, and the doctor said, 'Take him home, take two aspirin and call me tomorrow.' He went into convulsions that night from a high fever, and became cyanotic (the skin and mucous membranes were a bluish color because of an insufficiency of oxygen in the blood) (2). After that, Aaron began to have petit mal seizures, convulsions." He was taken to a hospital where a psychiatrist and several neurologists put him on Dilantin and Ritalin to control the seizures.

One day while in kindergarten, Aaron's teacher called his mother in and told her that his development, speech, and coordination were slow. The family headed back to the hospital where they were told that "'Aaron has fine motor coordination and gross coordination problems, he'll never be able to do this, this and this...that there was brain damage in the back of his brain'. Aaron's fooled everybody and still does. The mental part, Aaron is neither fish nor fowl...he's between 67 and 71 IQ.

"I took it pretty hard. It was tough to take because everybody I knew had normal kids, and why shouldn't I have a normal child? It took me a very long time. Paula took it more readily than I did," Garrett explained.

When Aaron was ten he developed a rare blood disease, ITP, "A condition characterized by the sudden, abnormal lowering of the platelet count." (3) Garrett explained, "The Dilantin was destroying all the platelets...he was lethargic, and if you touched him he would bruise. The blood vessels were deteriorating, and the blood was seeping through the walls. We put him into the hospital, and that night he started having seizures. They took him off the Dilantin, put him on Phenobarbital and he seized for 24 hours. (Garrett thinks the seizures caused more brain damage.)

"Aaron was in intensive care for fourteen days. He was comatose, developed a kidney infection...It was so bad that the doctors couldn't call it. We lived at the hospital; we ran 24 hour shifts. I would go for 12 hours and Paula would go for 12 hours. It was so bad that we actually called our rabbi and had him plan a funeral for us because we didn't want to deal with it when the time came." Fortunately, the crisis passed.

Aaron was enrolled in a local speech school in the Atlanta area, and then went into the first grade at Arbor Academy where he stayed about seven years. When he was a teenager he switched to a public middle school special ed program.

"We threw him to the wolves...he had to learn how to ride the school bus...had to learn how to survive in a large class room, and he had to learn how to survive going to lunch. He did remarkably well, and was pretty readily accepted by the group." Aaron graduated in 1987 from a public high school and was voted Special Education Student of the Year.

Aaron attended the *Havanah* Sunday school program. "We wanted him to have a Bar Mitzvah, we thought it was very important, and we thought that Aaron could handle it," Garrett, explained. They consulted the rabbi, and found a Hebrew teacher for him.

The parents chose a private service "with just friends and family, and Aaron was fantastic...Pat Conroy (the writer) came in late, and Aaron stopped in the middle of the service and said, 'Hi, Pat. How are you doing?' Then picked up where he left off. I think that Aaron was the second special needs child in the city of Atlanta that probably had a Bar Mitzvah," his father said proudly.

(I attended Aaron's Bar Mitzvah and cried through the service because I was so proud of him, and I believe that everyone in the sanctuary was similarly affected.)

"Probably the best thing that ever happened to Aaron was that he joined the AZA (a nationwide youth program sponsored by B'nai B'rith). The chapter took Aaron on as a special project. They said, 'You're a member, and we'll treat you like everyone else.' They made Aaron realize that he could do most anything."

Aaron was also active in Special Olympics where he won the Silver Medal for the City of Atlanta and the State of Georgia in the broad jump. "He had potential to be a fantastic distance runner but he was lazy."

After graduation "We were at a loss. We had looked for programs in Atlanta and there were none." Aaron was sent to a residential center in Chattanooga, Tennessee. For 12 years he lived in a group home with eight other individuals and worked either on site or out in the community.

"Aaron got involved with a group called People First which probably pulled him out, made him realize...that he was just as good as other people. He got to be the president of the chapter...and was on the state board for two or three years. He was flying off to Memphis to go to trials where People First were suing institutions...Aaron and his group were writing letters to everybody including the President (of the United States) about their special needs. He got pretty political. Because of People First, Aaron was nominated for the President's Council on Disabilities in 1997-98. He was one of 200 people selected to go to Dallas to this convention...Aaron came back knowing more about Medicaid than the people who run it do."

In the fall of 2000, "We brought him back to Atlanta and placed him in the Independent Living Program, a non-profit group offering family and career counseling. Aaron was moved into an apartment with a roommate where he literally paid his own rent. They got him a job in the community, and right now he's functioning as an independent living person...He works for Kroger, and I like to refer to him as a utility man; he's a glorified janitor.

"Aaron really doesn't know how to handle the situation (of dating). There was a very little interaction between the sexes at (the residential school)," his father explained. "Now he wants to get involved with going out with people." He's not interested in getting married.

When asked how he felt raising Aaron, Garrett answered, "That's a very emotional question. I think that we all start out in a state of shock. We all have trouble trying to accept it although we will outwardly accept it; inwardly, we all fight the fact that we have a special needs child. I think you also fight the social embarrassment of having a special needs child. You don't let anybody know this, but it's always there. It's not the child that gives a damn, it's the parents, and the siblings.

"You don't know whether you want to have anymore children because you don't know if (the problem is) genetic... DNA wasn't around then," Garrett explained. "It's a strain on your marriage. In my situation, I was traveling, so I had it on weekends and when I was home. Paula had to put up with all the crap during the week.

"All of a sudden you become very, very accepting of the fact that, hey, I have a child who has special needs. All of a sudden you start watching and you realize that you are learning as you go along, and it's not things you learn in school. It's not things you learn in life, it's just that your child is teaching you instead of you teaching the child about love, how to accept, patience, how to overcome. It's just that you learn constantly. And it never ceases to amaze me of the fact that you learn everyday, even in conversations. They touch the heart, they steal the heart."

Did it take a toll? "Yes. I didn't get the chance to see Aaron play football, or do normal activities, to go to college, despite the fact, that we spent enough money on him over the years to send him to Harvard 20 times, and still are. You miss the fact that he'll never marry and you won't have a grandchild, but that's minor. You can't dwell on those things, you have to take it day by day...after I accepted it, I just jumped in and learned. (As for his wife, Paula,) I think that Aaron's not being normal probably took a big toll. All of the kids on her side of the family are smart, creative and intelligent, and she sort of feels like, 'gee, what did I do?'

"It's taught me to look at things a little closer. It's taught me to be a little more patient with some people. It's taught me to be more accepting. It's the fact that I value the small things in life more than I would have. I've learned that it's not those things that we buy that are important in life, it's those relationships we have. I think that Aaron has taught me a great deal as far as learning how to live and learning how to face life. It's a challenge for him everyday."

Aaron's mother died in 2002, and his father worries about what will happen to him when he is gone. "There are no siblings, so what do you do? We drove it into him that *when we're dead and gone, you have to learn how to live on your own, and you better be prepared*. The first time I mentioned this to Aaron he asked, 'Do I get the house?'"

Robyn

While mother and baby were still in the hospital following delivery in 1968, Hannah became alarmed when the nurses brought Robyn to her to be nursed. "I noticed that she was drawing up, doing something funny, like getting stiff. I didn't know what it was, I thought it was peculiar. I asked the nurse about it and she said they noticed that she'd done something funny in the nursery and they weren't sure what it was. I called Eli, I was close to hysteria at this point...I knew it was different from my first child." Her husband called their pediatrician. He examined the baby and said, "'you're a new mother and you're overly concerned, there is nothing the matter with your child.'

"We came home with a nurse, and the nurse hadn't been in our house 24 hours when she said to me, 'Have you noticed something funny about Robyn?' I asked her what she meant, and she said, 'Well, she's sort of drawing up.' I said I did notice it and they told me it was nothing. She said, 'There is something the matter.'" They took the baby to the doctor, and when she didn't exhibit the unusual gestures in front of him, he again said there was nothing wrong. "But we knew there was something."

They admitted Robyn to a children's hospital in Atlanta for observation. Hannah tried describing her baby's symptoms to the doctor, "it's like she's having a fit." "He said, 'You mean a seizure?'...That is in fact what she was having." She was placed on Dilantin and Phenobarbital and stayed in the hospital for ten days. Meanwhile, Hannah ran back and forth to the hospital to nurse her child.

"I was in a great deal of pain, was very frightened, upset, and didn't really understand. At that point they really couldn't tell us what her future would be. Most of the children with infantile seizures do have a certain amount of retardation, but they couldn't tell us, we'd just have to take one day at a time. That's when we started her under the care of a pediatric neurologist," Hannah said.

"We were a mid-to late 20s couple with one normal child. We had no clue what the implications were of having what is now called a developmentally disabled child, then called a mentally retarded child," Eli explained. He reacted "with complete shock, had no clue what the implications were, didn't know what mental retardation was in the sense of knowing what those things meant, and had no idea at all whether we were talking about a months worth of mental retardation,...we had no idea what it even meant in terms of the future paths that we would travel. There were many stumblings along the way because there was nobody around to help you very much."

"We took Robyn home and every moment it was like, is she going to have another seizure?" Hannah said. "She was a terrible sleeper. She developed slowly. She started to sit up, walked late, and her speech was very slow. When she started talking, the first thing she said besides, 'Mama' and 'Daddy,' was 'Sammy hit me.'"

To make matters worse, Robyn's parents discovered a problem with their daughter's eyes. When she was two, she had to undergo a very complicated and serious surgery in Washington, D.C. "She had no fusion. She was seeing double images, and was cross-eyed," Eli explained.

Robyn also had speech and learning problems. Because she didn't fit in with a regular nursery school program, she was put into two private programs. After the federal law, Public Law (PL) 94-142, was passed guaranteeing public education for all special needs children, she went to public school. "Children in the regular part of the school system referred to her and others like her as retards. She spent some very miserable years there," Hannah said. "It was a nightmare. Every ILP (Individual Learning Plan) meeting was like a battle. It was like they were our enemy, and wanted to knock us down and make us pay for having a child that had developmental disabilities. There was no sense of 'we want to help you and let's see what we can work out.' We would sit for six hours in a meeting and come out feeling like they had beaten us to a pulp."

"I used to fight tooth and nail," Eli added. "It was like a battle to get them to do anything."

"I think the problem with some of the programs was that the

teachers didn't recognize the childrens' potential, or the level that they could raise some of the programming," Hannah said. Robyn went to the *Havanah* Sunday school program for years.

When Robyn was 14, she was sent to a private school in upper state New York. After graduation she spent an additional year there to learn independent living.

"We decided when Robyn was eight that she needed other experiences, and we were blessed with the economic facilities," her mother said. She was sent to a camp in Pennsylvania for eight weeks. When Hannah fought to only send her for four weeks, the camp director said, "'Someday you're not going to be here. Don't you want her to learn to develop some type of a life without you? I think that would be important to her.' I think it made me realize that she and Eli were right," Hannah said. "I was holding on and trying to coddle somebody that was someday going to have to be on her own." Robyn spent three summers at the camp, and then later went for five years to another camp that had "created a self-contained and integrated combination mainstreamed program for developmental disabled kids," Eli explained.

Robyn began working with Dorothy Miller, the director of the Elaine Clark Center, who was innovative in working with children with severe problems.

Then Robyn moved into an apartment with a roommate under the auspices of Jewish Family & Career Services (JF&CS). Through the work and financial help of several parents, an Independent Living Program was established at JF&CS. When that situation didn't work out, Robyn returned home until she moved into another apartment.

Eli was on the board of the Atlanta Group Home. "I didn't do that with any notion about Robyn, because she was very young at the time. There was a matter of believing in the concept of what at the time was surely a great alternative to institutionalization. I felt that if we could get this off the ground, then there's a future for other group homes and maybe someday there will be something there for Robyn. This was long before the new wave of thinking in terms of apartment living."

Today, Robyn is married to Philip (see next story) and works part time at a Kroger store bagging groceries and stocking items. "She's a very social person, everybody knows her...and she's like the mayor of the store..." her parents said proudly.

Hannah and Eli's son "had a terrible time. He paid a price because he was the total, central focus of being our first child, and in every way he got attention. He was her parent's first grandchild, and even though my parents had other grandchildren, he was sort of like a star. All of a sudden, not only does a sister show up, but a sister that required a significant amount of attention, particularly in the very early years," Eli explained. "It was a struggle for him and unfortunately, we weren't insightful enough to realize how much of a struggle it was. As he got older, 12 to 16, she was somewhat of an embarrassment to him around his peers." Hannah added, "He didn't want to bring his friends home, and was embarrassed when she was in the car during carpools."

"We didn't overlook him, we were active in every single thing he did but from his vantage point, it just wasn't adequate, it wasn't at a comfort level which he knew how to deal with," Eli said. "Part of that problem, which we only recognized later, was that not knowing exactly what Robyn's future was, we were trying to treat it as a normal family situation, which in fact it wasn't. But we were trying. We didn't prepare him for the fact that she was different, that she had major learning disabilities, and that she was going to have more problems in her ability to function normally. We kept thinking that if we raised them in a 'normal' environment, he wouldn't look at her differently. She would just be the way she was. I think that was a major mistake to not try to talk to him and help him to understand why she was different," Hannah stated. Eli added, "We discussed it at great length. It wasn't sufficient for his age and maturity to give him a grounding of understanding and acceptance. He's totally at peace with it today, and he's very good with her."

How has having Robyn affected the marriage? "It depends on what day you ask it," Eli answered. "On certain days it puts strains on it because Hannah's view is much more sheltering than mine. On the other hand, Hannah also spends bucket loads more time dealing with

Robyn's issues than I do because I'm off at my job while she's got a full time job taking care of Robyn, figuratively speaking. It's got to take some toll on the relationship, and you've got to learn to have views that you don't necessarily agree with, but that doesn't necessarily make them wrong."

Hannah explained, "It causes more of a strain on the marriage. It's just one more ingredient. Life is just not easy and marriage is work. It's like another job and you have to work at it. You're torn apart emotionally by the traumas…sometimes it takes more hours and energy than you feel like you're got, and it's got to weigh on a marriage."

Both parents are very proud of their daughter and her achievements. "I feel like I've grown a lot and learned a lot from her. She's a very beautiful person," Hannah, said.

"We're totally blessed with her attitudes, and her personality, and her desire to make people happy. We have to temper that because she will go off with any stranger," her father, Eli, added.

"I think we grew in a different way because we had a daughter like her. First of all, a lot of the petty things that a lot of our friends and people we know get involved with, we don't have the time and energy for that. We're to busy dealing with more serious things, and the other side of it is we learned a lot about life from Robyn. She's kind of a gift. It makes you realize that her goals, and desires, and needs are no different than yours and mine. She just expresses herself a little differently," Hannah said. "It makes us understand that there are fewer differences in people, and that human beings are more and more alike. Instead of looking at how different they are from you, it's an opportunity to see how much more alike they are and how much you can share together."

"There was plenty of stress," Eli admitted. "Here we are at our age, and when you think of your children grown and independent we're still dealing with it," Hannah added.

"We were so naïve and unknowledgeable about anything to do with a handicapped or a less than normal person that it created a sensitivity in us that was definitively a watershed in our life. Friends have said, 'We can't imagine what your life is like because of dealing with these issues.' We would say back to them, you're right, you can't imagine what its like," Eli explained.

Hannah said that it has made her "A more sensitive person, a person that sees life in a broader sense, not the narrow Walt Disney sense of living happily ever after. I had to play grownup earlier than I would have liked to. I think it's made me a better person in that I don't just deal with myself. My scope of what I do in my daily life involves more than my own personal needs. One of my expressions…I like to play dress up, I just don't want to play grownup. And I had to learn to play grownup."

Philip

Three days after going home from the hospital following his birth in 1970, Philip began throwing up his milk. "So we continued to change the formula on a daily basis. It got worse and worse, and then he started projectile vomiting. The sounds he made were scary to me and the noises got worse," his mother, Pamela said.

"One night about six while he was in his bed, I walked in and he was making that strange sound. His little foot was going up and down sporadically and his arms were moving…in the meantime there was also this wailing like a cat. I called the doctor, and said, *I want you to listen to this*. He listened to the noise, and said to come to the office immediately." After checking the baby and thinking he had pneumonia, Philip was admitted to a children's hospital.

A spinal tap was positive for blood, and the diagnosis was a subarachnoid (cerebral) hemorrhage, a stroke. Philip was placed in an oxygen tent and 24 hours later his condition worsened. Then the doctors informed the parents that their baby had taken a turn for the better, and was going to make it. "The next day they discharged him to go home. …that the hospital would let me bring him home 24 hours after they said he's going to die…that was really traumatic.

"I was scared. Here he is just seven days old." Pamela called her friend/nurse and "asked if she would come home with us. She stayed for 48 hours until we could get a nurse, because I was just so terrified. We didn't know when we walked in the room if he would be alive or not, or if we would see something that was horrifying. (He recovered from the initial episode) but did have severe and significant seizures that were treated with pretty high doses of medication. Giving it to him was traumatic because he was so fragile.

"It was devastating. Our first two children (14 months apart) are adopted and so this child was like a gift. And then for something to be the matter, it just wasn't fair.

"The outpouring of people coming to sit in the hospital room hours and hours with us, as tragic as his beginning was that's how beautiful his life (has been because of the love they received)... this was overwhelming."

Realizing that they needed help, Pamela called Dorothy Miller at the Elaine Clark Center. When told that one of her rules was having the parents relate their stories to the other parents, she refused because she felt her problems were private. "I needed advice and I needed to live with this terrible tragedy. To wail about it wasn't going to make me feel any better. And to hear such sad stories from these people, was no remedy, so I declined being in the program.

"Dorothy liked us and she seemed to love the idea of a challenge, and I was willing to work in the program." Philip was at the center daily from the time he was nine months old until he was three. During this time, his mother drove 100 miles a day to and from school, in addition to driving her other children to their schools and programs.

From three until he was six years old, Philip attended a private school. Then Pamela went to the county school board and they agreed to "provide a program under Public Law 94-142 if we could get two more children. And I got those two children."

Pamela became an advocate for her child. "Every year we adjusted his curriculum...I decided what the IEP's (Individual Educational Plan) would be... I was a parent representative to the Fulton County School Board, and advocated the best I could." She insisted on homework for her child and worked with him. Ineligible for a regular diploma, she pleaded with the school board that gave him a diploma after he passed a test.

Wanting her child to attend Sunday school, Pamela, started the first special education class at The Temple, a Jewish house of worship.

Philip played sports in school. "The only way he could be on the team was if I was on the team. I went out every single day during the season for soccer, and he and I played right wing. When the ball would come, we would run together. It was very exciting for Philip to be in a sports program just like everybody else."

After graduation, "We sent him to Warm Springs where he stayed for two years... (It also gave her a break) I was exhausted by this time."

Along with the independent living and job skills, she insisted that he receive classes in reading, writing, and math.

Philip returned home when he was around 20. "I went to the manager of a Wendy's restaurant and said, 'I'll come to work with him, and I'll help teach him the job,' and I did." He got a job refilling the salad bar, and for six months she acted as her son's job coach. "He was so proud and the people there were so lovely and willing…he was there a year. It was too hard of a job for him."

In order to make Philip succeed, Pamela pushed him to reach his level of achievement. "Learning how to be that way with Philip made me expect and treat my other two children the same way. And they were not achievers, and it's been a source of strife and stress with the other two." They said to her, "'You just never accepted me the way I am.' And I said, 'You're darn right, I don't. You can do better and should do better.' Her middle child cared so much for Philip that he wanted to share his bedroom with him.

How did this affect her marriage? "It must have been a problem," Pamela said. "I think the man I was married to had an affair. My preoccupation with the children, I guess it had a lot to do with it. We had a very structured house, it had to be, you have to have things a certain way or it's not successful.

"We could never go anywhere because not a single friend would keep Philip, they were scared of him. We couldn't trust babysitters. The one babysitter we did have, left him on the changing table when he was two, and he fell off and broke his thigh. He was in a full body cast for seven months. It was a gross time. I couldn't go anywhere; we couldn't get anybody to help us."

During their 21 years of marriage her husband was very supportive. "We got past all the worst parts. Then he went through sort of a mid-life crisis. He was a lawyer here, and he decided not to be a lawyer anymore. He wanted to help run the family business back in Alabama." The family moved to Mobile, and three months later he said he didn't want to be married anymore. He had a woman in Atlanta. Pamela divorced him and later remarried.

"I feel proud," Pamela said. "Phillip is such a great person. I found out what I could do. I had to put aside all of the organizations. I feel like the people that I've touched, who had special children who I think are sunk in the mud, feel like I've helped raise them back up." I told her that I've seen a lot of parents just sit and wait for things to happen, for others to establish programs for their special needs children. If nothing happens they continue to sit and wait. "That's one of the beefs that I have.

"As hard as it's been, I'm who I am because of him. I think that his sister and brother are who they are because of him. You bring out the best part of yourself when you have a chance to give. I'm just enriched. I'm so sensitive, empathetic, I read between the lines and watch the details, and I'm such a detail person. Being that way can only be good for you...You can't go through an experience like that without being different. I had a job to do and I did it. You don't get more than you can do.

"I'm tired. I've always been vivacious, enthusiastic, energetic, and I'm still all those things. I have a disease of the immune system that stress supposedly caused and I'm on steroids, and probably that (all she's been through) has something to do with it.

"You could never let your guard down, you could never relax. You couldn't just ride to the grocery store. (When my child was with me), I had to be talking about what color do you see, and what shape. 'I see something round, I see something red, what do you see that's moving?' It has to be teaching, it has to be stimulating, challenging. I believe that's why I have a success story."

"Because the damage to Philip had been so severe, we were told that he would never walk, never get out of bed, never eat anything but liquids intravenously. The pediatric neurologist told me Philip would be a vegetable; he would never be independent, that if he died, God would have given us a gift because he would never ever develop in any direction. That was the sentence." Fortunately, he was wrong.

Philip moved into an apartment and decided to invite his parents and some of their friends for dinner. When one of the ladies asked him if there was anything she could do, he asked, "'what did you have in mind?'

"She asked, 'Can I bring something? In the freezer I've got a meatloaf.'

"He said, 'That would be great.'

"She asked, 'What else can I do?'

"He said, 'Do you have a vegetable?'

"She said, 'I can whip up some beans.'

"He said, 'We love beans.'

"She said, 'Now what about dessert?'

"And he said, 'Is there anything in your freezer? We're going to need bread.'

"And she said, 'Do you think you can get the bread?'

"He said, 'It'll be a cinch.'"

Philip and Robyn got married in 2002 and his parents took them to Disney World on their honeymoon. The young couple lives in an apartment and he works at Kroger on a job he's had for over eight years.

Patsy

Patsy was anoxic and blue at her birth in 1956. "Her hand was all wrapped up as if some trauma had taken place to it. Her eyes were very filmy, and I remember saying that she looks like she might be blind," her mother, Lauren, said. "Nobody really knows what happened.

"At about five months of age she began having minor motor seizures. She became like a jackknife. It was like an electric current went through her little body. Her hair stood up, and when it was over with she would cry."

She was having seizures. "The diagnosis was that one out of 20 children with this problem would be something other than a vegetable. And Patsy turned out to be the one out of 20 that did develop, not in a straight line up, but plateau wise." Fortunately, the seizures were brief, and her husband, who was a doctor, medicated Patsy with a steroid. "She developed quite a bit slower than my four others like in speech.

"My husband thought she'll come out of it. But a mother's instinct knows differently. He was not as realistic in the beginning. He loved her dearly and was her best pal."

The family moved to Atlanta in 1970, and when Patsy was around six she was placed in a Montessori school on her doctor's recommendation. She lasted a year until her mother realized she wasn't working with the other children. She was tutored for awhile, and when she was eight or nine she was enrolled at Arbor Academy, "where she had a wonderful experience." After graduation she went to a public elementary school then to a public high school.

"I was very emotional in those years. I found myself in tears a lot. I just felt like I wasn't accomplishing what I needed to accomplish in getting my points across...one teacher in particular just gave me fits. We weren't on the same wavelength. Patsy graduated with her certificate; it was a good day for her," Lauren explained.

"With five children, I just got through the early days. Patsy was very easy; she was never a demanding child. If you tell her no, that's it, it's no. She is one of those people who wants to please...She's not able to stand up for herself a lot, she's easily controlled.

"I think some parents of handicapped children feel a lot of guilt. And they're going to do everything they can to assuage that guilt by giving that child everything they need, everything they want, making them the star of the show all the time, and that grates on me. They have to know their place too."

After high school, Patsy spent a year at a sheltered workshop that she got to by bus. "I never knew whether she got there. I picked her up at the bus stop in the afternoon. If one or two busses came by and she wasn't on it, I would have a breakdown. I was beside myself. For eight months that lasted." Then her husband got their daughter a job working in the kitchen of a local hospital. "Every morning and every afternoon for 11 years I took her and picked her up. I look back and think, *how did I ever do that?* When Patsy and others were let go (by the hospital) in July of 1997, "She cried, I cried, she was leaving something familiar to go to something unknown. I made a decision right before she was let go to let her move to a house that one of the other parents built.

"That was a big step. I had just moved Patsy over to the house with very little preparation for living on her own; I was not very good about teaching her about all these life skills."

1994 was a terrible year for the family. Lauren's husband died, she broke her back, and Patsy lost her job then got another job in a hospital kitchen. "They were awful to her. They called her names, and said, 'Why don't you just leave.' And every time I picked her up she would be so upset. That lasted for three months and I pulled her out. In January of '98 I got her a job at Publix... bagging and carrying out groceries.

"All these years I have been her advocate, her manager. I've been Miss Everything as far as Patsy's concerned." Lauren feels that living in the home is only temporary. "That's not the solution to the problem. When I'm gone, I can't envision Patsy staying where she is. She needs too much assistance. I'm open to the idea of Patsy living in a sheltered environment," where she would be part of a community. "I couldn't die easily unless I knew she was being taken care of daily."

How did having a special needs child impact her marriage? When the couple planned an out of town trip, "We always had to make special preparation. Even when it came time to empty nest with the others, there was still Patsy at home," Lauren explained. "We basically never had our own space...My husband was a very kind, step up to the plate type person. He would never have thought of leaving because of the handicapped situation.

"I feel like in a way it was one of our purposes in life," Lauren said about raising her daughter. "At the end of my life I think that's the one thing I'll take pride in, the fact that Patsy and I are friends, and that I've done the best that I know how.

"It has limited my being able to just pick up and go. I'm at the age that it would be great to pack my bag, go see whoever I wanted to see, travel wherever I wanted to travel, but I think twice about leaving. Nothing has ever happened, but I feel like I'm tempting fate."

Looking back, Lauren now sees that she should have done things differently. "I could have done a lot more to have Patsy be part of not only the family, but the community. I just protected her, babied her a little too much when she was growing up. I even had her be separate from the other children. I would've made the others be much more aware of her as far as including her more. I'm not reaping the benefit of that right now."

She has a daughter who lives nearby who worries about her mother. "I really do think deep down that she's worried about what's going to happen to Patsy when something happens to me, because she's the person in town." Lauren hopes that her children will be there for Patsy when she is gone.

"Now that I'm older and looking at my own mortality, it does scare me to think about what is going to happen to Patsy. Sometimes I wake up at night thinking, *where will she be, what is going to happen to her, will her siblings remember her at holidays, will they be kind to her?* I worry about those things.

"If I hadn't had a child with disabilities I would have never been at all aware of people who are like us but slower...I can see how I'm different from people who don't have a handicapped child. They really don't have a clue what is involved.

"I see them (special needs people) all so differently. They're just the same as us; it just takes them longer to do things. They still have the same basic needs as all of us, sociability, to hold down a job. They parallel the normal part of our society. But unfortunately society doesn't view it that way. Generally, society isn't kind." The frustration overwhelms her at times. "It never leaves you, you don't have a break from it, and it's always there."

Randy

Randy was a breech baby who was delivered by forceps in 1964. When he was five years old he had open-heart surgery. "He had anoxia to the brain, and a stroke a week after surgery. He wasn't able to tie his shoelaces, wasn't able to count to ten," his mother, Hillary, said. "The diagnosis from the University of Alabama Hospital was that he had had a stroke and would return to normal capacity," his father, Reed, explained.

They enrolled their child in a public school kindergarten. "In first grade they said we need to hold him back because he's showing signs of learning disabilities, and rather than do that, we started to explore schools for the learning disabled. We didn't know he was brain damaged, we thought he was just learning disabled," Hillary explained. At the time, the doctor prescribed Ritalin.

Randy attended a private school in Atlanta, and when he was about 12, some disturbing problems arose that weren't consistent with learning disability. As he approached puberty, he became very angry. Then his parents enrolled him in a school for children with learning disabilities in Florida where he stayed until he graduated.

"But it was clear to us that he really wasn't learning," Hillary said. "He went to a fourth grade level on reading and he never went any further, third grade level on math and never went any further. We finally said to ourselves, 'what's the sense of teaching him all this root work, it's not getting anywhere,' Reed added.

After graduation, "He came home and worked in various jobs with minimal success, and ultimately he came into my business," Reed said.

When he was between 19 and 25, Randy got into trouble for speeding and drunk driving. When he began having episodes of screaming, his parents sought help, and were told, "'Well here's the problem. Your son was head injured at five years old.' Well, you could have blown us over with a feather. Here's a child who looks perfectly normal, walking around head injured. We rolled with the punches. I think we did a complete 100-degree turn-around, and started to explore head injury. We were told that there is a neurological Behavioral Institute in Houston," Hillary said. So, off to Houston they went. "But there again, they kept telling us that he would be able to live a normal life. That was a myth. Someone whose head injured from age five gets into the kinds of patterns that Randy got into, including drinking, and doing the wrong things. And because of his own anger and frustration, he doesn't lead a normal life."

What was their reaction to a proper diagnosis? "Relieved, because now I knew what was wrong...It made sense to me when I understood he was hurting every day," Reed said.

"Their diagnosis was that Randy could ultimately go to culinary school. And we believed that he could go back into independent living," his father said. He stayed in that program (in Houston) for about two years then went to one in New Orleans before returning to Atlanta. At that point the family connected with a group offering services for special needs adults, and they placed him in an apartment with a roommate with supervision. "That worked, but not well enough, because he now had a history of all these years of inappropriate behavior that had become ingrained in him. He had varying degrees of success. We learned the term 'as good as it gets'...many times it was horrible," his father said. "He got into inappropriate buying and dialing 900 numbers on the telephone."

"He got in with the wrong crowd, toxic people, and we found out that Randy met this schizophrenic woman, 50 years old, and she introduced him to a friend of hers who was a drug pusher. So he got introduced to cocaine," Hillery said.

About three months before that, "He had really spiraled down to where he was going to lose his job...fighting, had problems all over. One Sunday I picked him up at work at a retirement home. He looked awful, dreadful, unshaven, and his eyes were bloodshot. He was irritable and jumpy. The next day Reed took him to see his psychiatrist and, up to this point, we aren't thinking drugs or alcohol." The doctor recommended that he go to a hospital for treatment.

After being told: "'It's either admit yourself, or you're out on the street,' Randy decided to admit himself into a hospital," his mother explained.

"The hospital detoxed him, and that's when we found out that our son was doing cocaine and drinking. Randy, being this little guy, and with his head injury, one bottle of beer is equal to two six-packs." Reed explained.

Randy next went to a local hospital that had a program for head injuries. After six or seven weeks there they recommended an AA program that he attended for seven weeks.

"He lives in a residential program for people with head injuries, and he receives occupational therapy. He will eventually enter their group home. We learned that some people are addictive and become addicted, or they are abusers. Randy has been labeled an abuser. He wasn't addicted but if he felt bad, he would also drink," Reed explained.

The parents are looking to the future. "That's why we're working so hard to find the right place. We are in a financial position to make sure that Randy can be independent. He is our lot in life, not his siblings' lot, they're not going to accept it nor should they have to. So we have to find where Randy is going to be. The hardest part was coming to the conclusion that Randy needs help 24/7," Reed explained.

Randy is his wife's child from a previous marriage. When she married Reed, he adopted her special needs son. "Hillary and I consider Randy a great blessing in our life. I believe that he was God's gift to me as a learning experience about life," Reed said. "I'm a better man for it."

The couple agreed that there is stress, but that they have handled the problems together. They don't feel that their son's problems have taken a toll on them. "It's your lot in life...we worked it together...It's heart breaking and emotionally taxing," Reed explained.

"I'm more understanding, more compassionate, and have a much greater sensitivity to making the world a better place for everybody. Hillary is very active in all kinds of community efforts," Reed explained. "We're community people."

Connie

Connie was a premature baby who was adopted at birth in 1981. When she was late opening her eyes, her parents became concerned; the ophthalmologist was not. When she was six months old and not developing normally for her age, the pediatrician said she was fine and would catch up. When she was 10 months she had a bad cold and began having seizures that her mother didn't recognize as such. The baby's body twitched, she had difficulty breathing, her body stiffened, and she stared. Her mother, Grace, called the doctor who said "'it's probably a reaction to the medicine she's taking. Don't worry about it, she'll be fine.'"

The following day the baby was worse. When the seizures began occurring every ten minutes Grace called the doctor who repeated his statement. "He never said for us to come in.

"I said, 'this is it, I'm bringing her in.'" Grace marched into the doctor's office without an appointment and said, "There is something wrong with this child. While she was there she had one of these seizures. He said **very off handedly**, 'Oh, yeah, she's definitely having a seizure.' They did a spinal tap right away, which was very traumatic for all of us, and at that point he determined that it was seizures, and that there was something wrong with her brain. We went straight from his office to the hospital and saw a pediatric neurologist. He said, 'I can't even believe that this child is standing up.' Her brain waves were so scrambled.

"She went on anti-seizure medication; it took awhile to find the right kind of medication for her." At about five she stopped having seizures. "The neurologist didn't feel that she was going to develop as a normal adult. He didn't feel that she would develop much past the mental age of six."

When asked what her and her husband's reaction was to this terrible news, she said, "We were destroyed at first, we totally lost it and didn't know what to do. My husband was very supportive. We felt mostly bad for her; I don't think we thought so much of ourselves as we thought for her and what her life would be like. We wanted to make her life as normal as possible, and provide for her in the future. That's our focus and our main concern.

"We started intervention immediately. Connie had speech, physical and occupational therapy, and was enrolled in a special education school. She started talking at three. When she was four she went into the county special ed pre-school program. She graduated with a diploma in special ed. Afterward, she went to the Warm Springs Institute."

Connie is now in an independent living program in a supervised apartment with a roommate. "She's very independent as far as doing for herself. Her mind is still very scrambled, but all in all, she does quite well." She attends a training center and is looking for a job.

"Because we sought help immediately, and talked to other parents, and became part of support groups, it made it easier to accept and to deal with Connie's problems," her mother explained. "We're great believers in support groups. I don't think I could have survived without them."

Grace and her husband have a daughter six years older than Connie. "We tried to protect her from Connie's problems and not have her worry much, but I think it did affect her quite a bit. She had been an only child for six years and this baby came and disrupted her whole life, getting so much attention. At first I think she was a little bit upset that this child was taking a lot of time away from her. I think that as she grew older as a teenager she was embarrassed by her a little bit. She never really talked about it... I think there was some resentment there. I think now they are closer and she's very understanding, but growing up pre-teen and teenager I think it was very hard on her," Grace explained.

When asked if Connie has a social life, her mother said, "Oh, yes. She's very much into dating. I don't think she's had sex, I don't think she's had an opportunity to have any sex. She's never unsupervised. We've spoken to her a lot about what's proper and what's not proper about sex." Her mother worries about her daughter getting pregnant. Connie agreed to have a tubal ligation but then she changed her mind.

"It was a real disappointment because we were really counting on that, it's a big concern to me. She likes the boys and she's got the hormones running through her body just like everybody else does. So do these young men." But as a precaution, she's been on birth control pills.

Dealing with a special needs child made Grace's marriage stronger. "It made us very close. My husband and I really worked together."

When asked how Grace felt raising a special child, she said, "I would feel very guilty about it. It's been very difficult and sometimes I feel, *why did it have to be so difficult, why did I had to go through life like this?* On the other hand, I think, *who would have taken care of her?* Maybe there was a purpose for her coming to us. I feel real good about that. But if I think about it selfishly, it didn't have to be so hard." Her husband didn't want to adopt a second child.

What kind of toll has it taken on her? "Great. Emotionally, physically, I really feel it…stress comes from this situation. I like to think this is my role in life. I don't know what my life would have been like without her. It's changed me from being a very free-thinking person, very optimistic, very outgoing and trusting kind of free spirit to a person whose kind of guarded, worried, not as free, not as happy as I would have been."

Kayla

Kayla, born in Raleigh, NC in 1974, is the second of four children. When she was two and a half she developed an ear infection and her pediatrician placed her on antibiotics; the doctor also noticed that she looked anemic. On a return visit the following week, the doctor noted that the infection had cleared up, but she still looked anemic. "She had been a real vivacious child and she had gotten so quiet and lethargic. She wanted to be held a lot. We ran a blood test, and her hemoglobin was low. Within an hour we learned that she had leukemia," her mother, Lane, said. "I was terrified because cancer for me meant it circulated everywhere.

"We're both devout Christians, and we immediately turned to God and told Him that we knew He was with us, and we would face this. That's the day I grew up. I was no longer a young mother of three children, I was a mother. We just went forward depending on God and taking one step at a time."

Kayla was taken to St. Jude's Children Hospital in Memphis, Tennessee. "She was admitted immediately as high-risk. It was like walking into hell. You could hardly bear the days, but we were surrounded by people who wanted our child well." Kayla underwent chemotherapy and "six weeks of cranial and spinal radiation because the first place that leukemia metastasizes is in your brain and on your spinal cord. It probably caused her head injury.

"I noticed that instead of going up steps one foot after another, she started going up steps one foot at a time. I was an educator, this was just when learning disabilities were first coming out, and I knew that was a backward progression. (At St. Jude's) I brought that up to them and they said, 'This kid has been thrown against the wall, leave her alone'. It didn't affect speech at all, it was motor, it sort of fried her wiring. When she was about four years old, she seemed to sense it because she kept practicing over and over.

"We lived in utter fear of chicken pox fearing it would kill her." The family hung a sign on their door for people not to enter if they were sick. "She got the chicken pox exactly to the month that it was safe for her to get it. She got it kissing her boyfriend who had chicken pox. She gave it to everyone we knew."

Kayla had a seizure disorder but her problems grew slowly. She went to nursery school when she was around five and a half or six, then into school. "But by the second or third grade we really knew we were dealing with something different." Her mother contacted someone in the California school system and received a program called *Score* that was used to teach Spanish-speaking children English. "It was how I taught Kayla to read. Math came slowly but actually that was robbed from her more as she got older because radiation doesn't just start and stop, it has an age. It progresses, and gets worse, it fries longer.

"In fifth grade she went into public school in a general classroom. It wasn't until Kayla was probably in the eighth grade that she moved into low, remedial work. And special dispensations were given to her at that time. She graduated with a special degree."

After graduation Kayla spent about nine months at the Roosevelt Institute in Warm Springs, Georgia. Though there were problems, she did get the experience of being away from home and living in a dormitory, which gave her confidence. The staff was not forthcoming to the parents because at 18 she was an adult. "Kayla was stolen from, (someone) wiped out her checking account. And they knew it was going on, but they couldn't reveal it to us."

When she returned home, she got a job as a dietary assistant in a nursing home. "She worked with a man who wouldn't talk, and she brought him out to where he was talking. When I'm really old, I hope someone like Kayla takes care of me."

Her friends became her sisters' and her brother's friends, but she lacked a social life with her peers. Fortunately, Kayla's parents discovered the Bregman Educational Series at the Atlanta Jewish Family & Children's Services. It offers educational information and socialization for developmentally disabled adults, and their family and caregivers.

"We were really stunned by the network of people in Atlanta. We learned a lot. We found out there was a night they bowled. She loves to bowl." They brought Kayla to Atlanta every Wednesday for three weeks then Kayla said, "'Folks, if Misty can live on her own, I know I can.' We sort of put that off; we said, "Yes you can." After about six weeks she came down one night and said, 'Mommy, Rosemary is grown up, Tina is grown up, Sidney is grown up (her three siblings), I want to grow up.'

"Cal and I talked late into the night...and decided that every fear that we had...money, roommates, jobs, being abused, were exactly the same fears we had for our other children when they were in college. But with Kayla it's exaggerated. We never kept our children from going to college because of our fears." They discussed the situation with the head psychologist at St. Jude's who laughed and said, 'She wants out of there.'

"We contacted JF&CS...she moved into an apartment with a young lady. And we began the tortuous days of letting go of our fears, and letting Kayla grow. I thought I couldn't go a day without talking to or checking on her." Kayla got a job at a Kroger store bagging groceries.

One day Kayla said, "'Well, I've done it, I've done it. I have bought something you would never let me have.' I couldn't think of anything I hadn't let her have except maybe a *Playboy* magazine. I said *Kayla what is it?* 'Tang (the orange drink). I always wanted Tang but you wouldn't buy it.' I call it the great Tang Rebellion."

Lane said that she didn't think Kayla embarrassed her other three children; the oldest was protective. "I think how you perceive your child and how you treat your child will be how your other children treat your special child."

Lane said of her husband, "I got a good one. We did not draw apart we grew closer. Actually, it was almost like going through a jungle together. Probably he suffered more.

"I would have never chosen this path. But it has made my heart so tender," Lane said. "It's so damned hard. Not hard on me, it's hard on Kayla. Once I told Cal that I have one really big problem with heaven. I know when you get to heaven everything's perfect. I want her perfect but I don't want her changed. It's immensely challenging, the great fear is when we die and leave them behind.

"I'm a lot more serious than I was. This was mortal battle; this was fighting a real enemy, a real dragon (leukemia). It could destroy her life, destroy her thought, destroy our family, and destroy a good citizen. I just threw down ribbons and flowers and picked up a shield and sword, and would do it again in a minute. The toll would be that I'm a more serious soldier."

Lane said that she would not have missed this journey. It strengthened the family, "We pay very close attention to people's needs. We've been there and we've been helped."

Chapter 4

Children with various forms of Palsy

"I was going to pay if the cake was good."

"Cerebral palsy is a complete or partial paralysis of the muscles [primarily of the limbs]. It is caused by a brain abnormality." In children, the extent of their disability differs. "Many of these children have some degree of mental retardation, although some others are highly intelligent. Children with this disorder may also have some degree of hearing loss, visual defects, most often crossed eyes and convulsions... Cerebral palsy may result from abnormal development of the brain or from brain damage that occurred before, during or shortly after birth." (1)

Ataxia results in "Poor coordination and unsteadiness due to the brain's failure to regulate the body's posture and regulate the strength and direction of limb movements. Ataxia is usually due to disease in the brain, specifically in the cerebellum, which lies beneath the back part of the cerebrum." (2)

Keenan

During her pregnancy, Elizabeth took Coracidin for her allergies. "I wasn't thinking about the labels...I didn't realize that aspirin was in there. In my seventh month I began to feel like I had the flu, I was getting pale...I was bleeding internally from the aspirin. Finally, when I collapsed on the bathroom floor, I was rushed to the hospital, and had to have nine units of blood. The remainder of the pregnancy and delivery (1971) were non-eventful, and Keenan was born with no obvious problems.

"When I took him into my office (at work) to show everybody, one of the psychologists in the office was tracking his eyes. At that time he should have been able to follow something from left to right, and he wasn't following it. As a mother it stuck in my mind, oh, no, his eyes were crossed. That was the first thing I noticed."

Keenan began developing slowly and the babysitters called it to her attention that he just sat and watched the other children. "The pediatrician wasn't picking anything up."

But by the time Keenan was three years old, his mother was not only concerned about his eyes, but with his speech and lack of coordination. The parents took him to the University of Nebraska Medical Center for tests. "A lot of times the pediatrician said he would outgrow it, and the ophthalmologist couldn't quite get a handle on his eyes." He was finally diagnosed with slight cerebral palsy.

A friend who worked with the handicapped took her aside and said, "'I think Keenan may have some problems, and you need to think about maybe a special kind of school.' When I told my husband, an experimental psychologist, he said, 'What! She must be a miracle worker if she can detect that. There are no tests to detect that. If she can detect that at this age then she ought to patent it.' He was in complete denial.

"I was sad. My style of dealing with problems is just to say *okay, here we are, here it is, what do we need to do next* instead of falling apart. We slowly accepted the idea that he was going to be slow and that he would need extra help." Elizabeth feels that the trauma of the prenatal hemorrhaging caused Keenan to suffer from anoxia that caused the cerebral palsy.

Keenan was placed in a regular preschool program where he was slower than, and not as aware as the other children. "All through school, my fear was that Keenan would be picked on, bullied, ridiculed, and laughed at. It just hurts you inside to think this is going to happen to your child. Probably some of those things did happen, but he had such positive experiences in school, and people tended to leave him alone. People didn't try to take advantage of him.

"He knows he's disabled, but he doesn't know how he looks to others. He's not aware of his body and how he comes across.

"He would love to find a girl to love." Though he has what his mother described as "acquaintance friends," she feels that "A big part of his life is missing...He would make somebody a wonderful boyfriend," she said proudly.

Keenan lives at home, participates in the "Just" People program, and has worked in the county library system for over seven years. "He loves his job and they love him."

Like other parents, Elizabeth worries about the future. "I've got to get him living independently with a roommate...probably with a caseworker once a week...I've got to get the finances lined up." Meanwhile, she's working with him to prepare him to live independently on such things as teaching him to cook and do his laundry.

Keenan's sister "has been very protective of him...I think there was some times when she was embarrassed, and might even to this day still be embarrassed in certain situations. Overall, I've seen her take up for him.

"I divorced in 1984, and a lot of it had to do with Keenan... His dad had low self-esteem. He would verbalize that he couldn't handle having a son like Keenan, it reflected on him. He wanted to be the perfect man with the perfect son. He is so into himself. He wasn't that good with kids. He basically loves him his son. I think it was just totally painful for him to have Keenan as his son.

"You carry the burden of, gosh, it's too bad this happened, but you don't think about that everyday, all the time. You just do it," Elizabeth said. "The emotional toll is that one of your children has to go through life with this set of handicaps. You go back and say, *why in the world didn't I know aspirin could do that to you, why didn't we go to the doctor sooner?* I don't dwell on that. Keenan is such a pleasant person, such a willing helper, such an upbeat personality that I can't say that it has taken a toll on me. It's a toll on him because it's a struggle, but he's making the best of it.

"It (the experience) makes you much more open to differences in people…I think I have a broader personality, and just an appreciation of different types of people. You don't have to be perfect, just be more open."

Blair

"We perceived Blair (born in 1968) to have no problems until somewhere around nine months when she started pulling up in the playpen and would fall over backwards instead of the normal crumbling. We decided it was either eyes or ears. So we had them checked and everything was normal," her mother, Gillian, said. When Blair tried pulling up on the furniture, "she would miss tables, and would miss the end of the sofa. Then we thought there was something wrong with her perception. I would've looked like an abusive mother because she always looked beaten up. Her speech was slow, but we didn't think too much of it because she was the third child." Her older sister and brother were all right.

When Blair was around 13 or 14 months old, her parents took her to see a pediatric neurologist. "He said that he really didn't see anything particular in her delayed speech, and her delayed walking that was obvious." So Blair was admitted to the local children's hospital for a 24-hour urine drip to see if there was a chemical answer to her problems.

The neurologist said her cerebellum was damaged. "'I would suggest institutionalizing her, you have other children.'" Shocked, Gillian said to the doctor, "Wait a minute!" Rod, her husband, added, "He was very rude and very cold."

"We stormed out of there, saying "we don't throw away kids in our family," Gillian said. "He said Blair was unable to put this puzzle together, therefore, she needs institutionalization. The only thing that we ever got from him, which didn't help us, was that she had a learning disability. We all knew that what she had was worse than a learning disability; it was across the board, delayed speech, fine motor, and gross motor. Rod and I basically did what we could do on our own.

"We cried a lot, we were devastated, we had to find something. We said that she needs to be with other children," Gillian said. "We had despair, we were young parents and it was pretty scary, and we thought there were no answers," Rod confessed. They finally got a diagnosis for Blair of ataxia palsy.

When Blair was three, they sent her to a private nursery school. "She (the director) said, 'There's nothing we can do for Blair, but you need a break.' Then I went down the list of pre-schools and found one that was receptive. I said, 'take her, she needs to be with other children.' The kids kind of helped her along," Gillian explained. "She was a little bit destructive just because of her gross motor problems."

Blair then went for testing at the local speech school in the Atlanta area, and the parents were told the program was not for her. "They were very arrogant. They said she would not fit in their program, she needed much more. Nobody ever said the word retarded," Gillian said.

"She looked bright, she was pretty, and she wasn't spastic. No one ever suggested anything. No one would ever tell us what to do. By that time we were so used to running the show and finding the places, we didn't even need them anymore," Gillian explained. She looked for a private school in the Yellow Pages of the telephone book, and found Arbor Academy, Inc. Blair was enrolled and completed the program. Afterward, she was placed into public school special education classes.

Blair's parents did everything possible to help her. They found a special education teacher and offered her a place to live in exchange for tutoring Blair while attending graduate school. The child had eye exercises to correct a lazy eye, and occupational and speech therapy. She took therapeutic horseback riding, and attended summer camp in the Poconos. "We did it all. But no one told us this is where you should go. Everything was from word of mouth from other people rather than from professionals," Gillian said. Blair still has problems walking. "She could be picked up for walking under the influence."

Blair attended a private school in New York for four years. "It was a great experience for her...she learned community living skills. When she returned home she got a job at Australian Body Works...she was a janitor...she did some day care...she worked three days a week...and I said this isn't enough for her," Gillian said. "Then she got a job at Kroger and got there by bus. Blair got fired from Kroger for stealing a cake and standing there and eating it. She said, 'I was going to pay if the cake was good.'" Then she got a job in another grocery store.

"I begged Rod, that while we were alive and had strict control, we needed to start moving her away from us and into independent living. Rod was very much against it." However, Gillian prevailed. They moved Blair into a house they owned, and got her a roommate, and a counselor, who lived there rent-free. The girls were taught to cook, iron and clean. Later a third girl moved in, and the counselor moved out. Then the parents swapped the house for one in a new subdivision.

"When Blair moved into that brand new, beautiful house, Leslie (their other daughter) who lives in a dump, said, 'I cannot believe that my handicapped sister has a Jacuzzi, and a two-car garage, and she doesn't even have a car. I've got a hand me down car, with no garage. Now, what is wrong with this picture? I graduated from Auburn with a double degree.'

"Blair made better choices than you, Leslie," her mother said. "Leslie said that Blair's been faking all these years," her father added, laughing.

Blair is involved in the "Just" People program. "She has a wonderful social life from this organization. It's the most important thing that has happened to her," her mother said. Blair now lives in an apartment in the "Just" People Village. "Nobody is able to depend on their other children. They have a life, they have kids, they can't do the job that we do," Rod said.

Gillian said her son "Tucker was a champion with Blair, even in junior high he would take her to the movies." But her daughter had problems dealing with a handicapped sister. "It was a little harder on her because she was at the age when most of her friend's mothers were very spontaneous." When they went shopping she had to drag Blair along. "That was very tough on Leslie...And she didn't know how to handle that...She was never unkind to Blair."

Both parents are pleased with how far Blair has come. "It's certainly not what you and I would choose, but from where she was when she was not expected to walk or talk, she's a tax-paying citizen with no government subsidies, and makes good money. We had despair when we were young parents. It was pretty scary and we thought there was no answer. Now she's still handicapped but we've grown with her, and we have a lot of confidence that she does have skills.

"I think in a way it brought us together in a more mature way. It was so hard for Gillian being with it all in the early years all the time. We had the normal amount of fussing. When we were worn out we'd get into arguments, but not about Blair's problems," Rod explained.

"It was very stressful," Gillian confessed. "My mother had never interfered in our marriage, never advised, one of those very smart mother-in-laws, she liked him more than she liked me. One day I got in the car, took off up that hill and left Rod with Blair, and let it all hang out on 400 (expressway). I was going whining to my mother."

When Rod called her mother and said his wife was upset and on her way over, "She said to me, 'Rod, why don't y'all just get divorced?'"

"We had some of those times when you just want to run. I never wanted to split from him," Gillian confessed. "Having a handicapped child is probably one of the most stressful things on a marriage. I would say that 70% of the people that I've known have divorced, it's just very stressful."

"Blair's my buddy. Gillian has to be the guide, the disciplinarian if she gets off tract," Rod, said. "I think Gillian and I both enjoy Blair in a lot of ways." Gillian added, honestly, "We enjoy her now because we don't have to be with her every day, and we know she's got a very good life. You still have fears that go on and on, but you have joy with the handicapped child." Rod added, "We're looking now to what will happen to her when we're gone."

When asked what toll it had taken on her, Gillian said, "Look at me!"

"There are a lot of people our age we see going to Europe and going on safaris, and we're limited somewhat even now," Rod explained. "We're not spontaneous with things that are big," Gillian added.

When asked how the experience had made her different, Gillian explained, "It has made me a more persevering person, one that doesn't like to see a job not all the way to the end. I find joy in Blair. The biggest crush in my life was not Blair, but Tucker (their son) dying. That probably changed me inside more."

"We had adapted to Blair. Tucker's death was almost the end of our lives. The thought of doing something that would have been stupid came to mind. Blair helped us in a way get through the crisis of Tucker because we were needed, and we were also involved with other people who had common challenges," Rod explained. "I see some of my peers... they have a lot of frivolous things that they are involved in. I'm not trying to put them down, but it kind of gets to the point where you say, 'y'all are playing fun and games, and this is serious, life has become pretty serious.'"

One of the funniest stories I heard was from these parents who were very concerned that their daughter might become pregnant, and made the decision to have her undergo a tubal ligation. After talking to her, they had a professional counsel her so that she would understand that she was going to have the procedure to prevent pregnancy. Blair agreed to have the surgery.

Then they went to the surgeon. "He said, 'Blair, you have to sign this waiver saying that you have been counseled, and this is of your own free will, and that you will go through the tubal ligation.' She said, 'Well, I've changed my mind. I don't think I want to sign. I love children.'"

Gillian looked at her daughter in disbelief, then screamed, "Sign the fucking paper!"

Brock

Though the umbilical cord was wrapped around Brock's neck, no problems were noticeable at his birth in 1970. "When he was about a year old, he developed a very high temperature," Conner said of his son. In the hospital emergency room his fever rose to 106 or 107 degrees and was finally brought down with ice water baths. "When he was about six or seven we noticed that he was not acting normally." His parents took him to a medical center where he was put through all the disciplines.

Brock was diagnosed with a minor case of cerebral palsy. "He doesn't really have good control of fine muscular activity." The doctors felt that the damage was caused by a spontaneous event and that there would be no further loss of functioning. Unable to recommend anything, they suggested letting him grow as he could.

"We went through a lot of soul-searching and we went through an awful lot of looking back and saying 'what have we done...what might it have been like had things been different?' You can only go through so much of that because you don't know what happened; you don't know what you could have done differently. The next thing is you accept it and say 'let's go on from here and let's do the best we can for Brock. Let's see how far he can go.'"

Brock went through school in special education classes. His speech is good but his money skills are poor. "His mental awareness is very good in a lot of areas. He will come out with words and phrases that you'd never expect him to know, but that he has heard somewhere, and he says them correctly. He has slight mental retardation, not bad."

When he was young, Brock attended regular Sunday school. When the family moved to Illinois "we fell out of the habit of going to church until one day Brock said, "'I want to go back to church.' It was Brock who got us back into the church," his father said.

When Brock was fifteen, he developed a very rapid form of scoliosis, a lateral curving of the spine. He underwent surgery and a Harrington Rod was placed in his spine. "It was very traumatic and there was a long recuperation period."

Afterward, he returned to school but had a terrible time. When he was expelled for behavior problems, the parents blamed it on the surgery. A home teacher was brought in to work with him. Then, as a result of his parents going head to head with the school system for not providing a proper education for their son, they were allowed to choose which school they thought was best, and the school system agreed to pay.

The high school intake coordinator said to them, "'We can put him into the school, but what plans do you have for him after he's 21?' We never thought about it. Then she said, 'We can keep him until he's aged 21 but then if you have no plans for him it's very, very difficult because most of these young adults will just sit at home and vegetate around the television set the rest of their lives.' So she took us over and introduced us to the residential part of Little Friends. We signed up then and there. There was something like an eight-year waiting list to get into Little Friends," Conner explained.

"He's three years older than his younger brother who he just idolizes." His brother left for college at the same time Brock got into the residential program, so their parents equated it to both boys going off on their own.

Brock lived in Little Friends housing until he was diagnosed with colon cancer at the age of 28. After surgery, multiple infections and chemotherapy, he moved into an apartment and works in the Spectrum sheltered workshop. He's been employed in the community as a hotel dishwasher, and at McDonalds, but his physical problems made these jobs difficult.

To celebrate Brock's recovery, the family took a trip to Europe. Because Brock loved his previous Disney World trip, they planned their tour around Neuschwanstein Castle, King Lugwig's fairytale castle in Bavaria copied by Disney for Snow White's castle in Florida. When they returned home he asked, "'Where are we going next?' He said he wanted to go someplace new."

Conner said that the three brothers are close, and the other two know that when the parents are no longer around that Brock becomes their responsibility. One son has even offered to have Brock come live with him, but his parents feel that that is not in his best interest.

Brock has not really dated, but does have a girlfriend at his sheltered workshop. "One of the girls at Little Friends, a number of years ago, latched onto Brock for some reason and wanted to get married and she gave him a ring. Brock really isn't interested in marriage," his father said.

"I think overall our marriage is probably stronger because of having Brock. I'm still here. I think it strengthens a marriage if it's something you jointly face. It's a challenge.

"You always regret that Brock's not able to do the things that the other siblings can do. And you always wish he could. The one regret that I have is that when he was much younger I didn't understand his difficulties. You always wonder if you've done the best for him, you always hope you have. As far as raising a special child, I think there is an unconditional love there, and I see the love that he has for his siblings and family...It's different experience," Conner explained.

"I hope it's made me more tolerant of others, and made me a better person. I look at Brock, and every time I see someone complaining about their life I just say, *life isn't fair. If you don't believe me, come take a look at Brock.*

"Brock has three siblings that are smart, capable, wealthy, and physically fit. And Brock has these problems that he didn't bring on himself, they were brought upon him. He knows he's different. He knows he's not able to go out and work and get married and have children. I think that it's difficult for him. It makes me cry at times to think about how unfair life can be to some of these people."

Chapter 5

Children with Encephalitis and Meningitis

"Meningitis is an inflammation of the meninges, which are membranous coverings of the brain and spinal cord… [and] occurs when the cerebrospinal fluid becomes infected, causing inflammation of the meninges." (1)

Lee

Everything was normal until Lee (born in 1949) came down with meningitis when he was seven months old. His mother, Judith, thinks he picked it up at the doctor's office. After spending a month in the hospital, the doctor "told me to forget about him and put him in an institution. He also said that Lee would be a vegetable because he'd been deprived of oxygen for some time. I told the doctor that he was as crazy as he looked. *Not my baby. What makes you think I'm going to put my baby in some kind of institution?* The doctor said he would never progress past the age of six years old."

Lee was the fourth boy out of 11 children, and they were glad to have him. "Everything he did we made a big thing of it...In a big family whatever happens, happens."

By the time he went to pre-school, "he was doing, developmentally, everything his brothers were doing at that age." Then he went to public school. "He was like everybody else...of course he wasn't really. We always considered him an exceptional person and we thought he was great."

When Lee's parents were told to look into special education, they chose The Northside School and he did well. When the private school folded, he returned to public high school and was placed in the special education program.

Judith was one of the founders of a Methodist church in Atlanta, and she made sure that there was a special Sunday school program for her son.

When Lee was 20 he went to work for the post office where, for 31 years, he sorted mail and loaded and unloaded trucks. He retired when he had what his mother called a ruptured appendix, but it was cancer.

Lee's siblings have been wonderful to him. Once when a friend came to visit his brother, Paul, the boy made some ugly comments. "Paul said he would never have him over again," Judith said. His siblings were very protective; they even took him to work with them.

"He was always expected to do his part in the family, and he did. He writes in a journal every single day, every now and then we get to hear it," his sister-in-law, Edith, said.

"I was just so thrilled that Lee was alive. He might've been handicapped to some people but he wasn't handicapped to me," his mother said proudly. The parents just threw Lee into the hopper with the rest of their ten children. She thinks that's why he developed so well.

Lee lived at home until he died of cancer in 2002.

Daniel

Daniel (born in 1969) came down with meningitis when he was six weeks old. "That's what left him brain damaged," his mother, Lillian, said of her youngest child. When it was diagnosed that he had hydrocephalus, water on the brain, a pediatric neurologist at an Atlanta children's hospital operated on him. The doctor told the parents, "'It's liable to go away and nothing will be wrong, we just have to watch him for two or three years to see how he develops…. Some of the cells around the casing of the brain regenerate and some don't,'" his father, Ivan, added.

By the age of three Daniel seemed to be developmentally normal for his age, but there were problems. "He was uncontrollable. He didn't accept discipline of any kind, was in constant motion, and didn't sleep. He spoke better and earlier than our other children; spoke in full sentences. But he'd take his mattress off his bed, stand it up, and strip the sheets off the bed. He dumped drawers. He couldn't play with toys, and didn't know how to play," his mother explained.

Regular nursery school didn't work for Daniel so he was placed at Arbor Academy. "I went to pick him up one day and they told me what a bad day he had, and I came home and was hysterical." She was referred to a child psychologist who, after an evaluation, said the child had some brain damage. "I was just glad that someone told me that I wasn't crazy, that there was something wrong with the child, because I felt that there was something wrong with me because I couldn't control him," Lillian said.

"In the beginning I thought it was just a behavior problem and there was nothing wrong with him," Ivan said. "More or less you have a guilt trip that maybe if you were here (his business frequently took him out of town) you could've prevented this but you don't know. At first I was denying it, figuring that he's just a rotten kid, spoiled. He's extraordinarily beautiful, precocious; he could have been a model."

Daniel went to the county training center, then to a class at the local speech school for a year. "It was a disaster," Lillian said. "I don't think they knew what they were doing," her husband added. "They said maybe its coordination problems, and then they saw he was well coordinated."

"The speech school thought he had psychological problems. They brought in a psychiatrist or psychologist who was a total incompetent. Daniel didn't know how to play because he couldn't relate to toys. So he would put puppets in the oven and they took this as some deep-rooted psychological thing, and told me we should go to a psychological facility. I didn't believe them. I didn't think they were correct, so I didn't pursue that," Lillian said.

"Later on they saw that one of the areas of the brain that was affected was his spatial orientation," Ivan said.

Daniel went into public school special education classes, and then boarded at a private school because of "his behavioral problems… where he would get a more structured environment. It helped a good bit, but in some ways, it was a hindrance because he was picking up other children's behavior traits," Ivan said. He returned to public school where, in the upper grades, he was taught job skills.

"When he got older we sent him to (a facility in) Pennsylvania. This place really got him on the road because they didn't take any guff from these kids. Very structured. It was like a farm. It calmed him down, he was a new person. He stayed there until he was 20 or 21." Then Daniel went to a school in Haddonfield, New Jersey for three or four years. "It was outstanding. They were the ones who said that ultimately Daniel could live on his own…they had told us that he could probably work in food service, a fast food place," both parents explained. While there he worked in a restaurant, and they secured a job for him in Atlanta before graduation.

Today he works at a Holiday Inn "washing pots and pans," Lillian and Ivan said. He lives in an apartment with a roommate and is affiliated with the "Just" People program.

Daniel's brother, Jason, is "very caring, very loving even to this day," Ivan said. "Once when he was young, a boy in his carpool said something negative about Daniel. Jason, who is very peaceable, took the boy by the neck and threw him out of the car when they came to the kid's house to drop him off." Lillian apologized to the boy's mother.

Daniel is "a very social person, I think he knows he's supposed to date. I don't think he knows how to handle it," his mother said. "One night he called us up...I said, 'Where are you?' And he said, 'K-Mart.' He was with his girlfriend buying her a ring," Lillian said. "It was a friendship ring," his father added.

"I think it affected it our marriage greatly in the sense of our freedom, our ability to do things when we want to," Ivan said. "He either has a doctor's appointment, or an analyst appointment. You're ready to ask why did this happen to me, but it happened. You woke up one morning and you had this problem."

"I think it plays hell on a marriage. It plays hell on your life. It's a drain, it's very difficult," Lillian said honestly.

"We made a decision that we didn't want to institutionalize our child. It puts a strain on a household, on a marriage and on a normal way of life. It's the cards that you were dealt and you can either be a quitter or you can be a stayer. You stay and make it work," Ivan added.

Lillian admitted there had been a toll raising Daniel. "I think it has determined what I did. I think I would have liked to have made more of my life personally. Gone back to school again earlier than I did, possibly to have been able to take different jobs, take jobs earlier. I didn't because I was responsible for Daniel's transportation and a lot of the daily activity."

Ivan worries about what will happen to their son when there are no longer here. "How is he's going to be able to take care of himself?"

Lillian heard a father of a special needs child say on TV something like, "'You don't want your child to predecease you,' but in Daniel's case it wouldn't be so bad. I hate to say it; at least you'd know he was taken care of."

Chapter 6

Children with Marfan Syndrome

"Handicapped people are surprisingly progressive and are doing things that people don't expect them to do," a parent

"Marfan syndrome is a disorder of the protein fibrous tissue known as collagen that gives blood vessels and heart valves their strength. This causes weakness of the heart valves, especially the aortic and mitral valves, and of the aorta. Children with this disorder grow tall and thin. The lenses in their eyes may also be displaced." (1)

Darren

Marsha and Gray noticed that when Darren was born in 1971, "His eyes looked like sunsets. He was long, and skinny and spidery. His ears were like cauliflowers, and there was a tendon that had not been released in his finger. We were told that maybe he had some chromosome deficiency. So we watched and waited to see what would happen. We were so scared and worried," Marsha said.

The parents had him tested at a local children's hospital. "He had every test in the book, and found that there was not a single thing medically that they could find wrong with him, including no chromosomal deficiency," Marsha explained. "We were worried because one of the doctors had said maybe his life expectancy would not be all that long. I watched him every day like a hawk."

Darren was developmentally slow. "He didn't walk or talk for a long time. We switched doctors when he was a year or two and that's when we discovered the Marfans, the spidery features of the muscular/skeletal system. Sometimes they can have heart failure; the heart valve stops working, (fortunately that did not apply to Darren). He plays sports, he jogs, and he walks the dog. He's really surprised us."

Even with proper diagnosis there was nothing medically that could be done. "No one wanted to put a label on him and say what his expectations were, because it was at a time when the doctors were leery about giving a specific diagnosis and saying what would happen. They were just discovering that handicapped people are surprisingly progressive and doing things that people don't expect them to do.

"Can you imagine, this is our only son. We had two older daughters. My husband, wanting a son...was totally wiped out and discouraged. We were unhappy, and there was nothing either one of us could do about it."

Darren went to a local speech school in the Atlanta area for further diagnosis, and they recommended a local private school where he stayed until he was around 11 years old. He was then sent to a school in New York City for about ten years. Next, he went to a residential school in Kentucky until 1998, "but that was marking time. He didn't get anywhere, he really just existed. So we realized the best thing for him was to be home and integrated into the community."

Back home in Atlanta he attended various sheltered workshops. "We were very, very pleased. They put him on work projects. Then they had a job coach who went out in the community with him to try and find a job. They found a job at Publix (grocery store)."

Scott lives at home but his parents are preparing for the future. "We're thinking group home or supervised living, apartment living, and I have two daughters who are going to be back ups. They are both fully aware of their responsibilities."

Darren's sisters, "were embarrassed by him when they became preteens," Marsha said. When Darren returned home from boarding school his parents indulged him. "Being a special kid, we have overdone it. We catered more to him than the others, and the other children resented it."

Darren is "crazy about girls, he's had three or four girlfriends and doesn't really know how to relate, or care about them, he cares about his needs...He's egotistic. We're working on trying to get him to think of others before himself."

How did Darren affect her marriage? "For years I was worried about the relationship," Marsha said honestly. "My husband left a lot of it up to me and avoided much of the interaction. My husband was a pilot, and when he came home he really didn't want to hear about the trouble Darren had gotten into, so I felt like I was alone much of the time. And I didn't appreciate that. It hasn't been a wonderful marriage, but whose is? I don't know if it had anything to do with Darren or not. I think he avoided Darren for a long time. Being a macho man, he didn't want his son to be like that. He couldn't handle it. But now that my husband is retired he's trying to make up for lost time.

"I feel like a heroine. I feel like, wow, I've done pretty well. There's still a lot of work to do, but people have told me numerous times, 'my gosh, you have the patience of Job. How do you deal with it?' You must when you have a special child. I always thought of myself as a very calm, patient person, but now I'm discovering that my patience wears thin. It seems to be getting harder at my age. I get frustrated faster. At times I would scream and holler.

"I have a wonderful understanding, and caring, and loving for special people which I probably never would have had. I can empathize and sympathize, go through all the emotions. I have a great respect for people who have handicaps, and to see their progress is unbelievable.

"We go to church every Sunday and Darren's the instigator," Marsha said. "When he was at boarding school, I asked during one phone conversation, 'Have you been going to church?' He said. 'Yea. I go on the van with lots of other kids and we go on Saturday.' I said, 'Saturday, you go to church on Saturday?' He said, 'Yes, and I wear a little hat on my head, and this is the song I sing.'…It was a Jewish temple…He wanted to go to church, and any church would do. He loves music and he sits in the front row and sings loud, it's not really on key."

Renee

Renee, born in 1969, was colicky and was throwing up. "She had that projectile vomiting (pyloric stenosis)," her mother, Marian explained. Concerned about these and other problems the infant was having, Marion went to the pediatrician.

"I said *she's not holding her head up right.* He kept telling me, 'Oh, your other (three) kids were just too advanced, she's just immature.' I said, *Okay, I'll buy this for a little while...but if we don't see some progress here, I'm going be pushing for more.* This is a mother's intuition talking here. I knew that something wasn't right. A couple or three weeks later I took her back in and said, *we need to find out what's going on here, something is very, very wrong. She should be holding up her head better than she is...she's eating...but she's not gaining.*"

The pediatrician admitted Renee to the hospital and it was discovered that her pancreas was not functioning correctly. The doctors said, "'She has what appears to be Marfan syndrome, and a little bit of cerebral palsy...' They said she will probably have a perceptual handicap where she'll try to fit into spaces that are too small, won't be able to see depth...They said her heart is very weak,...her muscles are not there. They called it congenital benign hypotonia. They said she would probably be a vegetable." Hypotonia is "Decreased muscle tone and strength that results in floppiness...(it) is a common finding with cerebral palsy and other neuromuscular disorders." (2)

"I wouldn't let them talk in the room with her, and they thought I was a little bit fluky for that. I said, *I don't want her to hear anything you have to say because I don't know that you're gonna be accurate, and I don't want this baby, who I know understands everything that's said, to hear anything.* So I made them do everything in another room. I said '*I don't buy that she's going to be a vegetable, and I don't buy that there's nobody at home in there, because when I look in her eyes she's very there. She's very alert and very much interested in what's going on around her.*

"Meanwhile I was questioning and reading everything I could get my hands on. I called everywhere including the University of Illinois, and finally got into their system.

"The doctors started her on an artificial enzyme, and she started to gain weight. They told me I was dreaming that she would be able to do more than what they were telling me. I worked with her. I did a lot of massage work with her; I kept moving her arms and her legs. I was studying as fast as I could about everything and anything having to do with her condition.

"When they said she would never roll over I knew they were all wrong. Within two weeks after they said that, she rolled over (at about six months). So I went trotting back in there with her and interrupted the doctor's whole day and *said I need to see you for just five minutes*. I put a blanket on the floor, and laid her down on the blanket. He said 'I don't understand why you're doing that, she's not going anywhere?' I put a toy just out of her reach and over she went. I watched his mouth go, 'whoa'. I said, *We're not done yet, we'll be back in a few weeks with a few more tricks, but I just want you to know that so far you've been wrong.* He said, 'Hey, I'm happy to be wrong. Whatever you're doing, keep it up.' So I just kept doing what I was doing."

Renee gained weight and continued to progress. Glasses were prescribed to correct her eyes. She was about two years old before she slept through the night and that left her mother exhausted and worried.

Then it was discovered she was hyperpyrexic. Her internal thermostat was broken, and she'd spike fevers up to 105 degrees. They were in and out of the hospital with each new fever episode. "Every time I turned around she was going to die, and she came close about three times." Marian continued to work with Renee. The doctors feel that there "is some kind of syndrome because she's got parts of several things; part Marfan, part cystic fibrosis, part cerebral palsy, part God knows what all else.

"I saw in a dream that she would stand, I had this dream over and over. I would go in her room and she would be standing up in her crib and holding on for dear life not knowing how she got there or what to do now that she was there. Sure enough, one morning when she was about 18 months old, I went in and there she was just as I had seen her. I stood there and cried. I said, My God you did it girl, good for you." She took Renee to Easter Seal for speech and physical therapy, and at three she walked.

Her husband's reactions to their child were adverse, and a year after Renee's birth, the couple divorced. "He spun out, he just kept saying, 'I couldn't possibly have had a child that's not perfect.' He couldn't handle it. He got very psychotic; it was just a nightmare. I left because he was getting extremely dangerous, and the psychiatrist said, 'you have to get out of there.' He said he could snap any minute and I could be dead...I reacted with fear.

"My whole fear was that she was going to die and I was not going to let her die. On one level I knew that with all the love that she could get, we would get her through. I didn't know what we would get her through to. I had no idea what the future was going to bring."

When Renee was seven, she developed scoliosis, curvature of the spine, underwent surgery, and had to wear leg braces. Today she is only four feet tall and walks without braces.

Renee went through school in special education classes. She has basic math skills, and reads on about the third grade level. During her last two years of school she began working at Little Friends' Spectrum sheltered workshop in Downers Grove, Illinois.

After graduating from school, Renee worried about her future. "She was all upset, she kept asking, 'Now what am I going to do?' She thrives on the social interactions of school and work...she was very, very depressed. When I asked her what she wanted to do, she said 'I want my own apartment and I want to work, and I want a car...and of course get married and have children.' "

Marian's first choice was Little Friends, and Renee was accepted in the Community Living Facility. Her dorm mates were so happy to see her, they helped her unpack, and threw her a welcoming party. "I felt so good. She was happy; she was smiling from ear to ear. And I said, *Oh thank you God, this is a blessing.* A piece of me felt a little bit concerned about how she was going to do this, but the bigger chunk of me knew she was going to do it. I thought *I'm so thankful*. Then this big sigh of relief came over me because I thought *thank God, she's now got a place where she can be, and become all that she can be with like kind of people.* I felt really good about it…She's loved it ever since."

Today Renee is in a Little Friend's group home and still works at the workshop. "At that point she met her boyfriend…about 15 years older and about three times her size…they just love each other. They've talked about getting married for years, I don't think that's a possibility. Neither one can live by themselves. She's on the birth control pill."

Marian said that her youngest son "was Renee's watchdog more than the other three." He would lie on the floor next to her "and share dreams with her. "The three older ones took care of her but at one point they resented her, they didn't want anybody to know. But everybody who met her, including their friends, loved her. My kids had to get over the fact that she was a stigma on them.

"Her older sister stepped away and stayed away from her for many years, and it's just in the last year that I put my foot down. She only lives ten minutes away and had never gone to see her."

When Marian was in Chicago a few years ago she confronted her daughter and said that she needed to do things for Renee even if it was just taking her out for ice cream. "I said, 'this is the real world, this is your sister. Fortunately, your children are all fine and normal. But had one not been, what would you have done?'

"At some point in time I think I came to a realization that the parents of handicapped children are chosen. You are chosen because of your own strengths and your own faith; otherwise, you couldn't do it. At that point in life I felt very honored. I used to scratch my head and think, *how am I going to do this?* My main concern was, *what am I gonna do when she gets older and I get older, where will she go?*

Marian said that when Renee was growing up, "I think I did pretty doggoned good. I was pretty stressed out. My other kids stressed me more than she did…they tried it all.

"In the early stages it took quite a toll. It took years off me. It wore me out. It was exhausting. I think I lost ten, 20 years off my life there for awhile, because I was really worried. Renee didn't sleep for many years and even after she did sleep, she didn't sleep very long. That part was very exhausting. Now, when she comes home, I find it very exhausting after a day or so, I'm really tired. I don't have the energy to deal with it.

How did Marian deal with her problems? "I think it's made me explore a lot of avenues spiritually and medically and esoterically than I would have before. I had a lot of natural healing abilities that came to the fore when she came along. I had used them unconsciously for many years. People used to bring me their kids and after I'd rock them, they would be fine. It wasn't until Renee that things started happening. I started paying attention. I thought, *I've got some gifts here that I've been ignoring*...that was one big thing she did for me, it was a wakeup call there. Spiritual growth I think was my biggest change, and opening those doorways."

Chapter 7
Kazmier Syndrome

Kazmier syndrome is a condition where some genes are broken.

Hoke

Hoke (born in 1959), the fourth of five children, was slow in his development. When he entered kindergarten at five years old, "He couldn't tie his shoes and would get very frustrated." After only one week, the principal called his parents and asked to see them. "My husband and I went in and she said, 'I have to tell you that we think Hoke is retarded.' It was like dropping a bomb. I was just stunned. I thought, I knew he was slow but couldn't imagine anything like that," his mother, Betsy, said.

"I immediately told a dear friend and she was a great source of comfort to me. She said, 'you know, the Lord doesn't drop these children just anywhere. You should feel very special because evidently you can handle it.' So I thought, *Hum, well, I'll see*. I didn't cry. I think it bothered my husband more. I think it's harder for a man to digest this kind of information.

"We went to a psychologist shortly thereafter, and had Hoke tested. The doctor said, 'Well, he's brain damaged, he will maybe achieve a sixth grade level. Intelligence-wise, he comes out about five years old which was where he was at the time. He said that Hoke will be able to get along pretty well.' He had no idea where the problem came from. He said, 'You can take him to Duke, and go through that whole thing, and put yourself and your family through it, but he's still going to be the same.'"

When Hoke was in first grade, their youngest son, who was in kindergarten, said to his mother, "'Mom, the teacher told me that Hoke's retarded.' I said, 'well, let's talk about it.' So, that night at the table we had a discussion. I said, 'Yes, Hoke is retarded.' Hoke said, 'I'm not retarded, I can hear.' We felt we needed to tell Hoke that he was special because his life was going to be so different than everybody else."

President John F. Kennedy was in office and developmentally disabled people "were just beginning to be taken out of the closet because of the information about his sister Rosemary. For the first time the mentally retarded were talked about publicly.

"So we tried to find services for Hoke. The only place we could find in Charlotte (North Carolina) that had any services for Hoke were for profoundly retarded children. He was there throughout kindergarten, and of course he came home with some of the behavior of the other children who were profoundly retarded. We never treated Hoke as retarded; we never treated him any different than the rest of the family. And we expected as much from him as we did the rest of the family."

The family moved from North Carolina to Atlanta in 1966 and Hoke was placed in a first grade educable (mentally retarded) class in public school. He stayed in that program until he was 22. During high school, he was in a vocational program that taught him independent living, and how to ride public transportation. Then they got him a job in the kitchen at a Marriott Hotel. Afterward, he worked in a movie theater, and at a Kroger grocery store.

A friend of Betsy's, also with a special needs child, urged her to move her son out of the house. "I said 'why does Hoke need to move out, he's doing fine?' She said. 'It's fine for you, but how about Hoke?'"

He tried living in an apartment with a roommate but there were problems finding the right combination of personalities and issues. Today he lives alone in a condominium. He works in the family business, and does part-time work for another company. When he was having problems at the family enterprise, Betsy was concerned they would fire him. She was told, "'We can't fire Hoke, he keeps us grounded. This is the population that we work with.'" He also participates in the "Just" People program.

"He never seemed to want to move back home, but he likes coming back home to visit and staying a weekend." Growing up, "As one of five he was just part of the scene. Hoke was very easy to raise. He was never a problem. He's very lovable, we were very fortunate.

"Hoke is socially acceptable. He's very good in social situations. I see him getting more frustrated as he ages because he has a much greater understanding of his limitations as he ages.

"Hoke has a lot of trouble with women being fickle. The girls call him and want to be boyfriend/girlfriend and that's fine. They go out and have a good time, and the next thing you know the girl is driving him crazy on the telephone, and trying to make him jealous and getting into all this emotional stuff. He can't handle it. I said, *The best thing you can do is be friends with all of them. Try not to get involved with any one girl. Just tell them right in the beginning you want to be friends. Play the field.* When one gal began pestering him, he told her to get a younger boyfriend." Betsy told her son, *Hoke, you will not marry*, and he realizes that." Her friend, who also had a special needs child, disagreed with her stand. She "thought they should have the opportunity to marry, and I said, *well, if you want to deal with it.*

How has this affected Hoke's siblings? "The youngest one has always been very close to him and has always been so much a part of his life. Because of Hoke, my daughter went into special education," as a profession.

"We didn't find out what caused the retardation until my daughter had two special kids, and my son has three special kids." Before her middle son and his wife decided to have a second child, he went for genetic testing, and "were told there was nothing wrong. So they went ahead and had the second child. Everything seemed to be fine so they went ahead later and had a third child. When this child got to be six months old and she still wasn't turning over, and was not developing, we (the family) went to Emory University for genetic testing."

It was discovered that the cause of the retardation was "a broken gene, the top of the fourth and bottom of the eighth genes are broken off. With the youngest child, it's just the opposite and she's more profoundly handicapped. She doesn't talk, didn't walk until she was four, she's just not feeding herself well, she doesn't chew. She's a fragile child." It took thirty years to find out what was wrong with Hoke. "I'm the one that started it evidently," Betsy remarked sadly.

How did Hoke affect her marriage? "It probably brought us closer together. Both my husband and I have deep faith and we just felt like this was something that we were entrusted with. We did the best we could."

Was there a toll? "I would not call it a toll. I would call it a growth. He has brought us more joy than he has sorrow, and it has helped us grow. Our youngest son said, 'We would not be the family we are today if we didn't have Hoke.'"

Chapter 8

Fragile X Syndrome

"I can either be pitiful or I can do great things," a parent

Fragile X syndrome is due to a defective X chromosome, and the "disease is caused by a gene that fails to produce a protein needed for mental and physical development." (1) It presents "with a characteristic pattern of physical, cognitive and behavior impairments (in boys), while a fraction of carrier girls manifest less severe symptoms." (2)

Adolescent boys display "an unusual, elongated face, large ears, and a prominent jaw. They usually develop enlarged testicles." (3)

"Fragile X affects children physically, emotionally and behaviorally. Their characteristics, according to the Fragile X Foundation, include impulsiveness, attention deficit hyperactivity, hand flapping, hand biting, poor eye contact, anxiety, and resistance to changes in routine and adverse reactions to sensory stimuli, which can lead to tantrums or aggressive behavior." (4)

This "developmental disability affects about one in 4,000 males and one in 8,000 females. The main cause of autism has been linked to Fragile X." (5)

Gary

"Gary (born in 1981) was not as responsive as my oldest child was when he was an infant, but I just thought he was a different personality, a different child. Then he was not developing language skills at age two, I guess that was the red flag. Physically, he walked, but he was clumsy; he talked, but he was hard to understand. He was developing, but was on the late side of normal. Even when he developed a particular skill, he didn't do it well," his mother, Ruth explained.

His mother took him to the pediatrician and said, "I think there's something wrong with Gary, he's not talking like I would expect a child in a language-enriched home should." The pediatrician said, 'Einstein didn't talk until he was five.' So we switched pediatricians."

When Gary was diagnosed as Learning Disabled (LD), "we gave him a lot of educational intervention." When he was four his speech therapist "told us she believed he was mentally impaired...The doctors basically told me he had specific learning needs, and physically he was fine. I think that because he didn't exhibit any physical problems, the doctors really took a hands-off approach.

"You're always searching when you know something's wrong. I didn't know where to get an answer other than from a pediatrician. So I started surrounding myself with professionals that worked with children with special needs, and created our own community of support.

"By the time he was five I put him in a private pre-school; it cost as much as a year in college. He got speech therapy, and occupational therapy. Because Gary had sensory overload, he also had physical therapy to learn sensory integration because changes in temperature, noise, and activity made him anxious."

Ruth's sister, who is married to a doctor, has two younger developmentally disabled children with problems similar to Gary's. When Gary was nine, his uncle attended a medical conference and heard a geneticist from Israel describe a syndrome called Fragile X (FXS) and explained the diagnostic procedure. "It just seemed familiar...So we all met with a geneticist and...all three boys have it." Her daughter is a carrier, and out of 10 grandchildren in the family, seven either express the FXS or carry it.

"I was disappointed. I wanted to think that he could be taught how to learn, or that he could be taught how to talk, be more agile. When I got the diagnosis that he was mentally impaired, it took away all those dreams that he would be normal. You want your children not only to be normal, you want them to be exceptional. I was never prepared to have a child that was exceptional in a way that prohibited him from having the same type of childhood or experiences either my husband or I had. I didn't like it at all. I was probably more emotional about it, although I didn't let it get to me. I considered it an instant challenge. For about five minutes I remember feeling pitiful, but after that I realized I can either be pitiful or I can do great things.

"I decided to learn who Gary was. He wasn't the person I thought he was. I thought he was more like a typical young man, like my oldest son, who had become my norm. Then I realized that I had to worry about who he was. It was a real quick lesson that kids are all different.

"My husband was very accepting of it. He said, 'That's the way it is, that's okay, we'll learn about FX, we'll do whatever we have to do for him.' Before the diagnosis, my husband was totally accepting of the fact that he wasn't talking. I don't think my husband really looked at Gary's future as critically as I did in terms of the development. I think he looked at the cute young boy who was playful and fine. And I was looking at the same child saying, *he whines a lot, he doesn't respond to me, and he has autistic-like characteristics.* If I went to him he would pull away as opposed to pulling towards me. So I was more in tune to those differences than my husband was." She admitted to moments of despair and sadness when her son was younger.

As Gary got older there were "delays in all areas of learning, especially in verbal expression. He doesn't appear at times to be impaired, his areas of strengths are so strong, but over all there is a definite delay." In children with Fragile X, their receptive language is higher than their expressive language.

Gary went into a learning disabilities class in public school for two years then switched to special education. "I remember crying over the idea that he wasn't going be able to ride the regular school bus, he would have to be in one of those little special ed buses. That probably upset me more than the label, because it would distinguish him as being different. But he loved that little yellow bus."

Ruth, with the help of the school principal, created a MID (Mildly Intellectually Developed) class in her elementary school. This was so successful that she did the same when Gary moved up to middle school. Wanting to create a grocery store in the elementary school, she worked with a Kroger grocery store manager and "developed a Kroger Store for Learning that became a hands-on learning experience. Now there are over 300 of these stores in schools.

"In middle school, we put in another Kroger Store for Learning and we incorporated a bank. I've been able to create systems to make the existing system work better." This mother, who is so optimistic and positive, repeated the programs in the high school.

Gary was in the *Havanah* Sunday school program for awhile. "I think religious training is very important. Gary's Bar Mitzvah was a great experience because we went to Israel. For him to be in front of 1000 people at the synagogue would have been a little daunting," Ruth, said. "He was part of a Bar Mitzvah group. Everyone was crying... He did what he could do. The 12 Bar Mitzvah students were so understanding that he did his best...Judaism is important. He loves the ritual, the routine. You don't have to have a lot of verbal skills to have faith."

When Gary was 18 "he entered the Community Based Vocational Training program and went out twice a week on a job site with a job coach to learn different vocational skills. He's worked at Media Play, Home Depot, Longhorn Steakhouse and K-Mart. It's been fun to create these programs. The system wants to serve the kids. They sometimes might not know exactly how, so they need a parent to serve as a support for the class."

When Gary was a teenager he wanted to drive a car, so "He used to get car magazines and circle every red convertible. He now realizes that that was a dream, that it's not reality for him. I think they know their own limits."

Ruth's eldest son, Martin, felt that "if I would be tougher on Gary or if I made more demands on Gary he would be able to read and write and do all the things he wasn't able to do. When Martin was a senior he wrote an essay for the *Coca-Cola* contest called *Triumph of the Human Spirit*. It was about when Gary learned to tie his shoes. It showed that he did have some compassion and some understanding of what a real triumph is.

"The younger child really didn't understand Gary. She expected an older brother to be smarter than her." After she passed Gary academically she realized there were problems. "She was embarrassed, but she learned to just treat him normally. When her friends were over she'd say, 'Oh, that's Gary, he's my brother, he's special'...or 'he does the funniest things'." This daughter has written a book about her brother. In December 2003 the family was the recipient of an award from the Points of Light Foundation, a national community service organization.

"He loves girls almost like fantasy girlfriends. He likes having a girlfriend but he really can't maintain a relationship because he doesn't have communication skills, or even the desire to maintain a relationship."

How did having a child with FXS affect her marriage? "In the beginning I think it was a stress on the marriage because I was so preoccupied with Gary that I didn't have enough energy left over to pay much attention either to my other kids or my husband," Ruth confessed. "Now, we've worked through the hard times because getting answers to questions helps a lot. The more information you have the better off you are. We look at his abilities not his disabilities. I think he has strengthened me as an individual, strengthened my husband and I as a couple.

"It's hard. The hardest thing is right now. I have been his cheerleader, his supporter, boasting about his strengths, I have parties for him... school projects, fieldtrips. Becoming an adult is going to be the hardest. Up to this point raising young children is a blast. You get involved, you have fun with them," Ruth asserted. "As long as they are happy and doing their best you feel good. But now that he's approaching graduation from high school, I need to prepare him for independent living. And it has to be independent living without me, and his dad.

"I never really felt sorry for myself, I felt like it was kind of extra work. I had to change my focus. But now I'm beginning to feel sorry for myself. Now I need to get him prepared to be independent from me.

"My mission was Gary. It took a toll, not only on my husband but the other kids. I just wasn't available to them. I think everyone just understood for that time period I had work to be done, and that I wasn't going to stop my work until I knew who Gary was, and placed him in a home, in a neighborhood that would support him.

"I think it's made me a better person. I used to see people and I would think, *if you would just study harder...play harder...*I now realize that people have different abilities, strengths, and different needs. It probably made me more open-minded towards differences. Because of that I think I'm probably a more tolerant person. It certainly has guided me towards my not-for-profit involvement with organizations, my friendships with people of diverse backgrounds, and people of color. I think I've really broadened my perspective as a result of having a child like Gary.

"Physically and emotionally it takes a toll on me. When he was younger, he was difficult to potty train, and I often had to leave an event when I first got there. (The emotional toll) is now, because I have my concerns; my fears for his future, and when I'm not going to be here."

Ruth and her sister, who has two children with Fragile X syndrome, established the Fragile X Foundation of Georgia in 1992.

Gary now lives with two of his friends and works in a grocery store.

Brandon

Brandon came into the world in 1980 with the help of forceps that is believed to have broken a bone in his skull. He was also jaundiced.

"I knew his development wasn't going in the right direction," his mother, Linda, said. "He had trouble feeding, he arched his back when you cuddled him, he had projectile vomiting...He constantly had a runny nose. He didn't interact with his toys in a developmental manner.

"So we took him back to the pediatrician several times then decided to go for a second opinion." Brandon's muscle tone was weak (hypertonic), and when he was a year old he was placed in physical therapy. Over the next several years he went to a developmental pediatrician, and underwent physical, occupational, and language therapy." At that time, the parents were still in the dark as to what was wrong with their child. "When Brandon was about seven years old, a neurologist diagnosed him as having pervasive developmental disorder with autistic tendencies."

When Brandon was 10, "We saw a TV program about families with Fragile X adults, and we knew right away that was Brandon. And so we investigated it. We went to the genetics department at a local hospital and had a work-up done. It turned out he has Fragile X syndrome. He was already getting all the services that we could have gotten for him. The right diagnosis validated everything and gave us a vehicle to latch onto to help him develop and get the right services, and do the right thing for him."

How did she and her husband react to the diagnosis? "We were thrilled. You also grieve a loss like a death for what you expect his life to be like. But then you move on. At different times in his life I've grieved for it again...when developmental stages come." It hurt particularly when she visited a college with her daughter and saw boys Brandon's age.

Brandon had attended the Adaptive Learning Center and then was placed in a normal pre-school class. After the diagnosis, he was placed in a special program in the public school while continuing his therapies. When he finished school, he went to Goodwill Industries for job training. When Goodwill failed to secure a job for him, his parents found for him a good employment provider. He's currently working in the mailroom at Cox Enterprises, and volunteers in the cafeteria at a private school.

Brandon was annoying to his older sister when they were younger. "He was embarrassing to her," his mother explained. "Once she matured and got older, she was very good about it. She stays with him overnight when we're out of town. She's there for him like a third parent if he needs it." She will become guardian when their parents are gone.

Linda said that raising Brandon, "made my husband and I stronger. I'm trying to put my life as a whole in better perspective. We're very fortunate that we could afford to give him a lot of opportunities that aren't available to the greater population. Our biggest concern was to get him a job, and for him to keep the job." She and her husband are exploring moving Brandon into a living situation away from home. Because Brandon is uninterested in sex, his parents are not concerned with his having a vasectomy.

When asked what toll it has taken on her, she replied, "He's so a part of our life now that it's hard to say what it would have been like had it been different. We're in a stage of our life like a lot of our friends who are starting to retire, or their kids are adults. They have a lot more freedom. I wish we could be traveling more, freer to do more things like that."

How has it made her different? "Hopefully I'm able to be calmer and put things in perspective having had Brandon. I can't even imagine what it would be like to not have him."

Her son has done commercials for special education events, has had his picture in the newspapers, and was speaker for the Georgia Special Olympics. "He's done a lot of neat things. If I hadn't had him, I wouldn't have had these experiences. It's probably developed us to be better people."

Lawson and Gil

Lawson, born in 1969, "had a pretty rocky infancy," his father, Elliott, said of his oldest son. The little boy suffered from colic, had difficulty eating, and experienced some projectile vomiting. His development was slow."

When Lawson, about two years old, became ill while visiting his grandmother in another city, his mother took him to a local pediatrician. "He was an old sort of grouchy pediatrician, and he just sort of blurted out that maybe he's retarded, or something like that." When they returned home to New York, the distraught parents took their child to his pediatrician. "He was totally noncommittal. He said, 'It's possible, but we don't have any hard data to support that. He's just missing his milestones.' He was slow walking, and he was slow talking.

"At that point I was in total denial. I had never considered having a child who was developmentally disabled," Elliott admitted.

The family moved from New York City to Albany, New York, and the distressed parents had Lawson examined by other doctors. None of the professionals they sought "gave us much advice. He seemed to be alright, we thought he was just learning disabled. It wasn't until we moved to Springfield, Illinois (when he was about 3 ½) that we had him evaluated at a medical school by a pediatric neurologist. (Because FXS was not discovered until the mid-1980s) it was just this vague thing... and they had some very strange theories as to what the problem was."

Until he was in the third or fourth grade, Lawson attended a Montessori school that also had other developmental disabled children. "It was a good experience for him. We realized that this condition doesn't manifest fully until they get a little older, then you realize that they are not progressing."

He was placed in a learning disabilities class in public school. Then came a meeting with school officials over Lawson's position in school: "The following year, we had some of those experiences where the special ed system gangs up on you. They bring six people to the table, and they slaughter the parents. You supposedly can do what you want but there's no chance to do what you want...they took Lawson out of that class (despite the parents' objections). So we sent him to a special ed school, and that worked. He was there for about five years and then they mainstreamed him back into public school. At that point he stopped progressing. " Lawson stayed in the public school until he graduated.

"He went to a supportable employment situation, and about the same time there was an opening in a residential home. Someone who had worked with Lawson at the developmental center was going to be head of this home. He said, 'this is it. You have to do this, this is the way to go.' And indeed, it was the best situation we've ever seen. He recruited the kids he wanted for this program. That is where he is now.

"He was working at Popeye's Chicken and he was actually doing quite a bit of the food prep, and he seemed to like it. Then unfortunately, Popeye's closed. He never really adjusted to another supportive employment situation. (Today Lawson is in a sheltered workshop.) He's the big man on campus, and he loves it."

When Elliott, a Ph.D. in neuroscience, and his wife wanted to have a second child, he and a geneticist "got a giant blow up of my wife's chromosomes, and we looked at them not knowing what we were looking for. Had we known what we were looking for we would have seen it."

The first time he heard about Fragile X syndrome was from a friend who was a pediatrician. "He sort of knew. He had figured it all out, and he said one day, 'I believe Lawson has Fragile X." Although they didn't know it at the time, his x-wife's sister had three Fragile X sons.

Their second son, Gil, born in 1975, also has Fragile X syndrome but "is much less affected, and has an IQ that's probably around 90. Even though you can tell that he's developmentally disabled, he appears fairly normal most of the time. We were much more alert to the condition; it took three, four, five years for it to show.'"

How did the family react to the second child having FXS? "Actually, it was not so bad. I was ecstatic that he was as high function as he was. He did pretty well."

Gil was able to attend regular classes in public school with relatively few accommodations. After graduation, he then went to work for three or four years at a grocery store where he bagged groceries. Then his parents got him a job working for the state of Illinois as a clerk.

Elliott said that both of his special needs boys were Bar Mitzvahed. "Since Lawson was the first, some people went out of their way to be incredibly gracious and nice." He went to Sunday school for a few years, and then worked helping the kindergarten teacher with the children. His brother, Gil, attended regular Sunday school classes.

"Gil lives with my ex-wife and spends time over here as well. We've tried all sorts of different programs to get him out on his own because we think that's best for him. After twice finding an apartment for him, he balked.

"Gil hasn't been happy with himself I don't think, and he sometimes has some problems at work. We worry about that a lot. Losing his job would be a disaster. We would really like him to get on with his life and maybe meet people, take a course. He's very sedentary, watches a lot of TV when he's not at work, and we would love him to do other things. But we're not making much progress." They are concerned with his future when they are no longer around. Both boys see a counselor to help them with their problems.

When asked how his former wife handled having two Fragile X children, Elliott said, "Probably a lot better than I. I was probably a lot more in denial than she was. By the time Gil came along I was probably okay. With the first child she handled it well."

His ex-wife has two siblings; she and her sister are carriers of Fragile X, and their brother has moderate cerebral palsy. "He is one of my heroes. He's just a super achiever. I knew all that he had overcome and I just thought, if we worked hard enough, we could overcome a lot of this.

"I think it put a lot of stress on our marriage. I think it had a major impact," Elliott confessed.

"I never even consider that you could have kids that were handicapped. It's been a huge part of my life. It's a burden that you deal with the best you can, and you try to help them the best that you can, anyway that you can," Elliott said of raising his two children.

Has the experience changed his life? "It's made me look at people in the world differently, for sure. I'm certainly much more sensitive to special needs people of any kind. I think it's, in some ways, made me more dedicated to my craft, to learn how the brain works. To look for answers…I would do anything I could to help people in our developmental disabilities branch learn as much as they can about Fragile X."

Chapter 9

Children Who Don't Fall Into a Specific Category

"Somebody has to drive the trucks and pump the gas," a doctor said to the parents

Lisa

While living in England in 1980, the Harrisons' first child, Lisa, was not rolling over and sitting up as was their friends' children of the same age. "We [wondered] at that point if maybe she was just slower." Her pediatrician told them saying, "'Children develop at different stages. There is nothing concrete that you could test.'" But Adrienne's motherly instinct kept telling her that something was wrong.

When Lisa was two, they attended a Mommy and Me program, and the pre-school teacher said she "obviously wasn't doing what she should...and suggested that she be tested." Though Adrienne realized her daughter's speech and fine motor skills were slower than normal, she hated the teacher who said "there was something wrong with my child."

Lisa was tested, and the results showed "an educational problem..." On the way home from the testing Lisa fell asleep in the car and Adrienne looked over at her little girl. "What I felt then was not so much pity for myself, but I was sorry for her as to what she was going to face. Lisa looks so normal, and when she acted out it looked like she was spoiled.

"I used to cry but fortunately I had a very good friend who was very supportive...I guess there was a lot of denial at first. I think I was disappointed." Her husband "denied it more in the beginning. He tends to be a good go-getter, so he was the one looking for the programs and fighting for programs for her in schools. He became very active and achieved a lot of things, set up a parents' support group...I guess the way he dealt with it was by doing something about it. I would talk about what I felt would be good for her in the class. I kind of look at something and I see a need, but I'm not good at putting feet to it, and he's very good at putting feet to it.

"There is a loss of a dream. When you lose a child to death, you have a loss and then you have a recovery process. If you have a child who is less than perfect, everyday you get up and face that loss of a dream."

When Lisa was around three, she was placed in a pre-school special education class with speech therapy, and occupational therapy to help with her slow fine motor skills. When the family moved to California she was tested and diagnosed as low to moderately intelligently developed. The remainder of Lisa's schooling was in special education classes.

The family moved to Atlanta where Lisa completed school, went into a vocational program, and then attended the Roosevelt Institute in Warm Springs, Georgia to learn community living skills. "She didn't learn anything new but it made her much more independent. She's ready to move on." Today she lives at home and is involved with the "Just" People program.

Adrienne has two younger children who realized early that their sister, Lisa, had problems. They enjoyed going to Special Olympics with her. One day, her sister, Gabriella, took a friend to the games and discovered that she was fearful of the different children. "That's when I realized that in some ways my kids had had a broader outlook on life because they'd been around these kids all the time." Gabriella told her mother a few times, "'I wish I had a normal sister...it seems unfair because I'm the second child but I'm really the oldest child.'" She was not really embarrassed by Lisa; her brother was more impatient with her.

"My husband and I went through some good patches and bad patches dealing with Lisa. I think it's because we're different personalities, we were able to support each other in that respect. At times it strained it the marriage," Adrienne said. "Looking back on it, it's probably made us less reliant on others. We're Christians, we prayed a lot about it, and through the years it helped us in terms of accepting that she's the way she is for a reason. That kept me going. I think it kept our relationship going. There was a certain amount of (self) blame...Not for anything I did, but for what I didn't do."

Amanda

The doctors told Bennett and Kay at the birth of their daughter, Amanda, that they had discovered anomalies in her eyes. The parents wondered if the problems were a result of a bout of flu that Kay suffered during her first trimester. When they brought Amanda home from the hospital she never cried. Having been in the field of developmental disabilities, at that time called mental retardation, her father became suspicious. They took their daughter to a pediatric neurologist who said that she was severely mentally retarded.

"I think I was more shocked when they told us she was blind," Bennett said. "Both of us felt like the best thing we could do was to get on with life and not take her to 27 different doctors to get another opinion about whether she does or doesn't have disabilities. We knew it, so our goal was to get her into the best program with the best services possible, and to get her development going so she could advance to the fullest extent possible."

Amanda, the youngest of their four children, "didn't walk until she was three years old…(and her) speech was slower," her father explained. "This child never cried, never acted out, was the easiest of all our four children."

When Amanda was three she was enrolled in a private pre-school class for children with disabilities in Fayetteville, Georgia. "So I went to the state department and asked if there could be some kind of support for families…and Amanda became the guinea pig. She was the first child in the state to receive educational monies to go to a school program. They literally paid her tuition even though she was just three years old. The state then set precedence and this is prior to the laws that came into play later on." Today special needs children from the age of three to 22 can receive free education through PL: 94-142.

"I would go and visit the school where she was attending and ask to observe. They were always so panicked because I would sit there and not say anything, and after class, I would remind them of certain things that they might try. Not to be critical but to help. I had a lot of expertise because of my background."

In 1972 the family moved to Texas, and Bennett went to work for the National Association for Retarded Citizens. Amanda was placed in public school where she did well and, despite the doctor's diagnosis, she never lost her sight. Shortly afterward, the parents divorced and Amanda and her siblings moved with their mother to Wisconsin. Her father spent as much time with his children as he could despite the long distance. "I wanted to be close to all my children, I love my children."

Bennett returned to Georgia in 1981 and remarried. When Amanda was 27 she went to live with her father and worked at various jobs. When he asked her what she wanted to do, she replied, "'I want to live in my own apartment with a helper and with a roommate.'" Before he could make arrangements, Amanda decided to return to her mother.

"Amanda's older sister (Belle) had gotten married and sought professional help for problems she was having. In the evolution of counseling, she disclosed that she'd been abused by her stepfather. My sons called their mother and said, 'You've got to do something about this. This guy has done something to Belle and we don't know if he's done something to Amanda. In the meantime, Amanda's got to be removed from that situation.' Her mother brought her to my house. She was in denial...couldn't believe it, although my daughter says now that she told her mother, she was oblivious to it.

"Amanda came to stay with us, and my wife, Roz, sat down and looked her in the face and said, 'Amanda, you've got a secret, don't you?' Amanda's eyes got real bright, and whenever she gets excited she rubs her palms together. My wife was able to get Amanda to reveal everything that had happened to her in great detail; horrifying details as a matter of fact. So she called me on the phone and said, 'your worst nightmare has just come true, Amanda just disclosed the degree of abuse that she encountered by her stepfather, mostly sexual.' He had threatened to kill her if she ever told anybody. She pretty much kept the secret."

The man was arrested, but the trick was to find a way to convince a jury that what Amanda had said was true. Her mother was a nurse who had spent 99 weekends out of town, so the man was charged with "99 counts of sexual assault, which was dropped to one probable count. They convicted him and he was given ten years. He went to prison and served six years." Amanda had had a hysterectomy when she was 13 years old. Her father thinks it was the stepfather's idea to keep him from getting her pregnant.

In 1995 Amanda took some cookies to an elderly man who lived in her mother's trailer park, and he too molested her. "She came home and told her neighbor, the neighbor then brought Amanda over to her mother. Her mother told her, 'Be quiet. We've had enough trouble.' When I found out about it I called the social worker in (their state)." After an investigation concluded that Amanda had been abused again, her mother was removed as her legal guardian, and she returned to her father in Atlanta.

"She's cute, and she's very vulnerable. She's not promiscuous, she didn't make any advances. She was incredibly trusting. I love her so much. I don't think it's taken any toll (on her) at all."

Religion has been important to Amanda. "She loves church. Amanda's very social and she loved the time between church and Sunday school when they have coffee, juice and cookies, and she could go around and say hello to everybody and talk to people. Everyone is very kind.

"I think parents relate to other parents who have a child with a disability better than with a professional who made a life choice to be a person working in this field. I have always had a very strong bond with parents. When they find out I have a child with a disability, I think that they see that I've gone through the same or similar things that they're gone through. They're more willing to say things to me, share certain things."

Norman

Norman, born in 1956, is the fifth child in the Bennett family. His parents first noticed that when he was about a year or 18 months old, "He was slow in walking, and he cried quite a bit. He wasn't developing like he should. The doctor said, 'Don't worry about it,'" his father, Emanuel, said. "When he was about four or five he was taken to a psychologist, and tests were run to find out what his capabilities were."

When Norman was in nursery school, he was hard to handle. "He cried easily, he wasn't potty trained, his speech was not good at all, and we ended up taking him to the local speech school in the Atlanta area to see why. They said, 'He's retarded,'" his mother, Adelle, related. "We were not familiar with retardation; we didn't know what it was, so we got books, and called people." The speech school gave them no direction.

"Nothing changed, we didn't change anything. He was brought up just like the others," Emanuel said. "We got him enrolled into a school (The Northside School for developmentally disabled children) for two or three years, then it fell apart. Then we got him into the county school system," Emanuel said.

When Norman became an adult, he moved into the Atlanta Group Home for a few years. Today he works for a private company and lives at home.

His parents' biggest worry is what will happen to their son when they are no longer around. They would like to put him in another residential program if they could find one, because they don't feel he can live in an apartment on his own.

Emanuel said that when their other four children were young Norman didn't seem to matter to them. "As they got older they accepted him." He said that Norman's older sister went into music therapy and worked with special needs people, and his second sister worked in special education. "He was just part of the family, nothing changed. When you have a large family you have to adjust overall because you can't just lead your life for one individual."

How did this affect their marriage? "It's just part of the adjustment in life," Emanuel said. "Anytime we go anywhere Norman either goes with us, or we arrange for someone to take care of him when we go on a trip. He's there, that's not going to change, so we just learned to live with it.

"It's given us a better understanding as to what life is. He's our child and it's our responsibility to raise him. We either accept it or we can go off the deep end. You can look around and there are a lot more critical children than Norman...That's part of the cards that's been dealt to you, so we didn't cry in our beer and say, *why did this happen to us?* We haven't allowed it to change our lives, and it hasn't changed the relationship between Adelle and myself."

Colin

Everything was normal until Colin was three and a half months old in 1960. His brother, who is three years older, had gotten sick and their pediatrician sent off a culture for diagnosis. The family had planned to go to the beach for a week, and asked the doctor to call them if there were any problems. There were, but unfortunately, the doctor did not call.

"Colin got sick while we were there, and when we got back the doctor said, 'I know what's wrong, he has salmonella and we need to get him to the hospital. He stayed there for five days with a temp of 105 ½," his mother, Letty, said.

"When I went to bring him home it was like they had given me a different child. There was a lot of excessive crying to the point of screaming. He seemed terrified of things. That was not my laughing little baby. From then on I kept noticing little things that didn't seem right to me." The doctor said, 'He was just a little slow in developing, but he would probably be okay.'

"We took him to a local speech school in the Atlanta area for an evaluation." The parents returned to hear the results. "I can picture the scene vividly. We were sitting around with the people who had been observing. They said, 'We've come to the conclusion that your son is mentally retarded. But, it's nothing to get totally upset about because somebody has to drive the trucks and pump the gas.' One woman kept looking at her watch.

"My world fell apart right there in that room. I thought it was the worst thing that could ever happen until our other son was killed. Their coldness, with no suggestions as what we should do from there. I know that they do a lot of good things, but I never could see beyond that experience. I think I knew it, but for somebody to just say it (coldly and clinically) it was cruel," Letty said.

Her husband, Frank, couldn't accept the diagnosis. "I don't think men really handle things like that. There was a long time when he didn't want me to talk to him about it. That was also bad for me. Not that he was ashamed; he just didn't want to talk about it. We were a long time getting to that point.

"A friend of mine was a kindergarten teacher and she said, 'Let him come to me.' She was good with him but he really didn't learn. He went to pre-school, then...first grade...regular school...then second grade. Lot of mornings I had to chase him down and catch him to go to school. Finally, the teacher said he just can't keep up, and suggested special ed."

Colin entered a public school special education class. "When you've got a child like this, nothing is permanent it seems to me. Everything changes." (When I offered that she was always waiting for the next shoe to drop), Letty said, "and boy does it drop."

When Colin was in high school, "We would give him lunch money. We found out after two or three weeks that we would take him to school, he would walk in and then leave, walk home and throw the money over the back fence. Nobody ever called us, nobody ever said, 'Colin is not in school.'"

Colin was sent to a program in Athens, Georgia for two years. When he was around 16, he ran away from school. "He was just so frustrated because he's got sense enough to know that there was something wrong and he didn't know how to cope with it. He has excellent verbal skills, really good sense of humor, but he's just so handicapped in so many other ways. He can't read, and we've spent a fortune in tutors. He can't write; he can print his name, but he doesn't know a penny from a thousand dollar bill."

He moved into a group home in Cartersville, Georgia for ten years. Then he started running away again. Once after a long walk, he laid down on the ground at an apartment complex, and when some people asked what the problem was, he said he was having a heart attack. They called an ambulance that took him to a hospital in Atlanta where his parents were called. "They said, 'We have a nice young man here who you might want to come and get.' They never charged us a penny."

Colin returned home and stayed with his parents for over a year. "That was horrible. That was like a nightmare." When he suggested living in an apartment, "We gulped and said okay." Over the next few years Colin went from apartment to apartment because of being thrown out for inappropriate behavior.

"My husband was a basket case because all these things upset him, they did me too but women handle it better."

Fortunately the parents found the "Just" People program. Today Colin lives in an apartment with two roommates, and works in the "Just" People office. "We've had our first real peace. He is the most delightful person to be around, sweet as all get out. I feel like that's best for him and for us. I think he's enjoying the interaction between the guys."

Colin once went to church and regular Sunday school. Then, something happened while he was there. When his mother went to pick him up, she found him crying. "He doesn't want to go to church now because he doesn't want to dress."

Colin has not dated, but he and a girl kissed a few times. His mother said, "To my knowledge he's never had a sexual experience; which is sad. He used to talk about marriage...never dwelled on it."

Letty said that raising Colin was very hard "I just tackled it like I do everything else. Do the best you can, hope its right. The first few years were hard for my husband to really accept it because he didn't know anything about anybody with a handicap. But once he did, then things were better...we were on the same page."

When asked if it took a toll on her she said, "I don't really know the answer to that question. I certainly got this head full of white hair at an early stage, but I think that's heredity. But it didn't hurt. But I guess because we have had a good marriage, we've been able to do things, fun things, and not dwell on the awfulness, the sadness.

"I don't know what will happen when something happens to us because we are his life." Plans had been made that their eldest son was going to assume responsibility of Colin.

Then her other son and his fiancée died in a car accident. "It was hard because I felt like I couldn't grieve like I wanted to because I had to take care of everybody else. You must steel yourself and go on."

Has this made her different? "I don't know. I hope it's made me a better person."

Melinda

When Melinda tried to came into the world placenta first (placenta previa) six weeks early, she was delivered by C-section in 1951 and put into an oxygen tent. "We were thankful she was born alive, and we didn't realize she had any physical or mental problems," her mother, Julia, said.

Even though Melinda talked and walked late, her parents weren't concerned. When she was five she entered kindergarten. The teacher suggested to them, "'Maybe you ought to have Melinda tested. Everything is all right but let's just see where she is.'"

Melinda was tested, and the doctor told her parents, "'she's got some problems, there's something.' It was said in such a way that we were in a complete state of shock," her father, Donald, said. Then the doctor continued, "'Lot of people have things like that, you know they have broom factories.' (He inferred that she would never be able to do more than work in a broom factory.) We were a basket case. We thought, did we do something wrong? Maybe she needs a tricycle or something...She'll never learn. What we have discovered since then is that it had to do with the oxygen supply (anoxia) at birth."

While in first grade, her teacher told the parents, "'Melinda's not learning as quickly as some of the other children, and maybe you ought to look into special education.' At that time there was no special education in the public school system," Julia said.

Her father, who was a social worker at the time said, "I know that there's something that will unlock that little old brain of hers and everything's going to be fine. We've just got to find what that key is. I made flip cards out of my business cards...and I started out with colors...We never knew if we were going in the right direction."

Melinda was enrolled in a county special education class until her parents found The Northside School. When that folded she went to Arbor Academy. She spent her high school years in a public school where she also attended a sheltered workshop.

Melinda worked in a day care center for several years then worked in the kitchen at a Morrison's Cafeteria. Since she is pretty and well endowed, some of the male employees made sexual advances to her. "She had two or three episodes that made us pretty apprehensive, but we got through that all right," her mother said. Several years later the family moved from Atlanta to Decatur, Illinois where Melinda got involved in programs for developmentally disabled adults. She participated in their activities and made friends.

"She is so close to normal but she has these deficiencies she can't overcome like counting money, she's not independent, and can't make decisions," her parents explained.

After returning to Atlanta, a friend told them about an out of state residential school. While visiting the campus and with her friend who lived there, Melinda told her parents, "'I'd love to go to that school.'

"We began to think that we're going to have to do something, after all we're no spring chickens anymore. Our son has five children, he's got his own responsibilities, and he doesn't need additional responsibilities. I had read this article about this young lady in her 40s who had been at home with her parents all of her life, and the parents were killed in an automobile accident. They put the girl in one of these government things. We heard all kinds of things of what happens in these government deals, some were pretty bad. So this got us to thinking," Donald explained. Melinda was accepted at the school and has lived there since 1986.

Melinda did volunteer work at a senior residence until she got depressed "because all these nice old people she got close to kept dying on her," her mother said. Now she works with day care centers.

Melinda's residential facility "won't allow any kids that have ever been sexually active," her mother said. "Melinda likes the boys." Though her parents have a fear of her getting pregnant, they considered a hysterectomy or tubal ligation, but feel the school protects her.

"I think it's been a wonderful thing for our marriage," Donald said about raising their daughter. "We were able to work out the stresses and strains together," Julia, added.

"We worry about her...there's the stress of how is she's going to manage in this world when we leave," Julia said.

Julia and Donald said of their son: "He is so attentive to her; he's been a wonderful brother."

"We've been more tolerant of other kids, more appreciative of our grandchildren. I think the Lord has blessed us. She has made our life fuller," Julia said.

Melinda was confirmed in her church. Their minister said, "'She's got the spirit,'" Julia said proudly.

Neil

When Neil (born in 1964), the third of four children, was not speaking at an appropriate age, Harriet, his concerned mother, had his hearing tested, and found there was no problem. When he was about three, the pediatrician "finally said, 'I think he's just going to be a little slow.'...I didn't really know what to do. I was 24 years old and didn't really know that much. I had all these other family problems, a husband who wasn't too helpful, so I just didn't' do anything. Neil just went along with the other kids," Harriet said. She said that her husband didn't pay attention, he didn't care.

"Neil played and didn't cause any trouble, he was a good boy. He went to kindergarten at a church school. He never misbehaved, and when they had a reading circle, he'd sit over in the corner, he wasn't interested. When he went to public school, he couldn't keep up." He was transferred to another public school and placed in a special education class. He did so well "that the teachers would come to me and ask, '"What's his problem?' I said, *you tell me, you're the one with all the degrees; I don't know, nobody does*. Sometimes I think he has some slight symptoms of the autistic...He functions, he works."

Harriet continued to have him tested. One doctor "was a ding-bat. She wanted to put him on Ritilin" although Neil was not hyperactive. When the doctor asked about weight loss at the next meeting, Harriet discontinued the medication. Then the doctor said, '"get him a dog.' So I never took him back. We did get a dog."

Neil went to high school in special ed. She asked his teacher, *after he graduates, what am I gonna do?* So we took him to the county and they tested him. His two older brothers weren't college material, so I put them into the Navy. Neil had this fear that as soon as he got out of school, I was going to throw him out and into the Navy. I didn't know he was so frightened as to what was going to happen to him. This doctor found out more stuff about him in 20 minutes than I knew his whole lifetime. He was the one who told me that he was borderline, that he could function, that he could work, could have a life, and never have a highly skilled job.

"So they put him into a workshop, and they taught him how to ride MARTA (Atlanta public transit). I did try to get him drivers ed at the school, but he was afraid. Then he must have lost 10 or 15 pounds, he looked like a skeleton. His daddy had diabetes, so we took him to the pediatrician to see if he's got it too."

The workshop was "suppose to find him a job, but they never did. Then her husband asked a local restaurant to give him a job. That was the best deal for them; they really took advantage of him. But he was happy there. He stayed there for about 13 years. He didn't have any vacation, any benefits. He was happy, they don't like change."

Neil wanted to go on a trip with his friends but his boss at the restaurant wouldn't give him time off from work. "I got very aggravated with them. I went up there and worked for him so he could go on a trip. It almost killed me, but I did it so he could go on his trip. Then he went to his daddy and said he was going to get another job. My husband, had spent 60 years in and out of St. Joseph Hospital, and knew everybody there. So he called one of the nuns to see about getting him a job." He went to work in food services where he gets benefits and vacation time.

Neil is with the Very Special People program. "He has his social group, they call each other up on the phone, they go to the movies, and they go bowling." He isn't interested in one-on-one dating. "Some of them are horney as hell. Their parents have had to have their daughters' tubes tied, and some girls have had abortions too.

"My Mother adored him, and he adored my mother and my daddy. When they retired they would come and get him and take him to the Varsity (restaurant). My mother-in-law didn't really have that much to do with him, but she didn't treat him any different.

"It didn't affect my marriage. My marriage wasn't the greatest marriage, but it had nothing to do with Neil," said Harriet who is now a widow.

"I never treated him any different than his brothers. I watched him a little bit more, I didn't smother him, and I let him go just like his brothers. And he's very independent, he's smart. I don't consider him handicapped, just with special needs at times. If it weren't for Neil, I wouldn't have any social life at all going to all those functions.

"When I see the others I know how fortunate I am. He's such a help to me. I couldn't keep this house without him. He remembers when to take the garbage out; he does the grass, my gutters... It's really like having a wonderful companion. I'm not holding him back from moving out, because he doesn't want to. He's not interested in independent living. He pays me some money, and I invest his money for his old age."

Harriet said that the house is in his and his brothers' names, and he has what he needs for now. She has no plans for independent living for her son. She said that when she dies, "Let his brothers take care of him. They would." She said that his siblings "Never treated him any different. He loves his brothers and they love him."

Jill

Nell suffered from a very painful carpal tunnel syndrome during her pregnancy in 1962, and was treated with cortisone shots; her pregnancy and delivery were normal. But soon there were problems with Jill. She didn't know how to suck her bottle, and this was followed by breathing difficulties. After undergoing a battery of tests, the pediatrician found nothing wrong with the baby. Later Jill was diagnosed as Mildly Intellectually Developed (MID), which the family feels was caused by the cortisone shots.

Jill attended Arbor Academy, and then went into public high school special education classes where she graduated. When "She walked across that stage, the family cried," her father, Hilton, said.

"Then we started looking around for workshops and vocational programs. She has worked over the years at a hospital for children in housekeeping and loved it. She then worked at a hospital in the kitchen. She's been working through the sheltered workshop with Coca-Cola, putting parts together for their machines."

There were no special education programs available in the church that Jill and her family attended, so Nell "fought like crazy to get these programs" for her daughter and others like her. In 1969 she began faith-teaching special children at the church, and gradually it attracted other children who were mentally as well as physically handicapped. This program led to the establishment of a camp that offers a camping program for one week each May for special needs children.

Jill "is a very outgoing person," Hilton said. "One of the problems is that these people are so trusting of other people." Her parents bought a condo that she shared with a roommate and with counselor supervision. Then a 55-year-old man took advantage of her. "It's a good thing I never got to him or my sons got to him or he wouldn't be alive today," her father stated. After a second encounter, she returned home to her parents. Nell died in 2000.

"Jill knows that there's something wrong with her but she can't put it into words," her sister-in-law, Paige, said. "Mom used to always tell her that everybody has some disability, then Jill would ask what everyone's disability was. It bothers her that people at work call her retarded. She mentions this quite a bit. She has got a great handle on life. She knows she can't do it on her own. It bothers her that Mom's gone, and possibly that Dad will be gone, and in her mind she wonders what will happen to her."

Hilton said that his other children, "treat her well, but they get frustrated like the rest of us." The whole family worries about Jill's future. "My kids keep asking me, 'What are you going to do?' I keep saying I haven't the foggiest idea," Hilton admitted. "I would like to see her go into a group home or some place, but I'm not ready for all the problems that would come about."

"That's an issue for the siblings," Paige said. "She wants to move in with us. Probably years down the road it wouldn't be an issue for my husband and me, but not now. I wouldn't do that to my children. My daughter has had more of a problem with Jill than my boys do. She's frustrated with the constant repetition."

Hilton said about raising his daughter, "It doesn't make me any different; it's probably made me a better person. I understand more." He said he's more tolerant but that, "I lose it now and then. It's probably made me an easier going person."

Glenda

When Glenda (born in 1969) "was about eight months old, she started losing weight. She only weighed 13 pounds and she wasn't holding food down," her mother, Ada, said. "She was put into a children's hospital to see why she was losing weight. They found nothing.

"When I brought her home she completely stopped trying to crawl, and didn't begin again until she was 17 months old." When her parents took her hands to help her stand up, "she couldn't put weight on her feet." Although she began talking before she was a year old, everything else in her development was delayed.

"The doctors didn't say a whole lot of anything when I asked. I waited too late to change pediatricians because he was not good with a child who deviated from his definition of normal. It wasn't until she was four that I insisted that we do something to find out what was wrong. When we had the testing done, she was diagnosed as hyperactive. The term didn't mean a whole lot to me...it doesn't fit what they like to describe."

When Glenda was two years old, Ada became very ill and spent three months in the hospital; the child went to stay with her mother's family. When Glenda returned home there were more problems. When relatives came to visit, the child was afraid that they had come to take her away again.

Because of her poor motor skills, Glenda was fitted with special shoes, and attended physical therapy classes at an American Red Cross program. "None of it worked. When she was six she had her eyes tested and found out that she had very bad depth perception. The doctor said she could have lost vision had she not had this corrected."

Glenda attended a regular pre-school program when she was five, and when this didn't work out, she went to a local speech school in the Atlanta area for a year. Afterwards, it was on to public school in special education classes. After high school Glenda tried various programs until she got into a sheltered workshop.

She is very verbal and talks a lot. "It's not the talking, it's what she talks about. There are people who know things about me that they shouldn't," her mother confessed.

Ada found a new doctor who was helpful and recommended therapists who prescribed medications for Glenda. "While on one drug, she began hearing voices, and at different times these voices would cause a great deal of problems."

Gordon, Ada's husband, "was very supportive." Even though he didn't relate well to children, "He did a lot of things for Glenda that were helpful to me." He died a few years ago.

It has been very hard on Ada who has had a difficult time finding programs that fit her daughter. At times she has felt very alone. She wants a program where her daughter will be safe. "I'd love to have Glenda in the "Just" People Independent Living Program, but at this time I can't afford to support two separate households."

Ada says of her daughter, "She'll meet someone and immediately talk of marriage. It concerns me that someone might force himself on her. I am more concerned about someone saying they want to marry her and then after awhile become abusive, or they expect something she can't give. If they could accept her, she would love that kind of relationship." Ada worries about her daughter getting pregnant, but she has yet to have a tubal ligation.

She doesn't think that her family understands Glenda. "My sister will make comments on what she thinks are helpful things, but that are hurtful to me. (As her father has aged) he's gotten less accepting of Glenda, and he's always felt that had I done something different, Glenda would be different." She is also angry that her in-laws never helped them. "They had full time help and could have relieved the situation by taking Glenda sometimes. "

Ada said that even though her friends have not pulled away from her, not once was her daughter included in things with their children.

"I wish there was something I could have done better," Ada said. "You do so many things. You say, *maybe this will be the miracle that might change her to normal...but will it help her fit better, make her less stressful and more enjoyable?*"

Does Ada feel different having gone through her experiences? "I'm not certain. Nothing went as expected with Glenda. No matter how much I learned about her problem, I never knew what to expect. And the sad part is that most of the time I've been disappointed because I always want more for her. And I haven't been willing to settle, and so I keep pushing and I don't think that's necessarily a negative. The problems are not going to go away, that's who she is; I just want her where maybe she can deal with things better."

Callie

"When Callie was four weeks old in 1969, I took her to the doctor for her first checkup and she hadn't gained weight, which was unusual with a newborn," her mother, Marie, explained. The baby also slept a lot. When they returned to the doctor a week later he decided to do a thyroid test. "They discovered that she had very little thyroid function. During the nine months in utero, the thyroid controls your physical growth and your mental growth...If she had been diagnosed at birth, the minimal brain damage that she has now would be next to nothing. If we had waited until she was six months old, she would have been severely retarded." She was placed on thyroid medication, and has been on it ever since.

When Callie was in nursery school, "I could see certain things that she did that were just not the same as the other children her age. Not just the talking or walking, but understanding. The teachers said she did things slower than other children. They more or less indicated that there could be some minimal problems."

Callie attended a summer program at a local community center and created problems in the carpool. Because she wasn't talking, she scratched the other children to get attention. "This particular mother called the center and said she wasn't aware that they allowed children like Callie to come to the nursery school. I pulled her out of that carpool immediately."

When she was five, Callie was enrolled in a private school in a class for hearing impaired and learning disabled children. After several years she went to public school special education classes, and graduated high school with a regular diploma. "She functions higher than her IQ...probably in the low 80s. She is highly motivated, more so than her two brothers."

I asked how she and her husband reacted to their child's problems. "My husband was really in denial. He thought she would outgrow it. With my nursing training I was a little bit more receptive than he; he said, 'she'll catch up...she'll be fine.' I was sad for her and for me and for my family members. I would daydream, *well, she'll probably never get married, and she won't have children, and it's so unfair to her and to us.* And there really was no one to talk to." She knew only one other parent with a special child.

Callie's father died of a massive heart attack when she was 12 years old. "She didn't understand death; she thought he was going to come back. Before he died she would call him every day…he spent a lot of quality time with her. Then after he died she was always worried about what's going happen to me."

For three summers Callie attended a program for special needs children at a camp in Palmer, Massachusetts. Her experience was so successful that she was invited to return to work there, which she did for several years.

Callie attended the *Havanah* Sunday school program, and when she was 13 years old, she was *Bat Mitzvahed*.

After high school Callie went to Warm Springs, Georgia to the Roosevelt Institute's vocational school where for two years "She learned how to cook and clean. She learned how to do computer-type work, and got a degree in that, so she really did well. She made some social friends, one she's been friends with for ten years."

Once back in Atlanta, Callie got a job in an office with a job coach paid for by her mother. After being fired for not working fast enough, she got a job with Jewish Family & Career Services.

At home Callie began to regress with her mother doing her chores. After going the apartment/roommate bit, she moved into the basement of her eldest brother's home.

"Two mothers came to me with young special needs adults, and said, 'Now that my kids are out of high school there are no social things for them.'" She went to the Jewish Community Center in 1983, and through their auspices the Very Special People program was created. Callie is active in the program. She has a lot of social friends, her social life is better than mine is. They go on trips, they go to the movies, and they go to the mall. They go as a group to certain functions, but those who can be independent, as Callie can, will meet some of them at a mall or at a restaurant." She's been given sex education and told not to go out at night by herself, but her mother still worries. She hasn't had a tubal ligation.

Marie said of her boys, "They were wonderful. We used to talk to them about Callie's condition and not to be ashamed or embarrassed. There was a little jealousy. I think they just assume that she can handle a lot more than she actually does. They never hesitated having their friends over."

How did this affect her marriage? "I think it brought us closer together. Harold was really the only one I could talk to. I think he accepted the fact that Callie has this problem. We were married later, we were more mature."

Marie said there has been a "certain amount of stress. Callie gives me more than I give her. I'm really proud of her; she's given me a lot." Marie has been a widow for some time now, and her brother-in-law feels the reason she hasn't found someone to marry might be because of her daughter.

Has the experience made she different? "I'm probably more patient with people, more understanding."

When asked how she coped, Marie answered, "You have to have a sense of humor or otherwise you'd die."

Kristen

During Kristen's first year in 1971, she "had fluid in her inner ear that caused her to fall down. Her hip bone socket was not fully developed, so she had to be in a splint at night or a good part of the time, so that when she did start to walk she wouldn't walk out of her hip," her mother, Mary Sue, said. "She didn't crawl when she was supposed to, but I attributed that to the fact that she was in the splint for a year." On top of that, "She was eating a lot of dirt. When we told the doctors about this they said 'that's a natural childhood kind of thing.'

"It was later that we discovered that she wasn't developing mentally either. When she was three or three and a half I took her to a neurologist and he said that it appeared that she had a calcium deficiency. It wasn't that she wasn't getting enough calcium, it was that she wasn't absorbing it. He bawled out the pediatrician for not knowing that. She had a seizure, so he put her on Dilantin, and she never had an episode like that again."

The neurologist told Mary Sue, "'put her in an institution.' He felt that her problems were such that she needed the specialized care that she would get in an institution. He said this was too much for me to deal with. I walked out of there crying and sobbing. I was totally devastated.

"My husband and I said no, we weren't going to put her in an institution. God gave her to us so we would raise her. He had a hard time with it, but he said we would take care of her and we did. He put in his full time at work, came home, and relieved me for an hour or two. He stayed with her because she was hyperactive."

Kristen was enrolled in pre-school, but when she was unable to keep up with the other children her mother had her tested. Two psychologists called Mary Sue in and told her that Kristen wasn't developing normally and needed to be in a special ed program in the public school. When she failed to fit into that program, she was sent to a private school in Illinois for two years, and then she returned home and went to public school.

"Socially she couldn't handle things and she didn't fit in. She would get very nervous and yell. I took her to all sorts of practitioners trying to find out what the problem was. They would tell me she was low on the B vitamins, so they started giving her shots and B vitamins. I took her to an alternative person who does homeopathy."

When asked about her thoughts on doctors, she replied, "The doctors need to educate themselves in the mental health area, in understanding that there are other things other than colds and flu. They need to expand their knowledge. I wish the doctors would get with it. They only heal the symptoms and not heal the body. The medical profession is so backward."

Kristen had vocational training in high school. Afterwards, she got a job, but there were problems because of her nervousness and not wanting to take directions.

While Kristen was in training for a job, an employee took advantage of her. She wasn't raped, "but he began the process. She had training here and at school, and she knew that what he was doing wasn't right. So she called me. I had to call in the police and go through that whole rigmarole. He was just doing the fondling bit and she knew what the body parts were so she knew what to tell me what he was doing."

The man's lawyer objected when the police wanted to give him a lie detector test. Since Kristen didn't seem to have any repercussions, the family decided not to go to trial. The perpetrator was not fired.

Finally, the parents found the Little Friends program, and Kristen will live at home until a spot opens in one of its living facilities. She works in the Spectrum sheltered workshop.

Kristen's father died recently. "She's taking it quite well, she asks me every day, 'Where's Dad, what's he doing now?' She can't understand the concept of leaving this world and going into the next."

Mary Sue said that her two older sons treated their sister "like a queen. They took care of her when they were little, and they're very good with her. One son said when other children wouldn't play with her, he wouldn't play with them so she would have someone to play with. The boys were never embarrassed."

Once when Kristen stepped onto a neighbor's yard, the lady "yelled, 'I'm not babysitting for your kid. Get your kid out of here, she doesn't know how to behave!'" Another neighbor yelled when the child went down the street looking for someone to play with, "'Get her away from here, I'm too busy, I can't be taking care of her.' The neighbors were not very helpful. It's not that we tried to pawn her off on anybody, it's just that she was seeking companionship." Kristen was very lonely.

"There wasn't much time to enjoy life," Mary Sue stated. "You couldn't go out because you could never leave her alone. (They had difficulty finding a sitter who could deal with their daughter.) We really couldn't enjoy life after that. You can ask your family to watch just so often.

"I feel that God gave her to me for a reason, and so I had to do everything I could to help her," Mary Sue said.

"Physically it's taken its toll on me and I'm tired all the time. Mentally it's taken its toll on me...physically, mentally and emotionally. After all, she's thirty years old now. When you're younger you can deal with it, but as you age and it's a longer term commitment, the more tired you become, the more frustrated you become because no matter what you do, it doesn't work. The doctors don't help. Fortunately we found Little Friends, they have been the greatest help.

"She's brought a lot of love to all of us. She made us realize what's important in life. Prior to having something like this, you live in a world where everybody has their problems, but I think you don't fully realize how many disadvantaged people there are in this world. When you get into the world of the handicapped you begin to grow in caring, and compassion, and love. I think she brought that into the family. I was headed in a different direction; I was heading into a job where I could write for a video company. She changed our lives and perhaps took us all into the direction we were suppose to go, and made us understand what we were really on this earth for.

"I think it made me cognizant that there's more in life than just having fun and going out and being care-free. It made me realize what true love is all about, what caring and compassion is all about. I think most of the world just doesn't get into that."

Arden

Arden was born prematurely in 1976, and her problems were noticed shortly after birth. The doctor told her parents that she would probably never walk or talk and "they were encouraged to put her in a residential facility," her stepmother, Holly, said. Her parents made the decision not to institutionalize their baby.

Her father's reaction was "obviously disappointment, hurt, frustration, confusion. Probably some anger, although I think he has worked through that, I think he's resolved that."

When Arden was three, the family moved from New Jersey to St. Louis where she was evaluated, and placed in a public school special education preschool class. "I was the supervisor of the preschool education program where she was first evaluated." She tested out as moderately mentally handicapped. She was not talking at the time, she was doing some little echoing, she was not toilet trained, and wasn't feeding herself. She had a lot of autistic-like behavior, although she was never diagnosed as autistic."

Arden's mother was an alcoholic and "died from complications of it when Arden was six. Her dad and I got married when she was nine, and we moved to Atlanta a year later."

Arden continued in special education, and while in high school she had some job training. She worked at PetSmart for four years, then at Atlanta Casualty Insurance. At the time of the interview she was unemployed. She is with the "Just" People program.

Arden's parents are hoping to get her into an independent living program. "They are few and far between here in Georgia."

Arden "doesn't date and isn't interested. When friends from "Just" People call, she says, 'I want to be friends with them but I don't want a boyfriend.'" Holly and her husband are worried that someone might take advantage of their daughter. "That's probably one of my greatest fears. Although, because she's so private, doesn't want anybody getting near her, it maybe doesn't worry me as much as if she was more receptive to it."

Holly said of Arden's brother, "He's pretty much run the gamut of emotion. He is very protective of her, always has been, but he also has experienced a lot of frustration, anger, and embarrassment."

Holly said that Arden's "mother pretty much rejected any involvement with her husband's family. There were times when his parents came and stayed with the children when she was sick and hospitalized. They were always very supportive but not always included. They have been very, very loving and accepting."

When asked about her friends, she said, "You don't include elements in your social circle who are not going to be accepting of your children."

Holly said that when she married Arden's father "I didn't know exactly what I was walking into. I thought I did, and that was maybe even worse. It has been a very enlightening, educating experience."

Has it put a stress and strain on the marriage? "Oh, I think at times it has. I think probably Arden's brother's problems put more stress on the marriage because he was more mobile." The parents had better control over her.

Has it taken a toll? "I don't feel that it has. Have I given up some things? We all do. We give up things for normal children. I think it has helped me grow.

"It has made me more tolerant, accepting. I think I am less tolerant of people who are intolerant. It's probably made me grow in my faith.

"When I get frustrated, when I get to a point of feeling I'm dead-ended, I make myself look at how far we've come, and then I'm okay. When we got married she was not feeding herself all the time, she was doing nothing, not bathing herself, not doing much for herself. She had no chores. She was verbal but only echoing. Today, she is verbal, she walks to work, and is a lovely young lady."

Frances

"Frances was born fine (in 1960), we thought," her mother, Leah, said. She suffered from colic, reflux and allergies. "Other than that she was fine and happy. She was a little slow. I guess when she was about six or eight months I just felt like something was not right. She's my oldest child. I really didn't have anything to compare it with except my friends' children. She was a happy baby."

When Frances was eight or nine months old her parents noticed that her legs were turning in. A resident at a children's hospital in Atlanta first said that she had "Hurler's syndrome, which is a devastating disease. It's a form of mental retardation where everything just goes, children die, the tongue gets bigger, and the stomach gets bigger. Then they said she didn't have that, but she was slow," Leah explained. Another doctor disputed the diagnosis and said a proper one could not be made until she was three."

We talked about how devastating the news was. Frances' father, Julian, admitted, "It was worse than that...for several weeks we couldn't look at each other." He was living in Mobile while his wife and mother-in-law were in Atlanta tending to their daughter's medical problem.

When Frances was 22 months old they took her to Ochsner's Clinic in New Orleans. "The first thing they told us was that she was retarded, but that she would never have to be institutionalized," Julian explained. Back at home they informed their pediatrician of the events, and he said, "'When she was born I felt like there was something wrong. But you will be pleasantly surprised with the outcome,' which we have."

What was their reaction when they heard the diagnosis? "Black. It was like three days of going from one doctor to another because they did the whole battery of everything. Had to go through psychological testing. How could someone who didn't know her test her? She was 22 months old. I was glad that we did it, but I did not put a whole lot of credence in it. I felt like she might be worse, but I had this hope. We had a wonderful pediatrician in Mobile. He was very encouraging and he got us into programs," Leah said.

Frances attended daycare programs, and because she was having problems with her leg, she underwent physical and occupational therapy. When the parents asked their orthopedist when she would walk straight, he replied, 'What difference does it make, she's retarded anyway.' I picked up Frances and ran out in tears," her mother said. Her pediatrician recommended another orthopedist.

Frances attended regular nursery school, but as she got older she was placed in special education classes. "She played in the neighborhood with normal children. When they get older it's horrible. You don't notice the difference until they get older. She reads and writes on a fifth grade level, but I don't know how much she comprehends. If she could just read warning signs it's worth it. She can tell you anything you want to know about the Braves (Atlanta Braves baseball team). She's a real sports fan," both of her parents said.

The family moved to Atlanta when Frances was twelve. Because her spine was beginning to curve, they saw a doctor who recommended surgery and explained there would be a long stay in the hospital. "I remember driving down the parking lot at the hospital from the very top, going round and round the exit ramp. Frances said, 'Is it bad Mama?' I said 'Oh, no. It's gonna be wonderful.' Meanwhile, I'm ready to throw up."

Surgery was performed, and she was in the hospital for eight weeks with a halo (a metal brace) on her head and two pins in her legs attached to weights. "It was a traumatic kind of surgery. She was a trooper. She never complained, except for the shots," her father said. While Frances was in the hospital, her mother began doing volunteer work at the hospital. She did it for several years then became a laboratory technician.

Frances attended special education class in public school. While she recuperated from surgery, she had homebound teachers.

"She turned out a lot better than we expected. Because of the surgery, Frances' self-image was shot, and she underwent some therapy. We had our horrible moments," Julian explained.

To discipline her they used a reward system. "We would have time-out, taking things away," Leah explained. "Even though we have always tried to coddle her and protect her, we've also tried to make her do the best she could to her ability and not get by with a lot of things," her father added.

When Frances went into puberty, her parents worried about her getting pregnant, and discussed it with one of the pediatricians. "He read me the riot act up one side and down the other that I would want to sterilize my child, that I would want to deny her the opportunity to have children. I thought *forget you, buddy."*

She changed doctors and he agreed that she should have a hysterectomy. Her terrible periods and fibroids were used as justification rather than her parents having to go to court for legal permission. "We had to explain to Frances that she couldn't have children, and she said, 'that's alright she would play with her cousins' children."

When asked what she thought about doctors, Leah said, "most of the professionals don't talk to her, they talk to me. When she was a teenager and adult, she could understand enough. If I go to a doctor with Frances I watch how they interact with her, and if they spend all their time talking to me, I go find somebody else."

"We always felt like the boys would see that she was taken care of, but we never knew, when they got married, what would happen with the spouses. We always wanted them not to feel like Frances was their obligation. As a result, they do everything they can for her, they are very good to her," her father said.

"It was natural in our family that Frances was different," Leah said. "Only my mother would not admit it. My mother dearly loved her, she would say, 'she's alright, she can do this.' But that was my mother's way of coping."

This family worked on the Atlanta Group Home project even though they were not planning to put her in the home because of prior financial obligations. Then their boys went to them and said, "'You and Dad have to do this now, we'll manage somehow, you might not have this opportunity later.' And thank God that we did, it's the best thing that we did. It was horrible for the first couple of weeks," Leah said. Frances does volunteer work at the nearby Jewish Home.

Before Frances moved to the home, "I would feel like I was running in 15 different directions. I'd drag her with me even if she didn't want to go; she was old enough to stay at home, but was too old to have a sitter. I felt like I couldn't just relax. I couldn't go out and not feel guilty," Leah explained.

(One night I went to a stage performance at the Fox Theater and ran into Frances and the other young ladies from The Atlanta Group Home. They were all dressed up, and Frances was wearing a mink stole.)

"I never wanted her brothers to feel like she was a burden. I always spent time with them individually. I didn't want them to feel like Frances was getting more. But she did. We had to because it took longer to teach her to tie her shoes, to go to the bathroom," Leah said.

"We have tried to develop Frances to her best ability and not pity ourselves and say *why us*?" Julian stated. "We always felt like we wanted, education wise, the best for the boys because they were overachievers. We didn't want the boys to suffer because of Frances. We tried to encourage them and they've done very well," his wife added.

"It probably made our marriage stronger. It either brings you closer together or pulls you apart. You have to accept it first. And then you just have to go on from there," Leah said. "I have always tried to support Leah, and I know that she has the bulk of the burden of everything," her husband stated.

"I would give anything if she had been normal, but I wouldn't take anything for her," Leah said. "She's the love of our life. They say God doesn't give you anymore than you can handle," Julian added. "There were plenty of times I thought He did. I think we've learned how to cope with situations," Leah added. "We've learned that there's other things that are not as important," Julian said.

"I'm a lot more responsible. I think we both are. I'm a lot more realistic about things that matter, and appreciate the things that are important," Leah remarked. They both feel that raising a special needs child has made them more compassionate and sensitive.

The parents had a family dinner at their house one evening and expected that Frances would spend the night. When a relative got ready to take her grandmother home, Frances said, "You know Mom, Aunt Dorothy is going to take Grandma home and she has to go right by my house. I think I'll go home.' It was like somebody had stuck a knife in my gut. Then I thought, *this is great. She thinks the group home is her home, and she's happy.*"

Jimmy

When Jimmy (born in 1970) was three and a half and having trouble in nursery school learning his colors, his teacher suggested having his hearing checked. When it was found that his hearing was normal, his teacher suggested having his eyes checked. "Our ophthalmologist told me that his eyes were perfect and asked why I was having him tested. So I told him that Jimmy was having problems with colors," his mother, Abigail, said. He inquired about Jimmy's class then said, "'If he were my child, I would have him (psychologically) tested tomorrow morning.' He was referring to IQ but he didn't say it."

Abigail called a psychologist friend and explained the situation. He said, "'I always realized that you were aiding Jimmy too much, but if I told every fucking person that I know what I suspected was the matter with their kids, I wouldn't have any friends left.' He recommended someone, and we had Jimmy tested immediately."

After the evaluation, the psychologist said, "'Your son has the most complex learning disability I've ever seen, but he's definitely not EMR (Educable Mentally Retarded).'" Then he recommended that they meet with a learning disabilities specialist.

The specialist said to the parents, "'I'm going to set up a series of academic exercises that you must use to work with him everyday after school like clockwork...It's like dog training. You never go to point B until point A has been mastered.' I thought about that...I said to her, *there's one thing I know for sure, that no matter what disabilities are involved, even if there weren't any, I can't teach him on a regular basis for several hours after school. I won't do that, and I'm extremely offended by the word dog training*...and that was the end of that."

Jimmy was tested at a local speech school in Atlanta. They said their tests showed that "this is open and shut EMR, and our school does not serve you. Here's a box of Kleenex.' She gave me a list of what retardation means; there were 12 of them. She gave me reality right up front and a box of Kleenex. I respected her very much; it really meant a lot to me that she called a spade a spade. She said, 'this is a terrible thing, it's much worse than if your child dies, because when your child dies, he's gone. This is the death of the mind. So you have this for the rest of the time.'"

How did she react? "I went home and called the psychologist and said, in my own inimitable way, just what I thought of the doctor he'd recommended who suggested training Jimmy like a dog."

She told the story of her sojourn through the medical maize, and of her anger and frustration to a director of a private school. The director told her of Dr. Elizabeth Kubler-Ross' studies on death. She said that Dr. Kubler-Ross "had a quote that kind of summed up my reaction. She said, 'You live in America. The underlying theme to everything is that no matter what is wrong it can be fixed, the refrigerator or a person. And the first time someone comes up against something that can't be fixed, a child or a husband, there is an immediate amount of rage because this goes against the unwritten American way, so to speak.'

"That just related to how I felt. I was just pissed all the time. It didn't show always, but I was aware of it."

She and her husband became closer. "We cried together. We accepted the diagnosis totally from the beginning, and we took immediate action to get him into a situation that would be best for him," Abigail explained.

"I'm not sure we have a true diagnosis yet," her husband, Dean, who is also a psychologist, said. "I had had an inkling at the time so I wasn't so surprised." He tried to support his wife who, like most mothers, had the lion's share of work with their son.

Jimmy was enrolled in a special program in public school. At a PTA meeting Abigail talked to a man whose child was also in the class. He said, "'my son just has a little bit of brain damage, but they're gonna have him fixed right up by Christmas.' He was stuck in denial."

Jimmy attended Arbor Academy then returned to public school. When he was 17 years old, "He went to a very, very well known, expensive private school on the East Coast," Abigail said. "He went because all of this takes a toll on your marriage and romance. We sent him up there so we could have some privacy."

While at school, and unknown to the parents at that time, Jimmy was physically molested. "Somebody sodomized him, and he went crazy. He thought he was living in a concentration camp during World War II, and that they were going to burn him in an oven. When I say crazy, I mean stark raving mad," his mother said. Unaware at the time as to what had happened, she went up to the school and got her son.

When they arrived home, her husband said, "'I just felt that if we could get enough medicine in him, he wouldn't have to go to the hospital.'" Jimmy became delusional. "He heard a young girl crying in distress across the lake (from their house), she was drowning, and calling, 'Jimmy, Jimmy, help me, help me!' He wanted to go across the lake to find her. Dean had to sleep next to the door to keep him from leaving."

Jimmy was finally admitted to the hospital where he remained for a month and a half. It was during his sessions with his psychiatrist that everyone learned that he had been raped at school.

Afterwards, Jimmy returned to a public school program that included vocational training. He graduated at 21 and was able to get jobs, but they only lasted for a short time.

His parents turned to the Very Special People program. "That saved my life," his mother said. His name was put on various group home waiting lists. "Independent living is the option everyone touts… we've been very skeptical," Abigail remarked. When she and her husband are no longer here, "Jimmy's brother will be his guardian, and we have a trust fund."

Jimmy has never dated. Though his mother says he is effeminate, he has had no "interest in homosexuality. Some retarded kids just aren't interested, they just masturbate and that's the end of it. I guess he kind of falls into that category," his mother explained.

They also leveled with their eldest son about Jimmy's situation. "We put it in terms that he could understand. We were always very careful to never ask him to baby sit. We made a gargantuan effort not to set him up so that he would resent Jimmy more than he would naturally. And it worked. As you know, it's very common for siblings of the retarded to suddenly decide they want to study Japanese, or maybe go to Alaska and stay for five years and check out the mountains and get fucking far enough away. One day something came up and I said to Jimmy's brother *you just can't understand what this is like.* He looked at me and said, 'Oh, can't I? Don't ever say that to me again that I can't understand,'" Abigail explained.

When Abigail described Jimmy's diagnosis to her mother-in-law she said, "'Why that's ridiculous, there's nothing wrong with Jimmy. He's just a little slow.' She could not accept the whole idea. And there was never a kind word to me like 'gee, you're doing good.' My daddy was realistic. When he saw the children at the Arbor Academy auction, he said to me, 'Abigail, I don't know how you can stand this.' I always felt he was on my side."

I asked Abigail about her friends: "If a friend didn't accept it that was the end of it. You know, goodbye, so long. My friends were wonderful."

Both parents use pottery making as a way to handle their stress. "I beat the shit out of the clay twice a week," Abigail explained. "The thing that got me through this was a sense of humor, because if you don't, you could go crazy. Stress takes years off your life. It affected my psyche in that I eat under stress."

How did raising Jimmy affect their marriage? "Well, we didn't get a divorce," Abigail said. "At one point we thought about it. There were times that we were so worn out and felt exhausted and depressed… We turned into the Bobsy Twins. I'm the fierce little bull…Dean would calmly and forcefully do something that would cause action instantly. We're a team.

"It made me far more compassionate to all kinds of situations that are different from any of mine. I don't judge people as much," Abigail said. "It's made me far more understanding."

Dean said, "I think it probably made me a lot more tolerant with people with short-comings." He feels that having Jimmy has helped him work with people in his practice. "In this field there are no experts. People who are experts are often more destructive than helpful.

I have been given such bad advice, such poor understanding. There are some shining exceptions. Some people offered warmth, caring and some common sense. They were far more helpful than the experts."

Dean continued, "This is not an area that gets a lot of attention. This is a group that is easily ignored. The way our political system works is that the squeaky wheel gets the grease." He said that after 20 or 30 years of advocating for special needs children, sitting on boards, pushing for programs, and raising money, parents get burned out. "I think in some ways that society was kinder in years back. They were much more aware of the burden on the family, and their solution was to put these kids in institutions. What's there now is so pitiable and meager, and you jump through so many hoops to get...Social Security... We live in Georgia and it's 50th in the nation in terms of what we offer for the disabled. Our Legislature is sitting on an enormous surplus and trying to figure out what to do with it. I'm disappointed in our society."

Jacque

Lila's pregnancy was normal, but when, during labor in 1982, the baby was in the breech position, the doctor opted for a C-section. "At six months Jacque wasn't sitting up. People didn't want to hurt my feelings but they were hinting that something was up. The pediatrician thought she was lazy and would out grow it." A radiologist in the hospital where Lila worked in Brunswick, Georgia recommended she see another doctor.

Lila, her husband, Joel, and his mother took Jacque to the doctor's office. After the examination he said, "'I have bad news.' So he tells us that he thought that Jacque would be a vegetable. He didn't think she'd walk, or talk. I stood there and started crying and the only thing that I said to him was, *was she going to die?* I didn't want her to die. I wanted to prevent her from dying. It took Joel and me a long time to have this child. It was the worst moment of our lives because he told us such devastating news. He couldn't actually diagnose her. I don't quite remember what else he said. The poignant part of this was walking out into the parking lot and the three of us bawling our heads off.

"Right after that we were referred to a developmental specialist in Savannah. She was more encouraging and told us that Jacque was developmentally delayed, and that she would not be as serious as we were told. She would be delayed." When Lila told the doctor what the specialist said, "He apologized and said he would never, ever tell anybody that again, that he made a mistake."

The family moved to Atlanta where their daughter could receive better medical services and special education. At the time of the interview Jacque was in her last year of school and working at Chuck E Cheese restaurant two days a week. She was in a program that helped her with on-the-job training and getting a job.

Even though Jacque "dates" in a group, Lila worries about sex and her daughter getting pregnant. She's had sex education classes, but doesn't fully understand the concept. Consequently, her mother is considering a tubal ligation.

When asked about her marriage, Lila said, "I think it's brought us closer because we've had to deal with it. It sort of takes off of us, and centers it towards Jacque and what we're going do for her, her future. I think it's made us stronger. It's always hard."

How did Lila and Joel deal with having a special needs child?" "It was hard for both of us but I think it was especially hard for him. It took Joel a very long time to accept this."

Lila told her husband about a new camp for special needs children, and that she wanted their daughter to attend. Joel said, "'Absolutely not.' He wanted her to go to a quote camp for normal kids." So they sent her to a regular camp that did not work out. "After that, I said to my husband, *you see, we're going do it my way*. Slowly but surely he's come around. I think he's finally seen that it won't change, that she won't get fine tomorrow." He sees that she's happy in her special programs and that they were trying to make themselves happy, not their child.

"I did everything to include her just to make her feel quote normal like any other child. I didn't tell her there was anything wrong." When they finally told Jacque she had a disability, "She wanted to know what a disability was. She said, 'Why do I have a disability?' I said, *each one of us has something we're disabled about.* Right now she cannot stand to be told that she's a special needs or disabled person. You can't shelter them forever.

"You always worry about the future; you worry what's going to happen. My biggest concern is where she's going to live. I want her to be able to go out on her own with supervision.

"I used to be shy and quiet but you can't be when you have a child with special needs. You can't just sit back, you have to go forward, it's always a fight, and you have to find the latest resources. It wasn't easy, but that's okay. I've certainly learned a lot."

Walton

"I had an excellent pregnancy, but I had had a difficult one before (with her first child)," Vivian said of her pregnancy with Walton. "There was an infection that had flared up during the pregnancy from the previous time. We figured that the reason he ended up retarded was from medication that was taken during pregnancy."

Walton's parents first became concerned when he was three years old. "It was time for him to start speaking and he didn't. He chattered with single words instead of talking in sentences." Vivian's husband was in the military and, because they were stationed in Norway at the time, they were sent to the medical headquarters in Germany for evaluation. Then Vivian returned to Norway while her husband remained in Germany with Walton waiting for the test results.

He was alone when he heard that "his little boy had mild retardation," Vivian said. "He was crushed. He was very distressed about it."

She added that she also was "Crushed. I said, *that can't be.* He had been toilet trained at the age of 18 months, both night and day, and he had done all the social things at an early age. It was just talking that he didn't do. We were very, very crushed. He did not have fine motor coordination."

When Walton was four years old, he attended a small private preschool in Norway, until he turned six. He then went into a regular class in public school. "The teachers were very understanding and very sweet. But he was definitely not able to keep up with the other children. Since his father was in the military, the first nine years of his life he went to seven different schools. He went to whatever school was available. Some of the teachers were great and would work with him beautifully, while others were unable to give him the right kind of attention. The unfortunate part of it was that every time he was somewhere long enough so that he was really getting somewhere, we'd move. He would start back over from the beginning. By the time he was nine or ten years old, we came back to the States to live. My husband retired and we settled down in Georgia."

The family moved to Milledgeville where Walton was placed "into special education classes in public school. Georgia at that time didn't have very much at all." Then Walton attended a school that was attached to the Milledgeville State Mental Hospital. "We got him into that as an out-patient and they were marvelous, they were just great with him. They turned closets into rooms for special ed, and I used to work very hard with the teachers to get them materials that they needed."

The time eventually came when that program was not the right placement for Walton, sending his mother on the hunt for a private school for him. She found one in North Carolina but did not want him going so far away from home. When she took him to a psychiatrist for an evaluation, and told the doctor her dilemma, the doctor suggested, "'Well, let him live with us. There's a little private school near us, and he can go there.' So for a year he went there."

When the family moved to Atlanta, Walton was placed in public school special education classes. "This was the best situation because he was not so retarded that he didn't know he was different and he didn't struggle to try and make himself fit in."

Walton speaks very well now. His main problems were reading, writing and counting. "He has no concept of numbers. We had private tutors for him. It concerned me so that he was going to go through life not being able to count money...he just doesn't have the concept.

"There's nothing he wanted more in his life than to read. We sent him to a reading clinic and discovered that he has dyslexia, as if he needed something more. He learned to read one and two syllable words. He can read simple words but he can't read a sentence."

Vivian found a program in California for special needs children and bought some of their teaching aids. "By the time he got out of high school he knew how to do his own laundry, and do a lot of other things for taking care of himself."

Following his graduation from high school, "He went into a work program where he worked as a busboy for a big hotel downtown. When they changed bosses, they didn't want to have handicapped people there. So the job ended."

One of the side effects of Walton's brain damage is his inability to focus on particular tasks. Over the years he tried his hand at different jobs; he worked for a motel folding clothes, and at a factory assembling paper cup dispensers. At each job "they liked him, he was good natured, he was pleasant, and they thought he was great. But he couldn't constantly deliver, he couldn't focus enough to deliver regularly." He worked in a hotel kitchen for three years.

One day when Walton was 24 years old, and living in a group home, he said to his mother, "'I've got a lump.' I looked and he had a lump on his leg. His lump grew three times its size in three days. They discovered that he had bone cancer." Walton's leg was amputated six inches above his knee, and then he underwent 13 weeks of chemotherapy. "He was fitted for a prosthesis, and placed in a physical therapy program for the disabled."

Afterward he got another job. "They wanted him to carry boxes full of vegetables. It was physically too much for him. So he decided he didn't want to go there anymore. It was the last full-time job he had.

"He now works Tuesday, Thursday and Friday as a volunteer worker at a daycare center in a church for seniors. He has a wonderful time. He works in the kitchen, he runs the big dishwasher, he cleans up the kitchen, and does anything they need him to do. They think he's just marvelous. They have been so wonderful and supportive of him."

I asked Vivian about her feelings regarding doctors. "Some doctors have been absolutely marvelous. Then there are doctors who don't know how to communicate with anyone who has a handicap. They don't talk to Walton, they only talk to me. Walton finds it difficult to ask questions and to explain what his problems are. So I sort of translate for him if it's necessary. It's just so frustrating. Walton's not dumb. He may not be able to function at the level that another person does, but he is not dumb. If he is ignored totally, he resents it.

"When he finished with his chemo, he was so angry with life that we got him some counseling. They worked with his anger and his frustration because his whole life had been turned upside down. They were really wonderful with him.

Walton's parents went the group home route again. Finally after a long struggle with living in group homes, he got a chance to live in an apartment under the auspices of the health department. He has a roommate. The whole complex has handicapped people. He's feeling so proud of himself, and is finally independent in his own way."

I asked Vivian if her son dates. "It's been a major problem. He says, 'I'm not like them.' He wouldn't have anything to do with other retarded people. When he made approaches to those who were not retarded, he got into trouble. They often see themselves differently."

Vivian said Walton and his problems did not affect her marriage adversely. "We hung on to each other harder. We were able to support each other more than if we had not had a problem."

Walton has an older and a younger sister. Vivian said they reacted to their brother "with frustration. With a great deal of protection. My oldest daughter was so angry with some young boy who was picking on Walton on and off the bus. She told him that if he ever came near her brother again she would let him have it. It scared him to death."

Did Walton ever embarrass his siblings? "Yes. What do you do? You have a brother who is not like others. They understood what the problem was, they understood what his handicap was, but that didn't mean that it wasn't embarrassing at times, that it wasn't difficult at times, but they really have been supportive of him."

How do other family members react to Walton? Vivian said they were supportive. "Walton was a very good-natured, cheerful, well-behaved child. He didn't act up; he didn't cause any problems as behavior went. But no one wanted to take care of him. I never had a night out. They would volunteer to have the girls over, but never to have Walton over. It was as if they didn't understand that he was not hard to take of. I would think *Oh, it would be so wonderful if they would just take him for an evening, and we could go out.* But no, one ever volunteered to do that."

As for friends, "Our military friends just loved him. Now, they didn't take care of him or anything. One of the first things they ask if they see me after a long time is, 'How is Walton?' And when he had his leg amputated, they were crushed. I had very understanding friends who cared about him."

I asked Vivian how she coped with having a special needs child. "Many nights I cried myself to sleep," she said tearfully. Like many other parents, her emotions are very close to the surface. Her husband "...dealt with it with a great deal of heartache, he was very understanding."

Did raising Walton take a toll on her? "It taught me a lot, and I won't say it's been easy, but it was sure good for me. I learned so much and became a much better person."

Does she feel different for having gone through the experience? "Yeah, oh yeah. You can't be self-centered when you have a handicapped child. You just can't. His needs have got to be primary, and you just can't indulge in yourself.

"We never, never spoiled Walton. We expected his behavior to be acceptable at all times. There could be no other option. And he did behave. Occasionally, the girls would think we were being too strict with him. My husband and I had decided he had to live in this world, and he had to learn how to behave to live in this world. And he was capable of learning that. We had to prepare him."

Vivian offered this advice: "Get all the help you can possibly get, because you can't do it all yourself. A lady called me and said she had a very disabled son who had been going to a special school. They could no longer keep him because he was too old. She was going to keep him at home, and wanted to have help in taking care of him. My advice to her was *find a daycare place and let him get out of the house and on his own. He'll grow and you'll grow.*

"Don't give up. Walton has gone through states of anger, stages of depression, stages of frustration, and so on, and I went through them with him. He has grown. Here he is 45 years old and he's now doing so much better than he was doing two years ago that you could hardly believe. So don't give up."

Tommy

Andrea was in an automobile accident around the 4th or 5th month of her pregnancy, and was not wearing a seatbelt when her car rolled over. "When I was able to get out of the car I was shaky and very nervous," she said.

A little over a year after his birth (1973), "When Tommy started walking, he would hold on with his index finger, and wouldn't let go. I didn't think anything of it, not having any children before, I just figured he'd walk when he's ready.

Tommy did not talk. He said "Mama" at eight months, then nothing." When he still wasn't talking at three, she discussed it with her father who was also her son's pediatrician. "He didn't say anything, and I didn't know the questions to ask. I found out later that he was concerned but he didn't tell me. He just wasn't sure what was going on.

"At the first school we went to, a little pre-school, he would walk around with his hands covering his ears. I knew he didn't like loud sounds, and he didn't like the sound of aluminum foil, that was kind of grating. I got a call from the teacher saying that Tommy has a problem. She said, 'In the morning when we're calling his name, he doesn't respond.' So I did my own little test. Tommy would be in front of the TV, I would talk as softly as I could, and he would hear me. Therefore, I dismissed the idea that Tommy had a hearing problem.

"At school, Tommy was always crying, not able to handle scissors, his fine motor skills were not good, he's almost four by then. I went to the teacher and she said, 'We think Tommy may have CP.' *What's CP?* I asked. 'Cerebral Palsy.' *I beg your pardon?* I was just flabbergasted. I couldn't believe what I was hearing. And I didn't know what to do.

"I went to my father and asked, *What's wrong?* 'I don't know what's wrong but I have noticed that he's slower at doing things,'" he responded. Andrea had Tommy tested through the county, and the psychometrist tried twice to test him and found him unresponsive and declared him untestable. She then took him to a doctor who tested him and diagnosed a learning disability.

"We were very upset. Not realizing that he had a problem, we took Tommy as the person and not as the disability. We didn't have any knowledge, we didn't know what to expect down the road."

They had Tommy tested at the local speech school in the Atlanta area. He tested "below average" but they were unable to diagnose any specific disability. They suggested giving him Ritalin, and his test scores came up just a bit. He was enrolled in their school and completed three full years.

Tommy transferred to a public school special education class and did well. "I remember in elementary school as the years went on, they would change Tommy's label. They would say he's emotionally mentally handicapped, mentally retarded with emotional problems, and I would just look at his teacher and ask, *What is going on here? Why are all these things changing?* 'Andrea, nothing has changed, it's the only way to keep him in the program. Don't be upset with the terminology because Tommy is still the same Tommy. He hasn't changed, he's not mentally retarded, or emotionally mentally handicapped...this is just where he fits' ...After all these years we still did not have a diagnosis," she explained.

Andrea said that Tommy embarrassed his sister particularly when they were on the school bus going to elementary school. He would talk to himself and talk about trucks, which he loved.

Tommy first attended a regular Sunday school then moved to the *Havanah* program. His parents also wanted him Bar Mitzvahed. "The day of the Bar Mitzvah there was not a dry eye in the place, and you could have heard a pin drop," his mother said. "I had a nightmare the night before that we were going up on the pulpit, but Tommy was still sitting in his chair. And the rabbi goes over and says, 'Tommy, what's the matter?' and he replies, 'I don't want to do this, I can't do this.'" The next morning at the Temple, "Tommy did a phenomenal job.

"We tried to do everything we could to put Tommy in sports...soccer...did Special Olympics. After that we learned to say, this is who he is and this is what we're gonna be proud of. And we got through it."

After Tommy graduated from school Andrea didn't know what to do. "I said, *Tommy, you can live here for four years and then after that you're on your own.* Not meaning it literally. He was petrified. "

Tommy received a little bit of job experience at Kroger and Burger King while he was in high school. Afterwards, he spent two years at a sheltered workshop. When he became dissatisfied, his parents sought the help of a program offering services in independent living. Then he decided that he wanted to work in a hotel. He went on an interview at a Holiday Inn, and got the job; he's been there for over eight years.

"We have been assured that through the Independent Living Program, Tommy will be taken care of for the rest of his life. He will need someone to always take care of his financial needs because of his disability...they assure me that that is in place. I feel very comfortable. My daughter lives out of state right now, and I don't know where she'll end up."

"In the beginning I felt that all of Tommy's problems were my problems, that they were always on my shoulders. I was the one dealing emotionally with it, and I didn't think that Jason (her husband) was dealing with it. Finally, we had a long discussion and I said, *Tell me what's wrong. Tell me how you feel about this...* "He said, 'You think I'm not upset? I wanted a son I could go out and play baseball with. I wanted a son who would play football. I wanted somebody I could really go hang out with.'"

Andrea said the things in life that her son has missed hurt her. "He didn't go to college, he didn't have quite the social life...it's different than what other men do. Even though he has his driver's license, he doesn't drive. He's in his normal life, not my normal life.

"We couldn't be any happier for the strides Tommy has made that I had no anticipation, no expectations of." He had the lead in a play, "and the words that came out of his mouth and the projection, I didn't believe my son when I first heard him.

"It's made me very aware of people's problems, and it has opened my mind up to all different kinds of learning. Everybody learns in a different way. Everybody is an individual."

As a teacher Andrea often talks to parents with special needs children. She says, "I had no expectation for Tommy, I didn't put forth any goals for him. Whatever Tommy did was his goal and now the goals just keep getting better and better because Tommy is making the goals and he is achieving the goals. And he is a wonderful, well-adjusted person."

Tommy went on a trip to Israel. "He comes off the plane and says, 'I have a girlfriend'" who he met on the plane going over. In the fall of 2003, Tommy married a young woman who has Down syndrome.

Brenda

There was a problem with the anesthesia during Brenda's birth in 1963. "In the back of my mind I've always had the feeling maybe there was too much anesthetic...I've never considered investigating, or suing, I'm not faulting the doctor, it's just the way we did things then," her mother, Esther, said.

"Brenda didn't talk, and I was the only one who could understand her." When she was around three, she was evaluated at a local speech school in the Atlanta area, and was turned down for their program. "The words they used and what they said at the time just didn't penetrate...I think one of the reasons that she didn't qualify was due to her IQ range, although I don't think it was ever put to me quite that clearly. It's only in retrospect that I realize what they were saying to me.

"When I tell you that was like a shock...It's almost like we sleepwalked through it. You're dumb, you're stupid, you don't know the questions to ask, or about what to look for. You don't understand what they're trying to tell you. It just blows your mind that there could possibly be a problem...Asher (her husband) and I were mostly in denial, we refused to believe it. Disappointed. My son the doctor, my son the lawyer, my daughter the whatever. You are beginning to see that these things aren't going to be. We were angry, why me, why us? This is a beautiful child."

Brenda was tutored several days a week by a speech therapist "and her speech problems resolved themselves beautifully...Then it came time to go to school. My boys were going to a private religious school, and I think at this point we were beginning to realize that that was not going to be the school for Brenda." She was then placed in a public school that wanted her tested. Afterwards, the parents were told that Brenda was educationally mentally retarded. They looked into various schools and found Arbor Academy.

Brenda's parents found the words *learning disabled* easier to swallow. "I don't think we ever really admitted to anybody that she had been diagnosed as educationally mentally retarded for many, many years." But they did explain the situation to Brenda's brothers so they could understand what her needs would be as she grew older.

Later, Brenda attended a religious boarding school in Denver, Colorado and received special tutoring. She had a good year and the family had a period of respite. The parents were told that she could be easily led, and "behold, she got kicked out for smoking pot. That was traumatic." She returned to Atlanta where she graduated from a public high school special education class.

Esther contacted a local junior college and explained that her daughter had learning disabilities and could not take the entrance exam, but she wanted to enroll in their early childhood program. "This gave Brenda the opportunity to say, 'yes, I go to college'...and I sat and worked with her every single night. We read the stuff together, and she finished the course. She achieved so much higher than they had told us she would, and it was partly because Brenda never had anything but normal expectations of herself even though she knew she had learning disabilities. She grew up a more compassionate young woman. I always told her we couldn't ever laugh at somebody or criticize somebody who might be different."

Esther also helped Brenda get her driver's license. "I spent a lot of years and a lot of energy with her. As a result, she had a profession, she's a paraprofessional."

Brenda's brothers were living in New York, so she moved there, got a roommate, and found a job as an assistant at a preschool. She dated and then married. When her parents discovered that her husband was into cocaine and had gotten Brenda hooked on it, they brought her back to Atlanta and got her into the 12-Step program.

Brenda has worked for over 15 years in a public school special education class as an assistant. The school authorities suggested that she go to Georgia State University to get a teaching degree.

She is now married to a man who is not developmentally disabled, and they have a child who attends private religious school. "They have a nice life," her mother proudly said. She also admits that their grandchild is the apple of her grandparents' eyes.

How did it affect her marriage? "We worked together hand in hand," Esther said. "It didn't come between us, didn't cause a strain between us, we always had a close relationship."

Chapter 10

Parents With Two Special Needs Children

"When challenges are presented to us...we can do all kinds of things," a parent

Courtney and Gene

Problems with Courtney were apparent at birth when she had difficulty sucking on her bottle. Next came problems with her physical development; she did not roll over until she was five months old, and did not walk until she was 18 months old.

The pediatrician "didn't really say anything. I had to practically beg him to tell me if he noticed anything wrong. He said that people develop at different times," her mother, Lucia, said. The pediatrician said Courtney was developmentally delayed, but her mother felt there was more.

When Courtney was three she was placed in a private pre-school program. "She was putting two words together, not three. They told me by the end of the year that she should be able to draw a face and she wasn't drawing a face. They referred me to a speech school in the Atlanta area," and she was accepted into their program.

After two successful years, Courtney transferred to a public school kindergarten class, and moved on into regular classes for the first three grades. When she was in fourth grade, "They told me that they thought she was severely emotionally disturbed, and that she should go to a severely emotionally disturbed class. I knew she wasn't disturbed. I knew she had learning difficulties and had problems with speech," her mother asserted. She then attended a private school until the eighth grade.

For four summers, she went to a camp in Pennsylvania. She made friends and "She started to feel better about herself."

Courtney spent her high school years in public school where she took some regular classes and some clerical classes. After graduation she went to work full time at the Internal Revenue Service where she works as a clerk in the collection department.

"My daughter lives in her own apartment by herself." People from a local program come every other week to monitor her. They help her with things such as "budgeting, transportation, and going to the store," her mother said proudly.

Lucia's second child, Gene, was born three years after Courtney. "He did things more slowly than Courtney did, didn't walk until age two and a half; he was potty trained at four and a half. He did well when he went to public school."

Because of his "severe behavior, he (six years old) lived with a paraprofessional from the public school, and then he lived with Dorothy Miller from the Elaine Clark Center. At age nine he became a residential student at a private school because he needed 24 hour care. He's been more difficult than Courtney as far as getting programs for him."

What is it like having two children with major problems? "It's very difficult. I divorced when they were three and six. You sort of got an idea that your kids weren't going to be rocket scientists. Going over to other people's homes where they had normal children was difficult because either my daughter would cry, or not play, and not get along. I felt like my kids didn't fit in," Lucia explained.

Her husband: "He's a person who just doesn't show any emotions. He's not a responsible person. When it came to the children, he wanted to ride bikes; be president of the Jaycees...he just wasn't involved.

"The problems with my marriage had nothing to do with my children," Lucia said. "My x-husband came home one day and said, 'I've always done what I had to do, and I don't want to do that anymore.'" She found an apartment and was divorced 30 days later.

"It's been difficult. Sometimes I feel like running away."

How does she cope with two special needs children? "How I beat the system is I plan for a vacation. I like to plan for a vacation about six months ahead so I can think about the vacation. Afterwards, for six months, I think about how wonderful the vacation was. I also have therapy once a month.

"It's important to have nice friends. I have friends who have children with disabilities, but most of them don't. I'm in organizations. But it's still fun to belong to groups that have nothing to do with disabilities.

"I guess what I worry about is what will happen to them when I'm gone. I only have a younger sister and we're not real close. I don't have any siblings to look after them. That's really my biggest fear.

Has she changed through this experience? "It made me more sensitive. At times I feel sorry for myself, but at times I think if I can do this I can do anything. I survived a divorce, having two children with special needs, and my mother died. I've done everything else myself."

Isabel and Christy

When Isabel was born, she weighed 9 pounds, 2 ounces. "Her head was kind of like a dunce cap, and the doctor said not to worry about it that was normal with big babies," her mother, Stella, said.

Two years later sister Christy was born. When Isabel was around three, she knocked her sister down a step and the youngster was taken to the hospital.

Later during a pediatric visit, the doctor wanted to know more about Christy's time in the hospital. He called the hospital physician, and then he handed the phone to Stella. Thinking that the pediatrician was still on the line, the hospital physician informed her that he thought that Christy was retarded.

"We had started to suspect that there was something wrong with Isabel because she wasn't talking. Isabel was drooling a lot and her tongue was enlarged so it was out a lot. The doctor must have suspected that she was retarded. I was young and didn't know anything.

"The pediatrician suggested having both girls tested. He got us into the Illinois Pediatric Center in Chicago, and at that point we hadn't even thought that there was anything wrong with Christy. We went through a lot of testing. In the end, they diagnosed them both as being mildly retarded.

"It was devastating. I couldn't believe it, especially for Christy. Of course I started to cry and the doctors were very cold. I remember at the time they just said, 'Well, you just have to get yourself together and accept this for the way it is and just deal with it. Don't even try putting them into a school or anything, they'll learn from their younger brother and sister at home. Keep them at home,'" Stella explained.

"My husband was a kind of quiet type guy and he was a lot better than I was, at least he didn't show a lot of emotion. It was hard for him to believe."

In the beginning, the girls' school situation was difficult, and they went from one pre-school to another. Christy had the hardest time because of her hyperactivity. "They never lasted very long. They would be in for a few months then for one reason or another they would not be in school anymore. They didn't look retarded so they could get by until you started talking to them." They attended the Easter Seals program for speech therapy. Despite the fact that the professionals kept telling their mother to keep the girls at home, she knew they needed schooling.

The family moved to Louisville, Kentucky from Chicago, and the girls were placed in programs where they began to learn. When the family returned to Illinois, both girls went to public school. Christy was mainstreamed, and Isabel was put in a special education class where she did very well, and graduated at 21 years old.

After graduation Christy went to Little Friend's Spectrum workshop, and at times she has tried different jobs. She lives in an apartment by herself. Isabel lives at home, and has worked for over 20 years in the dish room at a Marriott hotel.

"Christy and Isabel are totally different people. Christy is very open and friendly, she's very extroverted. Isabel is an introvert, she's very quiet, and she keeps to herself. She doesn't like to visit people, even family. She's crazy about her nieces and nephews."

The sisters fight with each other all the time. "Christy comes home almost every weekend, and by the end of the weekend I'm really tearing my hair out to take her back because they fight. Isabel feels like the house is hers, it's her territory and she doesn't want Christy invading it. "

Isabel has a problem with screaming and yelling. "When I took a bath, she had it in her head that I should never take my clothes off. She would be banging on the door with her fists, and yelling and screaming for me to get out of the tub," Stella said, her frustration showing.

"I haven't dated much since my husband died (in 1985) because she makes things so hard on me. If I wanted to go with my girlfriend to a movie or shopping she'd come out and follow me onto the driveway and scream at me, 'I don't want you drinking!' I don't drink, maybe a glass of wine at dinner. 'Don't take your clothes off!' She'd be yelling this out on my driveway." Fortunately, her neighbors are sympathetic and have even invited her into their homes for a drink to calm her down.

A psychiatrist is treating Isabel with Prozac, which makes things better for everyone. Her mother can now take a bath with her clothes off and go out with her friends. She is looking for the right residential facility for her daughter.

Stella has two more children. She said that her oldest daughter found it hard to deal with her two special needs sisters. "Even to this day, she can't tolerate them. She gets real upset if they start acting up or start fighting. She's very generous with them when it comes to birthdays, but she really doesn't like being around them for long periods of time. She says now that that's why she didn't bring her friends around a lot." She also doesn't want to come home with her own children because she doesn't want them to see their aunts' bad behavior. "My son has always been more accepting of the girls. He's more patient with them. He has no problem with the two girls."

Their mother doesn't think that Christy and Isabel have had real dates. Isabel was once asked to go to an office party. "The boy's parents drove him to our house, he came to the door and picked Isabel up and took her to his Christmas party. I was so excited about it. I thought it was so neat. She never went again. She doesn't want them touching her or coming near her. " She is not worried about Isabel getting pregnant.

"Christy is boy crazy. She has boyfriends all the time; most of the time they've been telephone boyfriends. When she lived at the CLF (Little Friends' Community Living Facility) she would have one boyfriend after another. They kind of change boyfriends all the time." Her mother feels that most of their activity is in holding hands and kissing. "Now that she lives in her own apartment it worries me because she does have different boyfriends. Christy is on birth control for that reason, you just never know what situation she would get herself into, and God forbid she would get pregnant. I know I couldn't live through it again raising her child. One of the boys has been trying to talk her into having sex. That scares me. She tells me everything. I try not to get too upset because I don't want her not to tell me."

Stella said of her husband, "He was really good. If I was getting down and out like I can't take this anymore, he would always back me up. He would say, 'It's God's will, what are you gonna do? This is the way it is,' and he talked me out of it. If he started to lose control because Isabel would be screaming and yelling, he would say, 'I can't take this anymore, I'm gonna kill her!' I would calm him down. We could always calm each other down when one of us lost it. It didn't affect our marriage. If we fought, we fought over the kids in general. We were always pretty much in agreement with everything except with Isabel's screaming."

What were Stella's feelings about raising two special needs children? "Exhaustion. There was nothing I could do about it. I felt, and to this day, totally hopeless. Isabel still lives at home, and Christy calls me three or four times a night. She wants to come home every weekend."

I asked her what toll there had been. "My life, I guess. I dated one guy after my husband died, and he couldn't deal with Isabel I don't think I've had a date in ten years...I don't have time for me." She's worried about what will happen to Isabel when something happens to her.

Burke Jr. and Melanie

Vera took her son, Burk Jr., to the pediatrician for his six-week checkup and "the doctor starts talking to me about the size of his head. He says, 'You know, this baby's head is really small,' and it just clicked to me what he was trying to say. And I said, *are you saying this child is microcephalic?* This is where the head is unusually small because the brain has not grown. And he said, 'Yes I am.' It went downhill from there. He said, 'Well, I think that you should look for an institution, some place for him to go because he will be a vegetable. There is no hope, and you need to find some place right away.'

"I was devastated, absolutely blown away. I didn't know anything about babies, but I had studied abnormal psychology in college so I had known the terms and knew what they meant.

"We kept him and tried to figure out what to do," Vera said. The family moved from Virginia to Atlanta and found the Elaine Clark Center where he began learning. From there he went into special education classes in public school. "He evolved from there, I got him all kinds of speech therapy, and he's done very well. He's like a sponge, he learns very well."

When Burke Jr. was about eight, his father "begged and begged that we have another child," Vera said. "I went for genetic counseling. And the geneticists said, 'You know your chances are like 5%, (to have another macrocephalic child)' but it was too late, I was already pregnant." Unfortunately, they were in the 5%. "Right away we knew that Melanie was also microcephalic." Vera feels that there is a recessive gene since no one on either side of the family has the same problem.

"The second was not so bad. They are so lucky to have each other. They have many friends because we are involved in so many groups. They get along pretty well under the circumstances; they have a great deal in common. A lot of his problems came when she was born. He was eight years old and was the life of everybody. There was normal sibling rivalry and jealously," Vera said.

Concerned about Burke Jr.'s behavior, his mother explained to him,

"You know, Melanie has mental retardation too. He was absolutely amazed. He never dreamed that his sister was also disabled. She'd gone through special ed classes like him, but she just seemed so normal, she's very cute, very outgoing, and very liked, and he always thought she was just fine and it was only him that had problems. And I think that it's made a big difference in their relationship, they're very close."

Burke Jr. lives at home and drives to work at Emory Hospital where he works in the landscaping department. "Every single day we say, *thank you, God, for one more day.* His bosses are very tolerant and very understanding, because he has behavior problems. I think his behavior problems stem from the fact that he is pretty high functioning for a retarded person. He's a very smart retarded person.

"He did live in an apartment for four years with help from two different agencies that offered independent living. In the apartment he had so much freedom and he didn't handle it well. He grew lonely and we finally decided he was really going downhill in a hurry. He had a roommate. I think the roommate situation is the hardest of all because of the strengths and weaknesses. My son needs a lot of structure with his time. He has a tendency to want to fantasize too much. He's very creative, very arty; I think if he was normal he would be a little weird because he's very bohemian and creative."

How has her husband handled his son? "That's been a problem. He wants the world for Burke. His whole life has been spent around gearing up and having things for these kids when we're gone. We've had a psychologist tell us that he needs to live for now instead of for later. He and his son clash a great deal because he wants so much for Burke, and Burke wishes he would bug off and leave him alone. He's kind of a drill instructor type with Burke, although he's softened up over the years. He would never have given him up in a million years."

Melanie went the same educational track as her brother though her education in the same school was of poorer quality. She too lives at home and works at a Publix grocery store.

Both Burke and Melanie are involved with Special Olympics. "It's great. I love Special Olympics. Because of the different sports, these people get a chance to get out and train to learn different types of athletics. They have coaches and volunteers who help them to learn how to do whatever sport. My daughter is big into ice skating. She just competed in world games with Russia, and China, and she won. I'm so proud of her it makes me cry. She beat everybody in the world." In the 2001 International Special Olympics World Games in Anchorage, Alaska, she won a gold medal in Figure Skating.

Burke "was an ice skater and was pretty good. When he moved out the first time into an apartment, he felt he was above all this. It colored him against doing a lot of sports and I didn't like that. He is on the Georgia Board of Directors for Special Olympics. It teaches them how to get along with other people, and that they're not the be all and end all."

In discussing the future of her two children, Vera said, "I know that they have to move out, I understand that. My husband would like them to move out. I don't want them to move out. They don't want to go, they don't even like to talk about it. Burke, Jr. told the psychiatrist just last week that it was time for him to move out. But I know the reason he told him that is that's what he thought he (the doctor) wanted to hear." But when someone else asked him about moving, he said, "'absolutely not, I can't go because my parents need me at home.'"

Vera has invested so much time, energy, and love in her two children that she wonders what will become of her when they are properly situated outside her care. "What would I do? I've never worked outside the home. I've always taken care of my kids."

When asked what will happen to her children when she and her husband are no longer here she said, "I don't know. They'll just have to be in an independent supported arrangement. There are several groups that we're looking at. It's a constant worry. What are we gonna do? That's all my husband talks about. I'm not ready and they're not ready. When it's time I'll know it.

"Melanie doesn't date because she's only interested in those so called normal people on television like In Sync, and Backstreet Boys. As far as the boys in the groups she's in, she's never shown any interest.

They haven't shown any interest in her. She's not even developed, she's like a 12-year-old girl." Her mother does worry about Melanie being taken advantage of, and feels that she is protected at her job and in the community.

Vera feels that having two special needs children is a plus for their marriage. "It's probably kept it together because everyone has times when they just don't want to do this anymore. But we have a special reason to stay together."

"I enjoy my kids, they're fun. They have a sense of humor. They're just a few rungs lower than normal," Vera said. "Socially they are not at all retarded.

"I wish that they hadn't been handicapped. I wish that they could have been normal. But when I look around me, I don't know that their lives are any worse than most of the normal people that I see. They just have different problems.

"I wish sometimes that I could be freer and that's nobody's fault by my own. I have access to respite and I've never ever used it. My husband nags me incessantly to use it." She said she only felt comfortable with her mother and mother-in-law taking care of her children.

"I never had an opportunity to have a career, which doesn't really matter a whole lot. I could have done something else. My family is the most important thing to me.

"I'm more tolerant of people, I think, than I would have been. I know that my husband is certainly more tolerant. You learn to not be so impatient with people."

Vera said there was very little religion in their home when her two children were young. "I hate to say it but, the Catholic Church never did anything for our children. I have to tell you I have a great deal of resentment. You couldn't put them in a Catholic school here in Atlanta. So we've kind of fallen away from the church." After she discovered the special Sunday school class at St. Jude in the Atlanta area, the children began attending. Now we go to the Baptist Church on the first Tuesday of the month, we're very ecumenical. We go to the Catholic things, and we go to the Jewish things."

Curtis Jr. and Ella

Eunice, an occupational therapist, became concerned about the physical development of her young son, Curtis Jr. who was born in 1959. "Everybody said I was overly apprehensive. He would crawl then fall over sideways and lose his balance if he happened to look up at you or something. He did not sit as well. And when I mentioned it to the pediatrician she said I had a very progressive daughter the first time so I was comparing him, and I shouldn't compare. He was a boy and he would respond differently." They changed pediatricians. "Years later she came to me and apologized. She said, 'I'm sorry that I didn't recognize it earlier, you were right, he did have a problem.'"

Eunice also noticed a difference when she would diaper her baby. "You hold their two legs and lift them up to put the diaper under; one of his legs didn't go up as easily. I would mention that to doctors, they would check him out, see that nothing was wrong with him, and then send him on his way.

"He didn't develop like other children did and nobody would say anything to me, nobody would agree that there was anything wrong." While at an occupational therapy meeting with the director of the Easter Seals Center, "I asked her to look at Curt and said, *Don't you think something's wrong with his balance?* She said, 'Eunice I think you're over anxious, just wait and see.' I said, *I don't think so, I think something's wrong.*"

Even though Curtis was still not walking at 18 months of age, "He had a good vocabulary, he knew lots of words, but his pronunciation was bad. The one thing that I probably should have noticed was he was not as good a nurser as his sister had been. He couldn't control his tongue well enough to nurse as well."

When Curtis was about two and a half he attended a preschool program at the Easter Seals Center. Still with no proper diagnosis of his condition, he attended the Center mainly for physical therapy.

When he was three, "we thought we would go on with our family, we didn't intend to limit it because of (his son's problems)," Curtis Sr. said.

Ella was born in 1962 and exhibited the same symptoms as her brother. "I thought, *Oh my goodness, what have we got?* But they are lovely, lovely children. The upper spine and the back of the brain are not fully developed," Curtis Sr. said. "The doctors feel the cause of the problem might be from a lack of folic acid that produced neurological problems. Fortunately, our fourth child was perfectly normal.

"I felt devastated, more so when our third child came along and we found out it was the same type of thing. Then everyone starts telling you that you're blessed, not everyone has a handicapped child, and you're the perfect parents to raise a handicapped child or children. You just bite the bullet and do the best you can. You wonder why it was you times two," Curtis Sr. said.

"I have a completely different attitude," his wife said. "Since I'm an occupational therapist I worked in the crippled children camp while I was still in college. We had these sweet little children, they were just adorable, and they were there for four weeks. At the end of two weeks they were supposed to have a parent stay with them. I was appalled because most of the parents didn't come. When we had our counselors' meeting that night, I said, *What's the matter, I would think they'd be dying to see their kids after two weeks?* The director kindly mentioned to me that some of the parents were anxious to get rid of these kids for the summer. This was not real important to them. They wanted to have some time away from them, and they didn't want to bother coming. I told my classmate *that's terrible. As long as there has to be handicapped kids in this world, I wouldn't mind having some because I would love them just for being themselves and forget about the handicap.* I really believe that. I have a different philosophy, and hopefully a little of it has rubbed off on my husband. But I cannot erase how he feels because he has his own feelings. I know it was devastating to him. Especially since the first one was a boy, named after him, you want your boy to be all right. Our fifth child is adopted is a boy. I hope we compensated," Eunice contended.

After Curtis Jr. left Easter Seals he went into special education classes in public school. He finally walked at 11 years old and uses a cane for balance. Upon graduating from the program he went into the Little Friends program. He lives in a townhouse with two other men, and works at the Spectrum sheltered workshop.

Ellla also went to Easter Seals. "When she got into public school, I wrote to the principal explaining her condition. I said that she was a very bright child, she just had this little problem with walking, and she needed her crutches to walk with because of her balance. She had a problem with her speech so we asked if she could have speech therapy. Because she was in special education she wasn't entitled to speech therapy, too! That was for the 'normal' children who were having immature speech problems," Eunice said. "We had to fight for everything for these kids. We had to fight for her to have speech therapy, too."

Ella resents not being like other children who are normal. "For a long time she wouldn't be in the same room with Curtis because he's handicapped. If we wanted to go to an activity she'd say, 'Well, that's for the handicapped kids. I don't want to go.'" Ella works at the Spectrum sheltered workshop and also lives in one of the Little Friends' townhouses with a roommate and support staff. "She blossomed...she loved it," her mother said.

"She fell in love with one of the boys in one of the other townhouses and wanted to get married. We had a lot of mixed feelings about that. Little Friends lets them get married," her mother said. His parents also had their doubts because the boy had been married before, and had two children. Eunice isn't afraid of her having children but doubts she can because she's so underdeveloped. But just to be on the safe side, they asked his parents to recommend that he get a vasectomy. Just before the procedure Ella said she didn't want him to have it, instead she chose to have a tubal ligation.

Eunice now works with the Parent Infant Program at Little Friends to show new parents what can be done for their special needs children. "When challenges are presented to us, with our faith in God and His help, we can do all kinds of things. I felt that having the one handicapped son was wonderful because as a therapist I could help other people. Having two was even better because people really paid attention to me. They said, 'Two children? I just have one, I guess I'm not so bad off.' I really feel that you can use any disadvantage to your advantage if you know how to use it and appreciate it.

"You wonder about the purpose of these children. Well, Curtis was the Easter Seals poster boy for 1965," Eunice said proudly. "His picture was up on billboards, fliers in all the magazines, *Readers Digest, Life, and TV Guide.*"

Eunice and Curtis Sr. were involved with the Farm Club in Hinsdale, Illinois, "where parents with handicapped children got together. My older daughter said she was so happy that when we went to places like that she could do things with her brother and sister," Eunice said. She would go along on the Easter Lilly drive with her sister who walks with the aid of crutches. "That made her feel special, because she was with her little sister who's handicapped. Psychologically it helped our normal child. She became a nurse."

Eunice feels that her special needs children embarrassed their younger daughter. "She wouldn't bring friends home because the kids were there, and she was really embarrassed to talk about them." The parents made sure their two other daughters had activities to compensate for the time they spent on the disabled children.

How has having two special needs children affected the marriage? "It's made it stronger, I think," Eunice said.

"Well, it hasn't driven us apart. 47 years," her husband added.

"When I worked at the Easter Seals Center, I was also in charge of the parent group, counseling them with a psychologist on marriage problems," Eunice said. "We had such a high percentage of parents that would get divorced. One or another couldn't cope; the wife would spend too much time with the handicapped child. One father felt guilty because he had thrown the baby up in the air playing with it and dropped it. There's so much guilt in some of these cases. And it would tear them apart.

"I knew from the very beginning that we needed something to hold us together forever and ever. My husband had always enjoyed going antique hunting, so I decided that this would be something that we would do together. Our parents would come and stay with the kids and we would go out for an afternoon antiquating or go to a flea market. We have to consciously work on it. I purposedly worked on it because I wasn't gonna let him go. I didn't want to have to have these kids by myself.

"I've often said I wouldn't change a thing," Eunice said proudly. "My husband has often said the only thing he would ever change was not having two handicapped kids. But as you see, we've adjusted. You have to go through a grieving process. These kids are not what you expected, not what you had hoped for, and are never going to accomplish things that you would like them to accomplish."

Curtis Sr. said that it makes him sad that his son will not be able to do the things he did growing up, nor will he marry and carry on the family name. When asked what toll it has taken, he said, "I don't think I would have gotten gray this soon."

"It made my life so much more enjoyable," his wife said. "I thoroughly feel important, useful. We've had to struggle for things for our kids that maybe they wouldn't even get to take advantage of, but we knew that for the next group coming up it would be helpful. I feel that it has been my main purpose in life."

It wasn't the same for her husband who is a teacher. "I've been the breadwinner, and I had other things that I've been doing. We've done a lot of the things together with the kids, but it's been mostly Eunice. It's taught me to be a lot more patient, I think, and I understand other people's problems a lot more than I would have. It certainly has given me an understanding. I've had kids in school who have had handicapped brothers and sisters, and I've gotten to know them. Every experience helps you in teaching."

Todd and Marshall

Todd's parents first noticed problems with him when he was six. His teacher told his parents that he was hyperactive, and had problems with concentration, coordination, and fine motor skills. She recommended having the child tested. "The diagnosis was that he is learning disabled and at that point he was hyperactive. His IQ was around 75. They prescribed Ritalin. It helped him focus but the poor motor control was still there," his mother, Bernice, said. It was suggested that Todd be put into special education.

"We were mortified. We were college graduates, this was our first child and a son. We said, *Oh my God, my child's not going to be able to go to college.* We were just devastated and really embarrassed. We felt like it was a reflection on us, what did we do wrong? When Todd was a baby I went back to work for a year teaching, and I hired this woman who was great with him. I felt like maybe I should have been there, I could have done something different, I had a lot of guilt feelings, that it was my fault."

A few years later Bernice gave birth to a daughter,"who is an over achiever (she has a master's degree in social work)." A few years later she had a second son, Marshall.

Todd went to a private school then to a public high school. After graduation, "We were in a panic situation, what do we do with him? He needs to learn a skill." Todd attended a sheltered workshop, and then went for three years to a private school in New Haven, Connecticut to learn a skill and independent living. He returned to Atlanta and went back to the workshop. He's on a tranquilizer and he sees a therapist.

The parents contacted a local organization that found him an apartment and jobs. "To this day he doesn't keep a job. His daddy is financially responsible for him and he knows it. He has problems controlling his temper, he's been married twice. To make money, he buys and sells pets.

Bernice's second son, Marshall, was born with club hands and feet. "This was just horrible. We knew we had to go through a lot of surgery and physical therapy. We went to Scottish Rite (Hospital) and he had surgery on his feet, and casts were put on his feet and hands. I had to put splints on each separate finger to straighten them out. He had a developmental lag, and ended up having a speech problem." He has had physical and speech therapy.

Marshall attended a private school for a brief time then transferred to public school. He then went to the Roosevelt Institute in Warm Springs, Georgia for a few years where he learned to garden.

Marshall lives with his wife and children in an apartment, and bags groceries at a local Publix grocery store.

Todd has been married twice, both times to developmentally disabled young women. "When Todd met the second one he said he didn't want to be married anymore to Regina. He got a divorce and went with April. They got married. Her mother insisted that they have a prenuptial agreement, which was okay. About two years after they were married they got into a fight and scratched each other, and April's mother came and got her and took her home. She was spending time on her computer on a chat line with other guys in front of Todd. He got angry and slapped her," Bernice, explained. April called the police because her mother had told her to if he ever hit her again. "They came and arrested Todd, and he spent the night in jail. Then they proceeded to move on with a divorce," his mother said, very exasperated. When the two saw each other at a dance, they went home together and April cancelled the divorce.

Then Marshall married his pregnant girlfriend, Clara. "The baby was fine. We told them to please not get pregnant again. She gets pregnant again and the second baby is fine. She got her tubes tied after that pregnancy. I still think my son needs to have a vasectomy."

Marshall's parents have been trying to get joint custody of his children in order for them to have some say in raising the children, and "because we are financially responsible for these babies. I say to Clara's mother, *Can't you and your husband buy a package of diapers every once in awhile?* Clara calls me and says, 'We're out of fruit for the baby, please bring some over.' We finance everything, they don't have enough money. We buy their car, we pay for car repairs."

I asked if the couple was able to take care of two normal, healthy children. "I don't think so. Not two of them together." His parents got a caregiver to help with the children in the house that they bought for them. "I have Britney four nights a week and a lot of times I take her more. Because Clara's and Marshall's judgment is poor, they don't know about schedules, and Clara didn't grow up in a good and nurturing environment. We don't trust them." His parents were concerned when the couple rode around at night with the children in the car when they should have been at home and in bed.

Bernice talked about her husband. "He at first was very embarrassed, like what caused this? I think in a way, it brought us closer together. He doesn't talk a lot to me about it. I feel like a lot of times that our communication is poor. He'll say something to somebody else and then they'll tell me, and I wouldn't have heard about it. I feel like, *gosh, couldn't he talk to me about it?*" It bothers him that they are raising the children of one of their developmentally disabled sons.

During the early years, "We traveled a lot," Bernice said. "We had this housekeeper, and we called on friends to carpool. Glenn and I ran a lot. I had counseling, he never did, and we just took a lot of trips to get away. We were running away.

"I just felt like, why us? One is enough, why did God give us two? We've been disappointed and it took a long time to get over that feeling. Why me? I'm embarrassed, and I'm angry. It's not fair. When I see other people who are in wheelchairs (or she sees children with terrible mental and physical problems) I say, *Oh thank God they* (her sons) *can drive a car and I don't have to diaper them. It could be a lot worse.*"

I asked what toll her two boys took on her life. "I think for some odd reason it's given me a lot more energy and it's made me feel younger that I had to stay healthy to get these children through life. It's been very hard, very hard."

This mother/grandmother's frustration was very obvious, and I asked how she felt about raising her son's two children. She said, "You know it really has interfered with our life. I should be spending more time with my husband. A lot of times I feel like saying, *I give up, let them go to their parents, I can't take it any more.* But I would not be able to sleep at night."

Emma and Jessica

Emma "was a beautiful baby. She seemed to be fine, but she was hyperactive and had a piercing scream when she cried. She was rolling over in the hospital and doing pushups. Didn't sleep well, but she looked perfectly normal. She was late crawling, she kind of dragged her body around, but she crawled around a year and walked when she was 16 months. She was beautiful but not very social and didn't talk (until she was around four years old). She had autistic behavior," her mother, Brooke, explained.

When Emma was about 18 months old her pediatrician said she "was retarded. I didn't accept it when he said Emma was retarded. We took her to a speech school in Atlanta and they said she was just a little delayed. I guess I never accepted her the way she was, and that she was going to be that way probably until she was 12 years old. (Her husband) was really supportive of me. Anything we could come up with, anything we could do...he was there and did things with us as a family."

Emma attended a program "for three year olds who had problems." At four she boarded at a private school so that the director, who thought she was severely aphasic, could work with her. She then went to public school. When hearing loss was suspected, she was tested at Emory University where moderate to severe hearing loss was diagnosed. She was then enrolled in the Atlanta Area School for the Deaf for two years.

When her behavior became a problem, she was sent to a school in Pennsylvania for about two years. "We had to think about the whole family and surviving as a family, which is one reason we sent Emma off for two years when we were having problems."

Emma returned to Atlanta and went to public school ending up in an autistic program even though she was not diagnosed as autistic.

Emma's parents feel she is severely aphasic and has difficulty expressing herself. They also think that their daughter understands more than she can relate because of the aphasia. (Her story is in this chapter because she also has a special needs sibling.)

"We talk very positively around her to help her be more than she would be. It's very important to her that she look good, be dressed well, and that she pick out the right clothes, even though she might choose to wear the same outfit every day."

Jessica was born when her sister was two. "She seemed perfectly normal. She didn't have the bizarre behavior or mannerisms that Emma did. She walked and talked sooner, but she was also late in her speech and had a funny pattern to her speech, it seemed slow. But she was an easy baby."

Jessica also attended private school. It was found that she also had a moderate hearing problem; both girls were taught sign language. Jessica was then placed in special programs in public school.

She began having problems with her walking when she was in the eighth or ninth grade. She has been diagnosed with "a mitochondria problem ("Mitochondria are the principal energy source of the cell..."), (1) and is unable to get energy to her muscles. Today she uses a walker and is in a wheelchair for long distances. After high school graduation, Jessica went to a school in Upper State New York for four years. Because of her ambulatory problems, she was anxious to come home."

In both girls "the hearing losses were progressive. They ended up losing almost all of their hearing."

The sisters get along well and are devoted to one another. Emma and Jessica are both employed, and live together in a group home. They both are involved with the "Just" People program.

The family has a son two years younger than Jessica. They have been realistic about the girls' future, and have made financial arrangements that their son will oversee.

"Peyton had a lot of anger about it but he completely worked through that," his mother said. "My son wasn't hampered; he could do what he wanted to do. He was extremely social, and outgoing. The only thing he would do is get in trouble, he acted out a little bit. He was good at home and then when he got out he did the teenage things. His friends were great, wonderful." The parents worked through much of his rebellion by sending him off to school.

Did his sisters embarrass her son? "Probably, but not any more so than he was about his mother and his father. Teenagers are embarrassed by their family, and his, probably even more so."

Emma has a boyfriend. "He's just devoted to Emma; he thinks she's the most beautiful, wonderful person. She says, 'Seth my friend.'…He buys her presents. Emma will allow a kiss or a holding of the hand or a hug," her mother said. Her daughter talks about getting married and having babies.

Jessica, "who is very social and loves the boys, can be quite manipulative. She has always had boyfriends, she's very sweet, and she's a good girl. Her boyfriend is an older man. At one time I would have worried about Jessica sexually because she just loves all the kissing and hugging. I took her to a psychologist before she went into the group home. She agreed that she didn't want to have children, and had her tubes tied. I don't think it was a necessary thing because she lives in a very sheltered, protected environment. She's happy to have a platonic boyfriend."

Brooke said of her husband, "He was very supportive emotionally of me, and always wanted us to continue to have a life. I'd get a babysitter and the two of us would always go off on a vacation every winter. I had good help. We continue to have a social life and to do things. It's probably made us closer, made us more dependent on each other. I really don't believe in throwing your life away or your family away for a handicapped child. I think you should be a good mother, but you have other considerations. You have a husband, other children, your life; I think some people can be a little sanctimonious about it. Carry it to the extreme."

On raising two children, Brooke said. "I handled it pretty good but I always had good relief. I had a maid everyday, I could leave the house. I had my mother here. My girls are attractive and well behaved, and I have a husband that's supportive, and money. For a bad situation we are very, very fortunate. I didn't plan to have a third child, but he's certainly been a blessing. He's married and it's helped me emotionally that I have a normal child in addition to two handicapped children.

"I wish I had known more about having children before I had them, as far as preventing their problems. I wish I had taken folic acid. I wish I had not done any social drinking at all, they didn't tell us that was wrong.

"I'm glad I kind of keep things in balance, I'm still married and my son has turned out well, and I think the girls are happy. I feel like it's added a depth to my life that my life wouldn't have had by not having handicapped children. There have been a lot of blessings. Everybody has their problems, and everybody does the best they can with whatever they are dealt. I love the networking, but I think the saddest thing to me would be to have a handicap child and not reach out, and not have friends, and not have the networking.

"I had two out of three. My mother always said I could have had three out of three. I would have loved to have three normal children, but I've had a good life in spite of it.

"I think it's made my perspective different, but I don't think I'm any different. I think people are the way they are no matter what happens to them. I see parents who complain about how their carpools drive them crazy. Gillian (another parent) and I drove our carpools, and it took us five hours, with five of these kids repeating the same words over and over again. All you could do was laugh about it. It gives you a definite perspective on what's important and what's not important in life."

Chapter 11

Siblings

"Chris is not a counterpart of my life…but he is my baseline," David Barnard

Being the sibling of a handicapped child is a difficult role. Besides the normal competition between brothers and sisters, and juggling for their fair share of the parents' attention, the sibling of a handicapped child has double duty. Most often they do not understand why their parents spend more time with their special needs brother or sister, nor do they comprehend why mother is often away dealing with doctors and hospitals. The dilemma of what is wrong with their sibling is coupled with wondering why he or she can't play with them like their friends' siblings do.

As adults, many are proud of their sibling's accomplishments. But if their parents have made no provisions for their future needs, many fear that their developmentally disabled brother or sister will be dumped on them when their parents are no longer alive, leaving them with the responsibility of taking care of an adult child.

Most of the siblings I interviewed have an excellent understanding of their brother or sister, and some have become guardians. Amazingly, they have coped quite well, though that's not to say that it has been easy. Other siblings have moved far from home in order to avoid the responsibility, leaving that to another sister or brother; creating a different kind of friction.

Most of the stories in this part come from siblings who have been guardians of their special needs sister or brother for some time. Even though the major disabilities of these young people would place them in another chapter, they are here because their sibling/guardians are the family historians. They demonstrate how many families' greatest fear has been handled.

Christopher

My oldest son Harmon, III (Tracy) was three when Christopher was born. Because Chris was so far behind Tracy developmentally, the two boys were never close.

"I knew that he was sick and that he wasn't going to be like the rest of us...I didn't have a problem with him being different. I probably had a problem more with his lack of communication skills. That was the biggest frustration, because you couldn't communicate with him. Even now I still have a problem talking with him," Tracy admitted.

Was Tracy embarrassed having Chris as a brother? "I don't know if embarrassment came into play, I can't remember any of the kids (his friends) teasing him. They weren't as cruel back then as they would be today, I think."

Would he have defended Chris? "Oh sure I would have. He's my brother...when you mess with my family you mess with me...I'll protect my brother till the day I die.

"The only two emotions that come up to me about Chris are a lot of frustration and impatience. Even today, Chris knows what he wants to say, he just can't always say it. He does require a tremendous amount of patience."

Tracy has a Masters degree in Special Education and in Business, and has taught special needs children for many years. He is also involved in Special Olympics.

"When I was up in Illinois in August (2001), I saw Chris through different eyes than I had ever seen him before. He really felt like my brother. I've felt distant from Chris for many years because we never really had a chance to bond as brothers; and we may not ever, unfortunately. He's still my brother, I still love him to death and I'll do anything in the world for him."

When Tracy was a child, he had behavioral problems that my mother-in-law blamed on Chris. "I was always Mema Barnard's favorite. I know she treated him overall differently than she treated me. Was Chris the cause of my problems? No. I am what I am because I had to go through life my way. I had my own struggles; I had my own ups and downs. Hell, I'm 43 years old and I finally figured out what I want to do with my life"

David, who is four years younger than Chris, said that as a child, "I didn't think Chris was any different than anybody else. At a young age you don't differentiate." He said that Chris not being physically handicapped made it easier. He had positive feelings about growing up with him, and remembers how frustrated Chris was because of his speech problems. "Chris helped me ride a bike. We used to sit in Chris' room and listen to records and sing the words."

David said that Chris never embarrassed him and explaining him to his friends or later to dates was never an issue. "Being an accident rather than genetics made it easier." But when David and his wife Cathy got ready to have children, we were asked to have Chris genetically tested just to make sure.

Harmon, Joann and I don't want Chris to be a burden on his brothers when we die, but we do want them to oversee his situation. Both have agreed. "It's the right thing to do," David explained. "We're trying to teach the kids (their two boys) that Chris is just a person. We want them to get to know their Uncle Chris."

David made a most insightful remark: "Society isn't accepting of the handicapped because there is high risk, and low reward."

When asked how he feels about his brother, David said "Chris is not a counterpart of my life...but he is my baseline."

Cynthia

Cynthia began having petit mal seizures when she was three years old and was diagnosed with epilepsy. Upset with their child's illness, both parents began drinking heavily, so during most of the early years, Cynthia was cared for by their kind and loving maid. Because of the problems, her father left and the couple divorced. Her older sister, Alice, took over guardianship of Cynthia when their mother was unable to handle her.

Cynthia attended a very fine private school in Atlanta that her mother helped organize. In the third grade, she began exhibiting behavioral problems and showing signs of mental impairment. When she was nine or ten years old, she was enrolled in The Northside School, at that time the only school for special needs children time in Atlanta.

Believing it must be more than epilepsy, Cynthia's parents took her to the Devereau School in Philadelphia, to the Montreal Neurological Center, Johns Hopkins in Baltimore, and Emory University in Atlanta. "Everybody came up with the same diagnosis: epilepsy caused by brain damage, unknown origin." Her parents were told, "'She must be institutionalized, you cannot care for her at home.'"

In 1960 Cynthia was sent to the state's institution for the mentally retarded. When it closed about thirty years later, she was moved to a group home near Atlanta where she presently resides; she also attends a Community Support Solutions program. "She really doesn't fit, but she's never really fit in any of the community programs," her sister, Alice, explained. Meanwhile, "She's provided for by the best care, and I make the decisions."

As children, Cynthia's two sisters were in the dark as to what her problems were. "We just thought Cynthia was spoiled rotten and mean tempered. We stayed out of her way."

Years later, when Alice took over the guardianship, she read Cynthia's records and saw the whole picture. "I was really angry at my mother and father for not keeping me abreast. I think I'm still angry because I was not involved in any of the decision-making all along and it's just been dumped in my lap because Mother's dead. It was dumped in my lap for five years before that, because she was sick. My other sister chose to leave Atlanta and lives in New Jersey; that was her way of dealing with it, I guess."

Caring for her sister has had a profound affect on Alice's life. "It's put a few more gray hairs on my head because I worry about her all the time. I'm conscious of a need to think about her needs as well as my own when I make decisions about work, about a job, and where I live. So, it has an ongoing impact in terms of how I function. It's kept me closer to home; I don't feel comfortable leaving the country as easily. I had to pick a place to live that would be all on one floor...that I made handicapped accessible so that she could visit easily. I chose a vehicle that could hold a wheelchair. It's just impacts every decision that I make."

Like many parents, Alice worries about what will happen to her sister when she and her other sister die. "I try to involve my children, and my sister's children. But neither of the two families are willing to take on my role, and they are resentful." Her children are angry that she has had 100% of Cynthia's care and has "been dumped on." They're afraid that will happen to them. "I feel it's been a privilege and an honor and I'm glad to do it. I will not dump on them. This is a topic of on-going conversation with my other sister about how we're going to make arrangements for Cynthia when neither of us is here."

Cynthia hasn't dated, but "She likes boys and she loves men. But I don't think she understands dates." She's afraid that someone will take advantage of her. "We've been through that. She's not been sterilized, my mother would not agree to do it."

When Cynthia was in an institution for the mentally handicapped in Georgia, "She had a couple of things happen at parties and things. They found her in the broom closet with some other resident and there was concern that she might be pregnant, but she wasn't. By the time I was guardian she was 45. I discussed it with my other sister and with the physicians, and we felt that the situation was such that she was not in danger because of the way that her life was being led. She was close to menopause, so we didn't sterilize her."

Cynthia attended regular religious school classes at The Temple in Atlanta, "until about the third grade. When they said it wasn't working, "Mother said that she had to find some place for her daughter." Because there was no Sunday school program for developmentally disabled children in the community, she founded the Atlanta Jewish Federation's Sunday school program that preceded its *Havanah* program.

Stephanie

Stephanie was born prematurely and spent the first two years of her life battling serious health problems, which included surgery. Her parents were concerned, when by the age of two, she was not walking and talking, but they were optimistic that these would come in time, which they did. Her parents visited a plethora of doctors trying to get a proper diagnosis, and to find an explanation of what had gone wrong, but they were constantly dead-ended.

One day when Stephanie was eleven, the anesthesiologist who had administered to her during surgery asked her father how she was. Then he said, "'We almost lost her on the operating table,'" her sister, Audrey, explained. That is when they discovered that she had not had enough oxygen during one of her operations when she was an infant. More poignant was the fact that their father was a prominent Atlanta gastroenterologist, a "physician who specializes in the diagnosis and treatment of diseases of the digestive system." (1)

"For all those years my mother had blamed herself. Maybe she used the heating pad too much when she was pregnant, or exercised too much or not enough. It was a cruel thing that they hadn't told her."

Stephanie was mainstreamed in public school for a short time then entered The Northside School. Later she attended a school in Philadelphia, then one in Tennessee.

When Stephanie reached adulthood, her parents saw the need for a residential village-type setting for adults with developmental disabilities. "They saw there was nothing like this in the South. My parents took a long trip to Europe to look at some prototypes over there. Then it became a passion with both of them." As a result, they established a very fine and well-respected residential program for special needs adults outside of Atlanta, and when Stephanie was 19, she entered the program.

Stephanie has flourished there, and "she's discovered that she is a good artist, our mother was an artist. She enters (her work in) art shows and she wins prizes, and gets a lot of satisfaction. She's happy.

She feels really good about herself. Mainly because of this art business, she has a definite sense of herself. She knows that she can't do things like drive a car, but she's very canny in a lot of ways. She has some pride of being the daughter of the founder...She thinks of herself as a talented artist.

"She has learned something she didn't learn at home. She's learned to care about the other people. Our mother tended to feel sorry for her, and babied her. Since Mother died she's been so much freer, because I'm not emotionally tied up with her. I love her and I care about her, I'm her guardian. But if she gets in trouble, I say to her, *well, it just proves you are a human being.*

"They have a social life at (the complex) and for years she would go from one boyfriend to another. Now she doesn't feel like she needs a boyfriend." Because there is sexual activity on the campus, Stephanie, like most of the residents of the program, has been sterilized, with her consent. Stephanie used to talk about marriage. She once had a friend who wanted to marry her so he could be a member of her family.

"My older brother had major health problems as an infant, had pneumonia and whooping cough, and Mother's energy went to this son who turned out to be spoiled because she gave him too much attention. My middle brother and I, grew up very resentful because we didn't get what we needed. We were never any trouble. "

She said of her parents, "They had a wonderful relationship because they were both so creative and they would come together in these creative projects." But Stephanie took "A terrific toll on their marriage and the family. Mother got overly involved with her. It seemed to me that they were much more carefree and frivolous before Stephanie, they had a lot more fun."

Audrey said that her brothers were less involved with their sister than she has been. "It didn't matter to me that she was slow. I just loved playing with her and mothering her and taking care of her. I was pretty much in charge of her because I wanted to be a lot of the time. I have never been embarrassed by Stephanie, and I think that's been a real saving grace for her and me."

Eleanor

Eleanor suffered from a lack of oxygen at her birth. By the time she was four it was discovered that she was developmentally delayed.

"We had a very unusual family situation," her sister, Addie, explained. "When I was three, my mother had a very tragic car accident, and was mentally ill the rest of her life...she was in and out of our family a great majority of the time," leaving her husband in charge of three children.

Eleanor attended public school in Fort Lauderdale, Florida in regular classes, but switched to special education classes in high school. When she was 12 or 13 she was placed in a group home. "That was probably as much to do with my mother's problems as to what it took to take care of Eleanor. She lived there for probably five years (then returned home). I really took over her care when I turned 18. Our family was really in crisis and Eleanor was the least of it.

"Eleanor has probably had one of the harder lives that someone in her population would have and yet she has the ability to forget the painful time of our mother being mentally ill, and our father being an alcoholic."

After high school graduation, Eleanor worked at Goodwill Industries for awhile and lived in another group home.

When Addie moved to Atlanta, Eleanor followed. "First impression, you don't always recognize that she's handicapped." Today Eleanor lives with two other young women in a house owned by one her roommate's parents, works at Chick-Fil-A, and is with the "Just" People program.

How has Eleanor affected her life? "I want to provide for her in every way possible, but I have to draw some lines. The best way is for her not to live with me, I feel that I needed to have my own life. I never had children, I think it must be the same duty a mother has for her child," Addie said honestly. "The biggest toll it has taken has been financial."

She explained that she tries "to look at the world through Eleanor's eyes...she has the joy of a child. It's so easy to do things for her, and you want to. We shouldn't take things for granted." Addie said she made a deal with God that she is to live one day longer than Eleanor.

"I have people say, 'I really admire what you do for Eleanor.' It's no way a burden. She provides a great joy in my life. I certainly get just as much out of it as she does.

"When Eleanor was in a group home she was kidnapped by the maintenance worker there, and for close to a year we had no idea where she was. The police tried to find her, there were no leads. In that year's time they were hitchhiking on trucks, they were going all over the country. They went as far as Colorado and the West Coast.

"They finally made contact with me to start receiving some money, wouldn't say where they were. I told them they needed to go back to Ft. Lauderdale. By this time they had gotten married. I wasn't sure if it was a legal marriage or not." When she spoke to Eleanor she "implied that she was happy, but I could hear this edge."

The couple returned to Ft. Lauderdale, and met with her mother and sister in a restaurant. "My mother and he are out in the restaurant and Eleanor and I go to the restroom. I have very little time to say, *Eleanor, if you're happy, I really can't change this. We all miss you and want to be sure you're okay.*' At first she said, 'Yeah, I'm happy.' I really didn't even recognize her as being my sister so to speak. Then she said, 'It's awful, he's hurting me.' We snuck out the back and left my mother with him. (Addie took her to a friend's house because Eleanor's husband) knew where I lived, so I couldn't take her there. It was like something you would see in a movie. He tried to get her back for a brief period of time. They were legally married, and it was a horrible time. He was supposedly of normal intelligence."

Eleanor was again taken advantage of by a neighbor and actually became pregnant." She had an abortion.

To safeguard Eleanor, she didn't get a divorce. "If she's married, she can't get married again," Addie explained.

Malcolm

Malcolm was born in a military installation in Kansas at a time when little was known about Down syndrome. "Lots of Malcolm's checkups were with the VA. Once a month or every couple of months we went into New York City from New Jersey to New York Children's Hospital for Malcolm to be evaluated. He surpassed everyone's expectations, he wasn't supposed to live past five," his sister, Grace, explained. "His main problems were always upper respiratory."

Malcolm attended special education classes in the New Jersey public school system and while in high school he was taught living skills. "When he turned 21, they didn't have sheltered workshops at that time; we were faced with what's next?" For three years Grace worked during the day and their mother worked at night, so someone was always home with Malcolm.

Then Grace got married. When the stress of working three jobs and tending to Malcolm took its toll on their mother, she had a heart attack. Over the next several years the extended family moved around because of Grace's husband's job, and the family grew again by three children.

Health problems developed when Malcolm was in his mid 30s. "Downs people get Alzheimer's...also when they're young males they may become schizophrenic somewhere between 19 and 20. Malcolm started to short-circuit a little bit, and got very paranoid and very fearful. They age faster and the brain chemistry depletes. When his symptoms got worse, we had to find the right medication." Their mother's health also deteriorated and she went into a nursing home. Malcolm went into a residential facility built by Tootsie Roll money in Tulsa, Oklahoma.

"It was very hard on my mother to do this but she knew that we had to do something. It was getting hard on my children, and it gave us a little break. Then mother died." When Grace and her family moved to Atlanta, Malcolm came to live with them, and went to work in a sheltered workshop.

Grace's children coped quite well having their uncle around, though it was hardest on her middle child. She was lucky to have a husband who helped and supported her. "It was a package deal when he got engaged to me. I give him credit. I don't know how many men would have taken that on."

Malcolm was not interested in sex. "He always liked girls. He would kiss girls on the cheek."

Because of the Alzheimer's, Malcolm "gradually went downhill… went into diapers…went from being self-sufficient to being fed." He aged very rapidly and lost a great deal of weight. He became frail and suffered several bouts with pneumonia and had seizures. He died in 1997. Grace thinks it was a stroke, the doctors thought it was from a seizure.

What had been Grace's biggest worry? "If I had become sick or was in a car accident, what would happen to Malcolm? There were a lot of issues that I just never consciously thought about, because the kids were so good about helping and my husband was so good about helping. "

Being the caregiver for her brother took its toll on Grace. "We didn't go away, we didn't travel. We would do day stuff. Things are very subtle. You get so used to doing something and picking up the slack. You never really sit down and think do you want to do A or F? You just lived it."

When asked how being her brother's guardian and caregiver changed her, she said that she learned to put her days in order so she could take care of everybody that included her husband and children.

Olivia

Olivia, who is the second of five children, was born in 1957 in Americus, Georgia. Her mother had measles during her pregnancy, but the baby appeared normal at birth. The first signs of problems came when she didn't begin to walk or talk when she should have. "Those developmental milestones just took a very long time to come about," Dale, the eldest sister, and a special education teacher, said.

"She had some other illnesses when she was small. She had some issues with asthma. When she was seven she was diagnosed with juvenile diabetes. She has always had a multitude of health issues (that have been) made worse by the diabetes over the years.

"The options for services were so limited then and the doctors knew less than they know today. There has never, to my knowledge, been a diagnosis. She's about 4' 8. She walks a little more stilted than other people. She talks with a lot of immature speech patterns, but you can understand everything she says. I would put her at a level somewhere at four or five years old, and she talks maybe like someone who hadn't been exposed to very good speech, like she didn't have someone good to model after."

When Olivia was ready for school, there was little to offer for special needs children. She eventually was placed in a special education class "that was sort of a catch-all class for physical and mental disabilities. This one class caught all ages, all ranges of disabilities, and these disabilities also encompassed some children who had some behavioral issues. Basically, it was just a place for children who couldn't fit into a regular classroom."

Olivia was removed from school when she was 15 because "she was making no academic progress whatsoever, and because some of the behaviors she was picking up were not suitable."

When Olivia was 18, she became eligible for adult services, and was placed in a sheltered workshop. "That didn't really last very long either because by then her health issues had escalated and she'd also taken on some emotional issues. A lot of difficulties came with her diabetes." She would get sick and become unconscious. "It was just a constant battle with her health and my parents constantly had to go to the shelter to get her."

From then on Olivia stayed at home and her parents hired someone to "come to the home and help train her to do jobs around the house. That helped some, because a lot of things she does today, responsibilities around the house, she's very good at, and does well."

I asked Dale how her parents reacted to having a developmentally disabled child. "My father, who was an only child, felt she was the heart and soul of our family. We couldn't have imagined her not being in our family."

What was it like for Dale when she was a child? "I can remember times, when I was very young, being placed in a position where I was told, 'take your sister, walk with her to here or to there.' And I would be embarrassed because I was kind of afraid of what other people might think. But that probably went along, maybe, with the age." As to the other siblings: "We've talked about it. I think sometimes they felt a little bit the same, but not overly so; it was just a twinge of that feeling.

"We've all kind of played a part in taking care of her. My father was very sick, he died of Parkinson's Disease. My mother has gone through a triple by-pass. When she was going through surgery, I took off work and went down and stayed with her and took care of Olivia. We all pitch in. We know that she's got to be taken care of.

"She's a very happy person, she's always laughing, she loves to do things for you, and she loves to talk to you. She knows lots of information; she knows all the family secrets, that's for sure. She's one of these people that everyone in the community knows." Even though Olivia has never dated, she talks of getting married and having children.

Olivia's parents decided that she would always live at home. When her mother dies, she will live with Dale and her family. "That's always been something that we knew. There are so many summers that she's come and stayed with me, and visited with me, and I've learned over the years to help her with some of her health problems. I can give her shots and I know about her medicines, and some of the things she's been through. I guess it's just being familiar with it so much, and we get along."

When asked how dealing with Olivia has changed her, Dale said, "I'm definitely more sensitive to people with disabilities, and their families. I think it's made me a more patient person. She gave me the desire to make things better." It also influenced her into going into special education.

"What I wouldn't give to have been able to turn back the hands of time and provide for her what's available to children now, because I think there are so many more things that she would be able to do which would have opened up more experiences for her.

"It hurts me when I see people make fun of people with disabilities. I just don't get it. I know that it's probably because they haven't had any experiences, they don't know any other way. Non-exposure is no reason to ridicule."

Chapter 12

The "Kids" Speak

"We're just regular people."

While interviewing parents, several of their special needs adults wanted to talk to me. I also interviewed people at the "Just" People program in Atlanta, Georgia, and at the Spectrum workshop in Downers Grover, Illinois. They all handled themselves with aplomb as they answered my questions. Some of what they have to say is very important. Please listen.

Darren

Darren, who is involved in the "Just" People program in Atlanta, said, "I go bowling next Wednesday night. I'm 29, almost 30. (He works) at the Publix (grocery store) near Lenox Square straightening out shelves and bagging bread, cleaning the outside refrigerators at night." He said that he likes working at the grocery store, and that the people treat him very well. Prior to that job, he worked at three workshops, which he also liked.

When asked about the schools he had attended, he reeled them all off one-by-one. "Right now we have my new "Just" People directory. I can't go on the cruise this year."

Glenda

When I asked Glenda how I should refer to her disability she said that "developmentally disabled" was appropriate.

This woman, in her early thirties, also works in a grocery store, but finds it quite stressful. "Some employees totally get the situation, but a lot of employees have a hard time." She had several clashes with the manager and admitted, "It was partly my fault."

She also participates in the "Just" People program, and has gone on two cruises, on a trip to St. Simons, Georgia and to Dollywood. "I went to Cozumel and I won a piece of jewelry. Someone bought an engagement ring for somebody so they gave us two for one. It's a promise ring for me and my father. A spiritual ring. It's one to keep promises I make to my father spiritually. As my father (who died several years ago) got older he was very spiritual. I was real close in my own way. Me and my mom are very close. We are bonded somehow. My dad was somewhere off in the distance…we (she and her mother) had to argue constantly."

Glenda lives at home and is looking forward to a time when she will have her own place. "Yes, I want to have my own apartment with a roommate. I feel very good because I do a lot of stuff here. I try to clean up and the best that I can. I still miss the mark sometime. In an apartment I think I would do better because I would be more conscientious and it would be on me to clean and not my mom to clean up after me all the time. I think that if she would say, 'I'm leaving this for you and you're gonna clean it, and I'm gonna leave it for you until it's right,' and not get frustrated, then it would be on me to do it. We get along overall very good. "

She has a problem not being included when her mother entertains her friends at the house. "It's sort of hard to be in my room and not hear stuff going on, or be somewhere else in the house and not hear stuff going on.

"I think it's very hard for people that are special needs to get along. It is a very big issue in the coming years. I think if President Bush keeps his word that he is going to make more equal rights for us... Will he keep it or is he just blowing smoke up everyone's rear end? It would be great, because there are things that need to be changed. The visibly disabled people get more fair treatment than the people who aren't visibly disabled people, because you can see the disability. You look at me and say she's not disabled, why can't she do this?"

I asked what she feared the most. "Something happens to my mom, that bothers me. Last year, when she got sick, it bothered me."

I asked if she had anything else to say for the book and she said, "I hope this book helps a lot of people."

Cary

Once, when my x-husband, Harmon, was in a hurry to get Christopher to the Chicago airport for a trip to Atlanta, he failed to give him the once over. When the plane landed in Atlanta Chris failed to debark. Panicked, I rushed onto the plane and there he sat. He hadn't shaved, was wearing a tee shirt and jeans, and he looked like a bagman. The flight attendants were supposed to look out for him, but because of the way he looked they treated him like a pariah. On the return trip, he was shaved, and wore a tennis shirt and khaki pants. The flight attendants were gracious and treated him like a person, not an unkempt, homeless person.

A few years later I was told that the Jewish children from an out-of-town residential facility were brought to The Temple, the Jewish house of worship in Atlanta, on Friday nights for religious services. It got back to me that Cary had showed up looking scroungy, much like Chris had looked on the plane. After I passed the information on to his father, I received a letter from Cary:

"My father called me last night and told me that you called him and that you were at Temple last Friday night and complained about the Villagers wore dirty clothes. Well I was there too but I didn't where (sic) dirty clothes and my roommate...didn't either."

I wrote him back and explained that it was very important that he and his friends look neat and clean when they were out in public. I said that they were special needs ambassadors, and how they looked reflected on the others. My new pen pal wrote back and thanked me for my letter:

He said he would tell the social worker "about this and she is going to see to it that everybody is dressed properly like you said.

"I will pass this information to my father. I understand that and know its (sic) important to be dressed properly."

Lisa

I asked Lisa, 22, how she liked her public school special education classes. She answered, "I liked it really good."

When asked if she felt different from her siblings, she replied, "Not really." Even though she feels there are things they can do that she can't, it doesn't bother her. "I learn different from them.

"I work at Northwestern Middle School across the street. I do cookies and stuff. I worked at Crabapple Kroger."

Lisa is a member of the "Just" People program, "I like it a lot." Does she date? "Yes. I go out to a movie, dinner." And she said she is interested in getting married.

She still lives at home but she's ready to move to the "Just" People living project when it is completed.

When asked what frightens her she answered, "Thunder and lightning does."

"Just" People Program

I visited the "Just" People program in Atlanta and interviewed ten people; six were the most productive. Even those who did not have anything to say nodded in agreement at answers that were given by their colleagues.

I asked what they liked people to call them. They answered, "Clients," or just "Regular people."

* "We're not retards, I wish people would understand that...We're no different than anybody else, God doesn't work perfection, we're all perfected," said one young man.

* "We've got learning disability and learning disability is same thing like handicap. Some people are in wheelchairs and they can't write or they can't speak, but some people can stand up, some can do more than others," said another.

* When asked about brothers and sisters, one man said, "I have a brother and sister and they kicked me out of the house."

I asked if their parents treat them differently from their siblings.

* One said, "Yes." Two said their parents treated them the same.

* "I'm the only child and I was spoiled most of the time," a fellow said.

* "I'm the oldest and they treated me like I was 13," a young woman replied.

When I asked what was the hardest part of growing up with a disability, one man said, "Trying to get a job."

Some in the group were interested in giving me a little of their history.

* "I was very, very sick when I was young and my mother was the only one I knew. I was sick half of my life."

* "When I was a little baby I had a real high fever at that time and my mom took me to the hospital. I had seizures, took medicine for the seizures and I had problems sometimes with reading or math."

* "When I was younger I had to go to special ed classes to learn a little slower than everyone else." I said that it must have been hard to be singled out and having to go to special classes and she said, "Yes."

* "I had to go to private school because the Catholic school I went to said I needed a little more discipline. I don't know what they did to me but they made me keep to myself too long and I got sick." I asked him if he had problems. "Not 'til later. I had a mental thing. It's just caused me limitations, and I'm trying to overcome these. I have things that I need to work on."

They all agreed that it was hard growing up.

I asked them if any of them took advantage of their situation in order to get something or attention. One used an excuse of being sick.

* "I used excuses like not taking the garbage out, part of it was not doing the dishes."

* "If I didn't do anything, my mother would punish me."

How do people react to you when you go out into the community, I asked?
* "Sometimes they look at you very oddly."
* "Sometimes we're driving along and people look at the vans (with "Just" People written on the sides) and people look at the vans a little strange...they look at the vans then look at us like we're not there."

They said that people get frustrated when they try to talk.
* "Like I have to ask a lot of questions. I like to have an explanation of things, and they (people) don't like it all the time."
* "One time I was taking my driver's license (exam) in Mobile, Alabama. I failed about two or three times 'til my mom had to talk to this lady. She didn't know that I had learning disability. Her son also had learning disability and they let me take the test again and then I passed it."

I asked them to tell me about their dating.
* "Movie...bowling, Pizza Hut."

What does dating mean to you?
* "Being friendship really."
* "Dating means when you go out with a girl, you just have fun

being out with them, because you care about them and love 'em."

* "I doubt if I'll ever be married. (He didn't think he was marriage material.)

What about sex?
* "That's bad."
* "Sex! Gross! I don't believe in that 'til after marriage." Two others agreed.

I asked them what their biggest fear was.
* "If something were to happen to my parents, cause no one in my family understands me. And I feel like that would be their opportunity to take advantage of the situation. I only have a sister, but I mean my aunts and uncles. They don't like me as it is. If something were to happen that would make it even more difficult than it already is."
* "My dad."
* "I fear that if anything should happen to me that my family will not see to my funeral at all. My family was close at one time," a middle aged man said sadly. "My mother had died and I lived with my sister for awhile. And I did something wrong and I was kicked out of the house three or four times. My two nephews and my sister and my brother-in-law...we used to be friends. We're not friends at all now."
* One young man was afraid of his grandparent's health, one was afraid because his father was not in contact with him.
* "I'm gonna be disliked where ever I go."
* "I have a fear that I may have another nervous breakdown."

Spectrum Workshop

I visited the Spectrum workshop in Downers Grove, Illinois and interviewed two men and two women; one couple was engaged and living separately in the same apartment complex.

I asked them to tell me something about themselves.

* "I try to help friends."
* "I like to help people…I didn't like it when they stare at me. It bothers me."
* "When I see trouble, I just try to stay away from it. That happens all the time here. (Sometimes people tease him out in public, and he doesn't like it when people look at him funny.) They can't help it, I understand that. I'm not gonna stare at them."

When asked if they felt different from their siblings, they said:

* "I get along with my sisters a lot." She also has a handicapped sister.
* "Probably the same. Maybe we do a little different stuff (than his sister)."
* "I feel like my sister helping cooking." Angie was the most handicapped of this group. One of her legs is in a brace and she walks with the aid of a walker. Her speech is very bad.
* "Same thing," said her boyfriend, Brian.

I asked if their parents treated them different from their siblings. Three said their parents treated them the same. But one said, "Sometimes. They can get on my nerves a lot."

They talked about dating.

* Brian and Angie have been dating about ten years. "We go to movies, we go bowling, we go out just me and her sometimes," Brian said. He has been thinking about getting married but Angie doesn't want to. They both live in the same apartment with four other people.

* "I dated with my boyfriend, Walter. He came over when his roommate was gone. We walked around downtown Naperville and we walked around the sidewalk sale. He likes Tinker Toys so we went over and bought some Tinker Toys for him. And I bought a stuffed animal. We went to the corner bakery and I had a sandwich and he had a pretzel sandwich. We had a great time together, then he went home. He didn't stay very long, just spend time together, and that's it," Christy said.

* "I go out sometimes, but one of my friends doesn't call me. I don't know why, so I'm just stuck home on the weekends, I don't like that, that hurts my feelings. No, I don't have a girl, I wish I did. I got to stay home on Fridays and Saturdays, I just gotta watch TV," Rory whined.

What do they think of sex?
* "No way," Christy said emphatically.
* "My parents would kill me," Rory said. "I don't think they would let me do it. They would be too serious."
* "I agree with Rory, " said Brian even though his parents are both dead.

None drive a car, and when asked if they wanted to, Rory said, "I don't know if my parents would let me."

* Rory lives at home but wants to move out. "Because my parents yell at me a lot for things I do which I didn't mean to but I mean I can't take it no more, it drives me crazy. I keep telling them I want to move out. I'm thinking about downtown Chicago somewhere, in an apartment not with one of my friends. I'm 24. I can't stand my dad."
* Christy lives by herself in an apartment and likes it. "I go home for the weekends. ...They asked me if I was interested in doing the YMCA parade (on Labor Day) so I said yes. I said this will be fun so they're gonna give me a tee-shirt, I told them I wear a 2x."

I asked them to tell about their biggest fear.
* "I think loud noises scare me the most, "Rory said. "It freaks me out."
* "Thunder and lightning," Christy said. "I usually hide underneath my pillow. I put the blanket over my head and go down underneath the pillow."
* "People talking around me at the workshop," Brian said. Angie echoed his statement.
* Rory said that when his parents are no longer here it "is a concern to me. I wonder where I'm gonna live or what I'm gonna do, or how I'm gonna get around. Unless I get new parents."
* Christy said her mother "isn't ready to go (die) yet. I really love my uncles and my aunts."

I asked if they had anything else they would like to add for my book.

* "Everybody's different, I'll say that," Rory said.

I asked Brian what he would say to an adult who hasn't been around people with problems; he said, "Go see a psychiatrist."

Chapter 13

Special Education Teachers

The Unsung Heroes

When people say that I'm such a hero for raising Christopher, I say I'm not, I just did what I had to do because he's my child. The real heroes are the special education teachers, caregivers, and the people who choose to work in programs for the handicapped because they don't have to.

Special education teachers give of themselves many hours a day teaching our children how to write their names, count to five, and prepare them for the future. Parents often take these people for granted when they should be grateful that they have someone who is there to help their child and wants to make a difference. Some of the teachers I interviewed have also been honored for their ingenuity in developing programs for their charges.

Thank you. My hat is off to all of y'all, you're my heroes.

Susan Feinberg

Susan Feinberg received her bachelor's degree in speech pathology at the University of Florida. She told me that she chose this field because, "My mother was a speech and dramatics teacher and had encouraged me to go into the field in some way, shape or form."

Her first job was in the Memphis public schools. She moved to Atlanta in 1966 and went to work in the Atlanta Public School system, and received in 1971 her Master's degree in Speech Pathology and Communicative Disorders from Emory University.

That same year she went to work for Arbor Academy as a part-time speech therapist, and my son, Christopher, was one of her students. She taught there for eight years.

After Arbor she did private therapy while getting a specialist degree in School Psychology. "That was about the time that Public Law 94-142 came into existence and all of these kids needed to be evaluated in order for the public schools to look at them," Mrs. Feinberg explained. "Once I got my specialist degree I did more school psych than anything largely in the public schools." Several years later she worked in a private school for six or seven years on a part-time basis. Today she is an independent contractor.

As the school psychologist, "I was the one who had to say (to the parents), *Look, we think that your child has some problems and maybe the Speech School or The Schenck School would be a better place.* I wasn't always their favorite person. Some parents were very gratified to hear that we were going to make life easier for the kids, and other parents probably wished we would go away and not tell them anything was the matter.

"I think that most parents know that something isn't just exactly like it should be. Some people are in denial and some people really want to zero in on it, get help and move forward."

When asked how working in this field has made her different she replied, "I would like to think I would be as sensitive if I had never worked with handicapped children, but maybe not."

She did not think choosing this field of work has taken a toll on her. "In many ways Arbor Academy gave me the stepping stones...I had the degree, I had the experience, I had the opportunity. And I had help at home (for her children) so I might work a couple of days a week. I don't think I really envisioned that I was going to be this life-long professional educator."

She said that testing techniques have improved. "We are recognizing more and more students...we are able to diagnose these difficulties much better at a much younger age. They've made progress, but things are always changing." She also feels that parents have made the difference, and have dragged some of the professionals along kicking and screaming.

Mrs. Feinberg also worked for awhile at The Atlanta Speech School. "There was a special ed class when I was there, I don't know that they ever truly admitted that they had that class. The Atlanta Speech School really tried to keep their school in terms of truly LD (Learning Disabilities) kids.

"There was a brief period of time between when 94-142 became law and the public schools began to start these programs. Until then, there was no place for these kids. Arbor was the only school in town that took that type of child." She feels that that is why the speech school broadened their program. "They wanted a child of average intelligence with a speech problem. I think that their Communicative Disorder Class, that they finally started, doesn't mean a whole lot."

Mrs. Feinberg had some important thoughts on pediatricians. "I think a lot of pediatricians are not as knowledgeable as parents trust them to be when it comes to a child that has problems. We don't do as good a job of training some of these pediatricians in terms of being knowledgeable. (Her pediatrician said) 'I see your kids, y'all bring them in when they're sick, and you bring them in for their well checkup. I don't see them in the classroom. The kid seems perfectly normal to me.'"

What advice does she give to parents? "I tell parents that they are their child's best advocate. It's easy to get lost in the shuffle. A child can just get lost, and if you're not there all along to advocate for what your child needs, it's not going to happen. They have to be involved in the school, in the process, they have to be knowledgeable about what their child's needs are, and they have to have good communication with their teachers.

"And if the child's on medication, there needs to be a triangle of communication between the physician, who is prescribing the medication, the parent and the teacher to monitor and make sure the medication is doing what it's supposed to do."

Dr. Linda McCuenn

Dr. Linda McCuen is a Special Education teacher at Henderson Middle School in the Atlanta area who won the Honor Teacher Award for 2001. She holds a degree in Elementary Education and Special Education, a Bachelor of Science Degree from Eastern Kentucky University, a Masters degree in Special Education from Georgia State University, and Doctorate from Nova, Southeastern.

When asked why she chose the path of special education she said, "I guess I have always been a care-giver, I've always rooted for the underdog. When I went to college I started out in Elementary Education and we had to have some outside experience. I volunteered at a Shriner's Hospital. What, I guess, influenced me the most was my experience there; I was impacted by a young man. That's when I decided that I could learn from the kids as much as they could learn from me. That made the difference right there and I decided I wanted to go into it."

The school she teaches in is very diverse economically, and it has a high rate of children who come from other countries where English is their second language. She finds that parental cooperation varies. "The parents who aren't struggling to provide a roof over the child's head usually are easier to contact and get involved in the school. Single parents who are trying to balance job and family have a real rough time with the child and the school. Priorities really make the difference."

Dr. McCuen feels that teachers who have limited experience with special education students are afraid of them. "When you put a student with a handicap in a large classroom you're always going to have bullies. And if a teacher is not fully aware of what's going on in the classroom, that bully will surface, and our kids are usually the victims." When this happens, she said the bullies should be confronted and counseled, and the special education student needs help in avoiding the bully. "I try to establish an atmosphere in my classroom where the kids feel safe. And either they'll tell me or I've even had students who will talk for other kids. It's wonderful. I tell those kids that it's part of their responsibility, we're kind of a family."

Dr. McCuen is involved in the Service Learning Program. "Service Learning is allowing students to apply what they learn in the classroom in the community. For example, we do a lot of environmental things. The reading of *The Lorax* (which is about monitoring and cleaning up streams) is service learning. Students with special needs find out what they can do, and that's the job they have. They work right next to a student who may not speak English or right next to somebody who is in the gifted education program. It's a wonderful bonding experience."

She believes she won the Honor Teacher Award because of the Service Learning Program. "Service Learning has caught on in the community and the parents have helped me in the process of starting a school that would be Service Learning oriented. It would be a public school. We would take the curriculum that is already established in Georgia and come up with activities that the kids would apply. For example, Habitat for Humanity, where kids can utilize their math skills, not necessarily going onto a site, they can build birdhouses, or flower boxes or mailboxes for the Habitat houses. We're going to try to instill in the kids some civic responsibility, a little bit of character, and make them good citizens."

How has this made her different? "My husband calls me a maverick. I think that's probably a good description of me because I operate a little bit different than everybody else.

"In special ed, one day is totally different than the other day and I can do so many different things, where if I was in general ed I would be much more limited. I like to step outside that box."

She doesn't think she has suffered any toll. "I think what it has done is to allow me to grow, and it's allowed my husband and my daughter to grow."

What advice does she have to parents? "Learn to be their child's advocate... but at a certain age they need to turn over that roll of advocacy to the kids. They need to learn to stand up on their own feet. I think when they're 13 and 14 years old they need to start accepting responsibility and being able to express themselves. I see too many parents who played the role of an advocate so well that they forget that they need to give that up sometime.

"I would love for the parents to occasionally recognize the teacher who has gone above and beyond. (When) the light goes off (in a child) and you don't get positive feedback from the parent, you sometimes give up. What keeps me going is that sometimes you just click with the kid and you get them farther than you ever expected."

Jessica Kasten

Jessica Kasten is a Special Education teacher in the Atlanta area who won an Honor Teacher Award for 2001. She has a BA in Mental Retardation from the University of Georgia.

"I have loved working with children since I was very young. One of my high school jobs was as gymnastics' instructor for young kids." At a birthday party, a parent of a child who was paralyzed from the waist down, asked if she would help "make him feel comfortable, to fit in as best he possibly could. I was really drawn to this kid... the mother came up to me afterwards and told me that I did great, and that I was a natural. I thought about this kid for so long. I thought I was really good at that and I loved it, and it was a great experience, one I would always remember. I had also volunteered at the Special Olympics every year... it was something that I knew that I was passionate for and wanted to do, and knew that I was good at."

When I interviewed her, she was teaching a special education class at Sentential High School in Roswell, Georgia where the majority of her students' families are well off. She tries to keep in close contact with the parents. She has a good relationship with her principal and the other teachers. "They have been a blessing. Without their support I don't think we would have been able to accomplish, over the past four years, the amount of things we have for special ed.

"It took some time for other teachers to get to know the kids. I've worked very hard to make our kids very well exposed throughout the school during any activity (such as lunch). I try to expose them as much as I can because I think that's really important not just for the administration and the teachers, but for their peers as well."

Ms. Kasten initiated "a Peer Facilitation Club, an after school program where our students get to go to all the events that other students go to (such as ballgames, dances, plays, etc.), and they go with the peer facilitators (who are non special ed students). It gives our kids the ability to be a regular student and attend programs the regular students attend. I have more and more students wanting to be a part of it."

As a consequence, some of her regular students have chosen special education as a profession.

"I opened up a coffee shop at the school in the teacher's cafeteria, called Sentential Perks. I got furniture donated, and I got enough money where I was able to hire an artist to paint a mural on the wall. I got t-shirts and coffee mugs made, we have six different flavors of gourmet coffees, and my students run the shop." They make the coffee, handle money, learn how to clean up, and acquire social skills. "I'm so proud. This is my baby."

Has she changed? "I've learned to appreciate the health and happiness that I have (and) the little things we take for granted. Working with these kids every day I realize I don't have it so bad. I see my life in a different perspective."

Has it taken a toll on her? "I definitely think so. There's a really high burnout rate for teachers in special ed and I can completely understand why. It can be very stressful at times."

She offered this advice to parents: "You have to be aggressive, you have to know your rights, and you have to know what your child can and cannot have. You need to know what your child is entitled to. Some parents may be in denial of where their child's real function level is, and don't push for things. Trust the professionals and be a little more realistic. We want to push your child just as much as you do."

Harmon L. Barnard III

Harmon L. Barnard III (Tracy) is my oldest child who, in his forties, decided to be a special education teacher. He dropped out of college and enlisted in the Navy and was on a ship in the Indian Ocean during the Iranian crisis. When his tour was up, he returned home. Unwilling to return to college, he tried a plethora of jobs, and married.

While he was a manager in training at Toco Bell, his daughter, Kristen, said that her teacher told her: "'if you don't have an education you end up flipping burgers at Micky D's.' "That really hit home. Toco Bell wasn't much different than being at Micky D's. That comment set forth the process of figuring out what it was I wanted to do."

While in the recovery room, following knee surgery the year before, the man in the next bed introduced himself and an instant friendship was born. As a teacher with a Ph.D. in Special Education, he encouraged Tracy to consider a teaching job.

"I finally woke up one morning and the idea of becoming a teacher became clear. At that point I started doing some research as to what type of teaching I wanted to do. It became apparent that there was a critical need for special education teachers. Not knowing exactly the whole term of what special ed meant, I researched it deeper and found that special education means learning, behavioral, hearing, and vision impaired, mentally challenged and a whole other cast of characters that fall under the term special ed."

While working full time, he returned to collage, got a degree in special education, and became certified. "On my first day in class working for my special ed certification, the professor stated two things. One, it will take you three to four years to be comfortable as a teacher, and two, you can't save them all. Although I understood that, my philosophy is, the day I quit trying will be day that I will walk away from teaching." Upon competition of his Masters in Special Ed, he went on and got a Masters' degree with a focus on Emotional Behavior Disorders (EBD) and Learning Disorders (LD). He later got a Masters' degree in Business Administration.

"Why did I focus on EBD (Emotional Behavior Disorders) and LD (Learning Disabled)? First of all I have a special needs brother who was near and dear to my heart. The other reason I chose special ed is because my oldest daughter is learning disabled. Going through the process of IEPs (Individual Education Plans), meetings, and getting frustrated with how she was being treated by the system, made me wonder if other children were being treated the same way. All that combined is what led me to into special ed."

Tracy got a job in a public school in Columbus, Georgia where he taught in an EBD class for children who had gotten into trouble. "You have to have the parents behind you. First they have to accept that they have a child with a problem. Some parents don't want to accept that they have a child who is not perfect. Not having a perfect child means they're not perfect. Some children go home and are totally lost in the household. They get no love, they get no pat on the back, and they don't get any hugs." He has had students tell him before they get on the bus when school is out, "'Mr. Barnard, I love you.' That's cool."

How did this career change him? "I feel more content with myself, I like myself. I think I grow every day, as the kids grow, I grow too. I think I learn as much from them as they learn from me. My patience has gotten a lot better than it's ever been. I think I've finally found my calling, I'm pleased and happy with who I am probably for the first time in my life.

"The most important feeling is the satisfaction of finally finding something I'm good at doing and seeing the differences in these children based on what I've been doing with them. I would see kids come in who had no hope of ever going to regular education class. Everyone had turned their back on them; they called them 'stupid and dumb,' and said 'we don't want you'. To take a child like that and turn him around and see him grow and realize that's because of something I did, there's no other feeling in the world. I am frustrated sometimes because you want to help all the kids and you can't."

What advice do you have for parents of special needs children? "You have to admit that your child is not perfect, which for some parents is going to be very difficult. Then you need to get the child help as soon as you can. The quicker we can intervene and break the bad habits the earlier the better. Don't turn your back on your child. You need to say 'what can I do to help?' Find the right program and get your child in as fast as you can. The law says you're allowed that, those are your rights, those are your children's rights, take advantage of it.

"Life is not to make ourselves happy, life is to go to the young ones, the ones who are going to be our future and say, *Hey look, we want you to be ready.*"

Janet Conrad

Janet Conrad is a special education teacher with an undergraduate degree in speech pathology from Southeastern Missouri State who did graduate work at the University of Illinois. She is also a speech pathologist who worked four years with a multi-handicapped population; this included non-verbal, mildly and severely mentally handicapped children.

"I wanted to teach. While growing up, my parents had some close friends who had a child who had Downs syndrome. She was my playmate. She was certainly an influence in my life."

The parents of Mrs. Conrad's students were cooperative. "I found that parents were hungry and eager for support and help." Working in the early childhood special education, "We were often the first people to tell a parent, 'your child has problems.' We saw the whole gambit from angry to frustration to devastation to disbelief to denial.

"I wish that as an educator, there had been a course in grieving. Because I think if you're going to be in the role of giving people bad news, you ought to understand the process."

Did teaching developmentally disabled students change her? "It made me more analytical, especially in the field of special ed where you have to break down to so many little steps. It made me able to look at any given task and break it down to its component parts. It gave me a lot of opportunities to meet people from all walks of life.

"It helped me truly understand Maslow's Hierarchy. It's just the hierarchy of needs in life. Your most basic needs are food, and water, and your physical needs. When you're working with parents who can't pay their bills and can't put food on the table, they aren't real interested in talking to me about their child's disability. You have to understand as an educator where the parent is before you put more on their plate than they can handle. If basic needs are not being met, they're not interested in talking to you about modifying their child's behavior. "

What advice do you have for parents? "Be an advocate for your child. You know them far better than any teacher can know them, or any doctor can ever know them, any social worker can ever know them. You live with them, you breathe with them, and you eat with them. You know them. Be their advocate.

Miriam Smith

Miriam Smith, a special education teacher in Atlanta, Georgia at North Atlanta High School, has a Master degree in Mental Retardation from the University of Alabama, and a degree in Behavioral Disorders.

Why did she choose this path? "Because I had been teaching elementary education and I especially liked the children who were retarded, and decided I would like to do more."

What does she like about her job? "I like that every day I come to school and I'm met with something different. It's hard to get burned out in special education because every day is different. Their needs change daily."

What she dislikes about the job is "the parent participation. We have many parents I've never meet, and that makes me very sad." At her school there is a "higher mix of blacks and Hispanics. The special ed parents of white children in the Buckhead area (of Atlanta) find private means to educate their children."

Ms. Smith talked about a child whose life she improved. This child lived in Macon, Georgia, and the parents were told that she would never read or write. Ms. Smith worked with her and her parents, and the child passed the Georgia Graduation Test and trained in computer processing at a vocational school.

"I think children of special needs need two things, organization and consistency."

How did her vocation impact her personal life? "Positively, because the friends that I have in this large metropolitan community are people I work with. I have a close support group, and loving friends... But if I had known how my life would have turned out I would have chosen another profession. I would have chosen interior design."

She feels that the Georgia legislators should visit the schools and properly evaluate the role of teachers, and give them all the support they need to make sure they stay in the profession.

Heather Lubeck

Heather Lubeck is a special education teacher at Atlanta's Seaborn Lee Elementary School. She has an undergraduate degree in Educational Psychology, a Masters in Learning Disabilities, a teaching certificate in Learning Disability, and she received the Honor Teacher Award of 2001.

Why did she choose special education? "I enjoy children. I'm the type of person that likes to get to know everyone, whether they are an adult or a child, on a fairly comfortable basis. I like to joke with them; I like to know what makes them tick. As I grew older, I found that students with learning disabilities, or behavior disorders, or mild intellectual disabilities had an extra something that I was drawn to. Their challenges made me appreciate them even more."

At her school, over 90% of the students fall into the lower socio-economic group, and receive free or reduced lunches. It also has a highly mobile student rate. "Many students come in and out of the school very frequently. If their mother moves, they go and live with grandma, so grandma might live in a different school district. Then they might come back to live with mom, and they come back to school. So many times education doesn't mean anything to them because they really don't have a safe roof over their heads. These families' priorities are not school.

"I've never had any parent challenge my decisions or the way I was teaching their child. This was because there was no parental supervision at all; the parent wasn't involved at all. It was like 'well go ahead, do whatever you want to do.' There are a few students who I could never successfully contact the parent.

"At the other extreme, I have had some parents who were very dedicated to their child and to their education, and I made myself available. I called them frequently and gave them my home number so they could call me." She also spends time with some of her students on the weekends and shares her personal life with them. "I think it makes it easier for them to come to school, hopefully it's kind of like a family setting within the classroom.

"That's what's so neat about special education. The classes are a little bit smaller. And as a teacher you are able to work a little more individually with the students."

Ms. Lubeck took on the school garden as a project for her students. "It was already there when I came, but it was dormant. There were weeds covering it all. You could tell there was a teacher who had really taken some time to lay it out."

The first year she and her students talked about things that could be planted, the second was going out on nature trails, and the third year she got help from the Georgia Extension Service to rejuvenate the garden. "We got the kids out there and we weeded, planted, and we talked about all the things you could talk about with a garden." They used subjects such as math as they planted their garden. After harvesting the fresh vegetables, a teacher took the food home, cooked them, then brought them back to school for them to eat. "It was a cycle for them to see from the weeded piece of land all the way up to something good in their tummy, and they were part of all of it...it was something that they could look forward to. It taught them some patience. It taught them that they didn't have to be totally dependent on other people, that they did have some self-control. They could make their own decisions if they wanted to grow some food." She feels that she won the Honor Teacher Award for 2001 because of this project.

Did she think that teaching special needs children has changed her? "I think it's made me more patient. It's given me more self-awareness. It's made me more aware of how difficult it is to be a teacher. The reward is having a small classroom, having students who are more willing to share or are very trusting of you because of the relationship you formed. The benefits outweigh some of the possible negatives that might come out of a classroom."

Has it taken a toll on her? "I don't know if special ed has taken a toll on me, but I think teaching in general has (the early wakeup, long hours of teaching). My ideal situation would be if school started at 10:00. There's also the constant threat of falling into a routine that you know you might not necessarily be the best for the student. But out of ease or convenience, you just teach the lesson this way. If you're having a bad day, or you're not feeling particularly dramatic, interesting or fun, you realize that you can't do that every day, otherwise you become a tired old teacher, and I don't think that's really doing anybody any good." She worries about burnout.

What advice would she give to parents? "Students need parents to be involved, because they can achieve a lot more than a parent might think. It just takes the parent having a routine at home that supports the school, and the teacher having a routine at school that supports the parent. If you get both of those together, then that child will learn things such as how to use the bathroom or dress himself. If the parent and teacher have a similar understanding and they're not fighting against each other, the child will learn how to do many things. You really can tell the student whose parents talk to them because their vocabulary is higher. Even if the parent isn't the most educated, you can tell the ones who might have taken them to the zoo, who might have exposed them to more opportunities out there."

She said that she knows that some of her students of both sexes have been sexually abused. It was usually done by someone within their family or an acquaintance.

Chapter 14

People Who Provide Services for Special Needs People

As stated in the above chapter, the people that I most admire are those who do not have handicapped children who give of themselves to work in programs whether it's teaching or providing programs such as "Just" People and Little Friends, Inc.

There are programs for people with special needs in almost every community. Some work with their clients on the social aspect of their lives, such as residential, job placement, and sheltered workshops. The people that I interviewed gave me a sampling of what services are available for the developmentally disabled adult.

Becky Dowling

Becky Dowling, Director of "Just" People in Atlanta started the program in 1996. She has also served on the board of the Special Olympics for over 20 years and was a substitute teacher in a special education classroom.

Ms. Dowling's adoptive father, her mother's second husband, was in a car accident and suffered a head injury. When she was six, he was diagnosed as paranoid schizophrenic, and manic-depressive with suicidal tendencies. "So, growing up we spent a lot of time as children with a mentally challenged man in a situation probably just like you all as a parent. His family was ashamed of him, his father was chief of police in Miami, his brother was president of a Ft. Lauderdale bank, and another brother was head of the Water Department in Miami."

When she was young her friends' parents did not want her in their home, and her family was "also shunned at our Catholic Church. I grew up constantly wanting to fix it, that's my father...I loved him and it was returned."

Ms. Dowling married, had a family, and became a "professional volunteer....Special Olympics...convalescent homes...with people with mental illness." Then she went to work at Creative Community Services (CCS). "I had this drive that I couldn't explain to anybody, to make a difference with this population. You don't have to have a degree to treat people like human beings. And common sense with this population is half the battle."

After leaving CCS she thought about starting her own program. She sent out letters to about 12 families to hash out the possibility, and about 50 or 60 people showed up at a meeting. They wanted a program. They raised over $6000 and Ms. Dowling's unnamed program began with 12 clients. One evening while her family sat around the kitchen table discussing the program, her daughter said: "'since I was this big, all I've heard is that they're just people." They had their name.

The "Just "People program is a family affair with Ms. Dowling's husband, her children, and their spouses working there. "We do independent living, social and job coaching, Social Security, and food stamps. We interact with their families. We just manage their whole life, and keep their whole life in some kind of order. I prefer people who are 21 and older. We have autistic, Down syndrome, mentally retarded, cerebral palsy, learning disabled, attention deficit, emotionally disturbed, schizophrenics, OCD, whoever wants to be here...(if they can handle them).

She finds that parents are her biggest problem. "I make a joke that a lot of times our people would do so much better if the families would just drop them off to me and go. I spend a lot of time doing group therapy with our people and the majority of problems we run into are things that went on with their families; not being accepted by their parents, and parents wanting them to be cured and fixed. Sometimes they don't even accept that they have a disability. Absolute denial...it was the wrong medication when he was a child.

"There are some areas that they are never going to improve on or ever understand any better than they do. So take what they do know and make that their strength. And work with that. And accept their flaws. The ones that excel and do the best in this kind of program have parents who have accepted their responsibility as a parent, and have accepted the fact that their child is going to have limitations for the rest of his life, and is going to have to have supports for the rest of his life.

"I tell parents when I meet them, that I don't fix anybody and I don't cure anybody, nobody here is sick. They're here because they need supports and I will provide them to them for the rest of their lives. And when you accept that they are going to need you for the rest of their lives, this will work. But if you think they're going to be here for a year or two and you're going to have a changed child, take them somewhere else. I will push them as hard as I can push them but I will accept their limitations. Some parents are looking for a cure.

"I see the biggest problem is with a parent still having a child at home at 39 because they didn't know where to go. They get frustrated, and it is simpler to keep them at home than to keep looking. Start looking when they're 17, don't start looking at 45." She suggested they call United Way and other programs.

At "Just" People there were dogs and babies of the employees all over the place. Becky explained that the animals fill a need "that we all have. The babies teach them warmth and caring. They show them love unconditionally. They don't get that in the outside world."

Traveling is part of the "Just" People program. Ms. Dowling has taken her group to Alaska, Las Vegas, the Grand Canyon, the Bahamas, Jamaica, skiing and camping. "I totally believe that they have a right to be out in the world, a right to be working, a right to be socializing, and a right to be shopping, all of the things that you and I do. They also have the right to go home and be themselves. I can't make the next door neighbors be their friends, so, I'm going build my own community."

Finding the right property and dealing with zoning has been the hardest part of developing this project. Dealing with contiguous neighbors and zoning committees is very frustrating. People would say, "'the basic bottom line was that it's a great idea, we think what you're doing is remarkable, but not in our backyard.'" She persevered, and her complex is completed.

What advice can you offer to the parents of special needs children? "Acceptance is the biggest key, accept your children. Love them and understand them, understand that they have needs for friends, socialization, nice clothes, and getting married. That's not what they're getting. They want a companion. They want their parents to participate. These are people who will never ever be mentally older than 14 years old. 12 to 14 are the worst time of any child's life, and they are stuck there. They need more support than your teenager or your infant child. Parents can change the whole quality of their child's life because 'if mommy accepts me anybody can.'

"Agencies need to work closer together. Psychiatrists and psychologists need to work harder to find support systems so programs for these people will have a chance."

Kelli Salyer

Kelli Salyer, Becky Dowling's daughter, was an education major in college, and works at "Just" People. "One day when I was in elementary school I went to a special ed class and asked if I could help out, I was in the third grade. I worked in the special classroom from the third through the fifth grade. After that, I was still hanging out with some of the people I'd met because they weren't really different to me. They enjoyed having 'normal people' around them. I started working with my mom when she was working with CCS."

What does she get out of it? "It's very rewarding, because they are like big children, and it's always rewarding to be around children. The greatest reward is seeing them accomplish things that they want to do. The things that we take for granted, like driving a car or getting your own furniture for your apartment, or making your first dinner, is for these guys a constant effort."

She said having the dogs and children around is done to make their program as normal as possible. "Most all of our clients will probably never have children. So we bring our children to the office and they think of these kids as their kids too. They enjoy being around them, and it's very beneficial to our children because from the time they've been able to walk and talk they've known that these people are just like you and I. They are never going to see the difference. It's a very good thing for them. Also I bring my dogs because many of the clients don't have the mental capabilities to care for a dog properly. They take care of the dogs while they're here and they think of them as their dogs.

"A lot of them enjoy coming here on their days off because it gives them the socialization that they need. They all pack their own lunch, and we also have a canteen.

"My mom does this for no other reason than because she was raised by good parents. She was lucky in her life; she just became a very compassionate person. She does this because she loves these guys. And everybody who works here is afraid of what will happen to them if we no longer exist, and that's why she gives so much."

When asked what she would say to those people in the community who are turned off by people who have special needs, Ms. Salyer said: "I have a hard time understanding it. I really can't comprehend why they're like that. They are missing out on so much. These guys remind you to be a child, they remind you to have fun. Those people who are embarrassed around these guys, or are afraid to touch them or talk to them, they're the ones that are going to live their life for no one but themselves.

"A lot of parents call and say 'my child is 30 or 40, and we're ready for them to be independent.' They're so embarrassed. What they don't realize is that these guys are dying to get out of their house... and the parents need their own life too.   It's very difficult to find people you can trust to take care of your child forever when you're gone."

Webb Spraetz

Webb Spraetz is Developmental Disabilities Director of Jewish Family & Career Services (JF&CS) that was started in 1992. "There were a number of parents who felt the need for services in the Jewish community. As a result, they pressured the planning and funding sources to start something. I was the first person hired.

"Today we have three agencies that are involved...JF&CS, Jewish Education Service, and we have the Jewish Community Center. They offer more programs for the handicapped now. We have residential programs, we help people find housing. We have a vocational program, and we help people find jobs. We have a respite program, family support, and do family counseling.

"80% of the population has mild mental retardation; we are doing a better job of diagnosing; I think the schools have helped a lot... Things have changed; choice has become a bigger issue now. Instead of parents making the choices and the decisions for their adult children, we are allowing people with disabilities to make their own choices."

When asked about what advice he would give to parents, Mr. Spraetz said, "Advocacy is a big issue. These people aren't generally spokespeople for themselves; other people must speak for them."

Ginny Riley

Ginny Riley was a parent of a special needs son who was in his teens. Like many of the parents in this book, she was honestly looking at the future, and realized that the group home concept was the way to go for the special needs adult. When she set out to find a group home in Atlanta, she discovered that the county program in her community had a bad reputation; so she decided to establish one.

Her son was in the North Fulton Training Center. She got together with other families struggling with the same problem, and they formed their own corporation. The North Fulton County Group Home Association applied to HUD for funding for two group homes. They received their loan reservation in September 1979, and the homes opened in June 1982. In addition, the Association created a strong supportive employment program.

Tammy Niemeyer
Little Friends, Inc. and Spectrum Workshop

Little Friends was established in 1965 as a pre-school class by parents who asked a pre-school teacher to teach the class. This special education program was conducted in a school in Naperville, Illinois. In 1968 "another group started the Naperville Sheltered Workshop for adults with disabilities...later they merged to become Little Friends Sheltered Workshop and then just Little Friends, Inc. Over the years... as families and parents have come to us with different needs, we've just tried to meet those needs by adding different programs and different services, Ms. Niemeyer explained.

Tammy Niemeyer has a degree in Journalism. After working for a newspaper for several years, "I really wanted to do something that could help people, and when I saw an ad for this position and learned more about the organization and what they did, I just knew it was something I wanted to do.

When asked if the experience has made a difference in her life, she said, "I think when you work with people and you build a relationship with them you start to see past the disabilities and start to see the people. Even when I'm in the community and see disabled people that I don't know, where other people might be turned off, and avoiding them, I tend to be more interactive with them; I recognize the person not the disability."

Ms. Niemeyer said, "I really admire the parents I see for their perseverance and for the dedication that it takes to raise a child...love their kids, and help their kids achieve to be the most that they can be the best that they can be. I really admire that."

Matt Verscheure
Vice President of Community Services
Little Friends, Inc.

While in college, Matt Verscheure worked with people with disabilities in a hospital. After graduating, he wanted to go into the corporate world but, "I ended up taking a case manager position in Rock Island, Illinois, and I've been in the field ever since." In 1999 he got a job at Little Friends, Inc. working with adults to get them into the community.

At the time of our meeting he said, "I oversee all of the adult residential programs, we call them community living services, coordinating all of their life outside of vocational. I oversee the directors of all parts of community living. This includes homes, apartments and group homes that serve 116 individuals."

He told me that he never envisioned doing this kind of work. "It makes you appreciate other people, whether they are disabled or minorities. It has definitely impacted my view of who is in the community with me. What I realized is what I do for a living is putting these people out in my community and they're just part of my community." He does not think it takes a special person to do his job. "It's just being human and working with people who need assistance."

When asked what advice he had to offer to the parents, he said, "I would tell parents that just because their child is moving into a home and they're living as independent as possible, and there's a provider, it doesn't mean you're off the hook. We can't do everything. Families should never be out of the picture if they can; that natural support only makes our job easier and the family's' job easier when we work together. Don't be afraid to call us if you have a concern."

Mr. Verscheure feels that Little Friends "is truly a partnership between the staff and the individuals in the homes and the families that choose to be involved. Every home has its own personality, based on who's living there, who's working with them. And even though it's a group home, it's a house and they're like a family. We may own the house but it's their home."

Kathy Schildback
Social Worker with Little Friends, Inc.

After getting her degree in Social Work, Kathy Schildback began working "with disabled children at Easter Seals in Illinois. Then I went to the schools for five years and worked with special ed as a social worker. Then I came to Little Friends in 1989, where she is with the Community Living Services, the residential program for adults.

When asked why she chose special education, she said, "I get as much back as I give to the clients I see. So it isn't only selfish, I get some of my own needs met that way. It's an altruistic type of thing. The adults appreciate any type of help that you can give them."

I asked her about my son, Christopher. "He's doing terrific; he's made so much progress since I've known him. When I first met him he was kind of troubled. We were still trying to figure out what was going on inside of him. Because of his aphasia, he had such difficulty expressing himself, and I think that was a big part of his frustration and his mood back then. He's blossomed I think. When I first met him he would get frustrated and would try to hurt himself. (At that time he developed ulcers.) He was hitting his head. He would say he didn't like himself, and would talk negative toward himself. We don't see any of that anymore. He's much more patient with himself, and he tries to talk to people and people notice that and they'll give him time. I remember when he came back from one of his first big vacations, I think he went snorkeling, he was so thrilled and couldn't wait to sign up to go on vacation again.

"Getting them (the special needs adults) into the proper program in living and working takes so much of the pressure off them." She said that when all the things fall in place about who they are, "where they're supposed to be and what they're supposed to be doing they feel safe and secure.   The Naperville community has been very accepting of this program and our clients, and they support it financial as well."

What advice did Ms. Schildback give? "The system doesn't always react as fast as you would like it but it does work. Learning how to work the system or finding someone that will help you to find your way around is really important...Don't give up...Get together with other parents, there's strength in numbers."

When asked how she changed, she said, "I have made so many wonderful friends it's hard to describe...It's incredible watching people with these challenges keep succeeding and watching their joy. You think about what problems you might have and they're miniscule compared to what they're facing. It gives you a lot of respect."

Janette Antink
Community Support Specialist (house manager) at Little Friends, Inc. Cape House

Janett Antink spent 15 years working in human services with people with chemical dependencies before going to Little Friends, Inc. She also was a therapist and a volunteer at a center for handicapped infants.

At the time of our interview she managed Cape House, the group home for four adult men, one was my son Christopher. "Working around these clients, they're delightful. The simplest things are very appreciated. They enjoy the very simple things in life that they get excited about. They just enjoy somebody paying attention to them. We have so much fun. We go so many different places, and do so many things, all of which they want to do."

Is there a downside? "No, none at all. There's no downside because they do the littlest thing to improve themselves, then you're just as excited as they are. And it doesn't have to be big things to be appreciated.

"When things come up, we try to work them out. The idea for them is to be happy and safe... When they do the slightest thing, we make a big praise out of it. I think all of them are a lot smarter than people think they are. They can really kind of manipulate you in one way and then they're very appreciative in another way. It's a wonderful experience."

I asked Ms. Antink what advice she would like to offer to parents, she said, "Be very open with them (their children), everybody likes praise, it doesn't make any difference if you have a disability or not.

"I give guidance on some things with some of the guys. When they can do things themselves, they feel really good about anything they do, whether it be housekeeping, going for a walk...It's making goals that they can achieve that makes it fun for them and it makes it good for me because I know that they've accomplished something they didn't do before."

When I asked about the parents of the men she works with, she offered some excellent advice. "We still have parents who are trying to control their sons, but they have to let them go, let them get to their full potential. When you do, you'll you see they can do a lot more than what you thought they could. And they'll feel good about it too."

For parents whose adult children still live at home, she said: "Eventually they're going to have to let them go because they (the parents) are getting older … The last guy I got was 65 years old. His dad could no longer take care of him. Because his dad and his aunt had taken such good care of him, he didn't know how to do simple skills that everybody knows how to do like his laundry, or make a bed. Here he is 68 years old now and he can do these things. He feels good about what he can do; he might fuss about it because he's so used to being taken care of. These parents that hold on to them are really holding them back for doing more. I guess coming from where he was before it's called tough love."

Tom Pendziszewski
Vice President of Adult Day Services
Little Friends, Inc.

While working on his graduate degree, Tom Pendziszewski heard about Little Friends, Inc. and interviewed for a job as a job coach.

What drew him into working with the handicapped? "It was a totally new experience for me. I really wasn't sure what I was going to run into. I figured I'd get my couple of years in and then move on somewhere else. The kinds of things that kept me here are the clients themselves. I find that with all the people I work with here there is some kind of genuineness with them. What you see is what you get. They are very happy with who they are, they tell you the truth...No airs, no pretenses. It's a completely different kind of population, and it's really endearing. So I stayed around."

When I interviewed Mr. Pendziszewski he was in charge of all day services for adults. "I basically supervise those people in the sheltered workshop, the developmental training...vocational skills for those still in school...and the Color Burst program...transportation...supported employment. A good part of what we do back there is getting the people to the point where they can leave here and go into a more competitive environment, which would be regular work."

I visited the workshop and watched while my son, Chris, worked assembling multiple parts for an item. I was very impressed with the level of intensity and how fast he was. Mr. Pendziszerski commented that Chris was "staying on task and working hard."

What was his advice to parents? "The best thing for parents to keep in mind is to focus on what their son or daughter can do, and keep emphasizing those skills...Too often earlier in life we hear the litany of k nots. K not do this, k not do that, k not do the other. Our whole focus now is the cans, can do this. It's a whole mind set that's starting to change all over. People with disabilities who we thought k not do things really can do other things. If we accommodate them correctly, they can do a lot, accomplish a lot.

"Parents need to know that they know their son or daughter best, and they need to be assertive enough with the people who are working with their son or daughter to say let's try this, or I know that might not work, let's try this. Advocate for their kids along the way...Prepare them as much as possible in the younger years for adult services... 21 comes so quickly and public funds for school ends in a flash."

Mr. Pendziszewski said that parents need to prepare their child early for independent living. I added that parents of young children need to start being realistic about their future. Because in short order, they'll turn around three times and their child will be an adult. They must make plans for the time when they are no longer around. You can't leave it up to the gods to work it out.

When asked if working at Little Friends has made a difference in his life, he said, "It makes me less tolerant of people without disabilities as far as their pretenses or their interaction in public. It's made me more tolerant and understanding of those people who have different needs. I think I've even mellowed in the past 10 years, so they tell me.

"I'm hoping I spend the rest of my days working here or working in an agency similar to this. It's been so rewarding to me to see progress in some of the people we serve."

Case Manager for Supportive Employment at Spectrum Vocational Services

This Case Manager asked that her name not be used. "I have my teaching certificate in Special Education. At a break in college, I worked in a group home for kids with disabilities. After I graduated and got my teaching certificate I just kind of stayed along with the social services because I enjoyed helping these people.

"Our program is helping people find and maintain employment in the community. So we have job developers who help clients find jobs and job coaches to help maintain their employment. [Finding jobs is] relatively hard and the pay's not great. You really have to find somebody who's interest in working with this population instead of doing it for the money factor.

"Sometimes employers are reluctant to hire somebody with disabilities, and sometimes there are people who are looking for a person with a disability...Sometimes I think parents might think that we have a magic bag of employers and we can pull their names out of a hat, but we have to help the clients find a job like anybody else does. We get mixed reviews from employers in the community. Some are real interested in working with people with disabilities other ones aren't interested."

When asked what advice she had to parents about putting their older children out in the community, she said it should be done, "As early as possible. Get them acclimated to the community, learn problem-solving skills, and what to do when their transportation doesn't show up...They have to learn good social skills so that they're able to maintain a job in the community where they have to interact socially with customers. Everything that the parents can do to prepare them early on to be integrated in the community is a plus."

How does she feel that working with special needs adults has impacted her? "I think I'm maybe more open-minded with people and their differences and accepting people for who they are. I know what potential they have and I realize everybody's the same."

Erika Detrick
Floor Supervisor, Spectrum Vocational Services

Before going to work at Spectrum Vocational Services, Erika Detrick worked at a health department "working with mentally ill clients in their group homes. She returned to college and got a degree in mental health. Afterwards, she went to work at Little Friends.

"I like working with children...I heard about a therapeutic playgroup for children whose parents are mentally ill. I thought that would be interesting. So, I became a mentor mom. The mothers were mentally ill, most of them were single mothers, and they know how hard it is to raise a child especially 2 and 3 year olds. I was paired up with a mother and we went to McDonalds and to parks where we let the kids play. Then I started working with a therapeutic playgroup, which is where we watched the children and observed some of the things that they did. If we noticed a lot of hitting or a child was extremely shy, we would document it and talk to the parents while the mothers were in group therapy. From there I went into the group homes and started working with adults, and at this point I had no experience with working adults. And I loved it. From there I started getting paid for it and then decided to do it full time. But I had never worked with this population...developmental disabilities. When I came here (Little Friends) I found my place."

Spectrum "is a sheltered workshop where we do subcontract work. We bid for our work, we do have competitors, so we're very careful about whether or not we meet customer standards. We try to get whatever jobs we can, then we try to find appropriate jobs for our clients, like training and evaluating the client. We have three units and two programs. One is regular work and the other is developmental training. Regular work consists of the front unit and the middle unit. They get work the most often. They also get the most difficult work and they also make the most money."

Ms. Detrick talked about my son Christopher. "Chris is regular work. He's capable of doing the work. He's also able to go in the building as freely as he wants, he doesn't need any assistance. He's a pretty responsible person...Chris is a good worker, he really works hard...his work is almost always 100%...it's almost always up to customer standards. He is capable of making good money...If he wants to make more money, he has the opportunity. I think it meets Chris' needs. I don't know how he would do out in the community. I think he is happy here. One of his favorite things is to watch other people interact and that's when you'll see him laughing when someone does something goofy across the room. You don't notice him because he's quiet but he's watching.

"Chris can be a real clown. When I first started working with Chris I didn't know how to talk to him because he always seemed so angry. When he would hand in his work, I would say *Good job, Chris*. He would say, 'Mam' and mumble and walk away like he was angry with me. People told me that's the way Chris gets sometimes, and I would think I'm only saying *good job*. I tried to encourage him to do better and tell him I am proud of him. That went on for awhile, and then I decided that there's got to be something (I could do). Chris likes to read the *TV Guide*, so I started asking him when certain shows were going to be on... It was amazing, because it was the first time that I had ever seen Chris actually light up and not be angry. He would try to find the words to tell me, it would take him a couple of seconds, he would stutter and then he would tell me."

Epilogue

In 1978 I became president of an organization called "Promise" that was comprised of parents whose children ran the gambit from the ultra bright to the most severely handicapped. The goal was to find parents who needed help and assist them in finding support.

In order to assist parents of mentally and physically handicapped children, meeting with obstetricians and pediatricians was crucial to our program. Since many problems such as cerebral palsy, Down syndrome, spina bifida, and physical deformities are identified at birth, we wanted these physicians to contact us so that we could send a parent to the hospital or their homes to try and help the new parents move forward.

I wrangled an invitation to speak to doctors at an OB/GYN meeting. As I stood at the front of the room, I looked out into the audience, happy to see a large percentage of doctors that I knew. I felt I had a friendly audience. After the first several sentences, their eyes glazed over; they had shut me out. Realizing I'd lost them, I quickly said what I came to say then asked for questions from the floor. Receiving none, I left.

Two days later one of the doctors came to my house to drop his son off to play with my son, David. I asked him, *What happened at the meeting?* He answered very matter of factly, **"We weren't interested."**

How dare you not be interested! I challenged him. I was irate that an obstetrician would deliver a baby to parents that he knew had problems and then blithely walk away. I told him I thought it was horrible that the obstetricians had no interest in helping families in need find resources and comfort. All they wanted was their check. He shrugged his shoulders and got back into his car. He was finished with me.

When a doctor, with war-like precision, drops a bombshell on parents that there is something wrong with their baby, then walks away, he leaves behind a devastated family. His backside heading for the door is the last thing they need. Their world has collapsed and they desperately need help. They need to understand that the new parents are looking to him or her to provide that assistance. Unfortunately, parents are at a terrible disadvantage because they don't know the right questions to ask.

Equally wrong is when the doctor suspects a problem but fails to disclose it. This only keeps the parents from seeking the help they need, and magnifies the feeling of parental guilt when they struggle on for years with a child they know is not normal. Parents need to be told the facts, and doctors need to learn how to mix compassion with test results and not to take hope away. Like Mary Poppins said, "A spoonful of sugar helps the medicine go down." They need to be prepared to help parents with special needs children find appropriate services, specialists, psychologists and schools.

And doctors, in most cases where we were told to put our child in an institution or were told there was absolutely no future, we have proven you wrong. The steel in our reserve to do the best for our child, to challenge them, school them, to try and find a place in society for them, has brought out the best in our children, and in us. It is my hope that this book will act as a desk reference to every pediatrician, neurologist, speech school, psychologist and psychiatrist who deal with parents of special needs children.

Everyone deals with problems in their own way according to their personality, financial means, religion, family and friends, and perhaps with some magic ingredient they can't quite put their finger on. We parents of special needs children, for the most part, didn't spend time dwelling on the whys and what ifs because finding the right doctor, the right diagnosis and the right schools were paramount in helping our child. A few of us had mini nervous breakdowns along the way but they were short-lived because we realized we had a family to tend to. None of the parents I interviewed ended up hospitalized, even though we could have all used the rest.

The way I see it is that parents have two choices when faced with a child with any kind of mental or physical handicap. They can sit at home and ignore the disability while dreaming that their child will end up at Harvard or Yale. Or, they can be realistic, and see their child for who she or he is. Then they can face the challenges of giving their child every opportunity to be prepared to live independently, or semi-independently, to manage money, shop, take public transportation, and work at a job or in a workshop.

To this end, parents have created, revised and pushed or enhanced school programs, started Sunday school classes in their churches and synagogues, and put together group homes. After all, one day we parents will be gone, and it is our responsibility to prepare our children for the future.

When author Pearl S. Buck was asked how she bore the sorrow of having a handicapped daughter, she said, "...endurance of inescapable sorrow is something which has to be learned alone. And only to endure is not enough. Endurance can be a harsh and bitter root in one's life, bearing poisonous and gloomy fruit, destroying other lives. Endurance is only the beginning. There must be acceptance and knowledge that sorrow, fully accepted, brings its own gifts. For there is an alchemy in sorrow. It can be transmuted into wisdom, which, if it does not bring joy, can yet bring happiness. (1) She also said that sorrows "which cannot be assuaged are those which change life itself..." (2)

Our stories of raising our special needs children have ended. It is hoped that they will help the next generation of parents who are faced with children who are out of the norm.

Footnotes

Preface

1. Nesmith, Jeff, Surgeon General assails discrimination, Atlanta Journal Constitution, newspaper, Atlanta, December, 17, 2001, p. D20.
2. Pueschel, Sigfried M., M.D., Bernier, James C., M.W.W., Weidenman, Leslie E., Ph.D., *The Special Child,* Paul H. Brookes Publishing Co., Baltimore, 1988, p. 3.
3. Ibid, p. 3.
4. Buck, Pearl S., *The Child Who Never Grew Up,* The John Day Company, New York, 1950, p. 18.

Chapter One: Children with Speech Problems

1. Batshaw, Mark, M.D., Editor, *Children with Disabilities*, Fourth Edition, Paul H. Brookes Publishing Co. Baltimore, 1997, p. 276.
2. Ibid, p. 280.
3. Doman, Glen *What To Do About Your Brain-Injured Child,* Paragon Press, Honesdale, PA, 1994, p. 114.
4. Ibid, p. 114.
5. Roberts, Alice, ScD., Thomas, Charles C. *The Aphasic Child,* Springfield, IL, 1970, p. 5.
6. Hecht, Frederick, M.D., F.A.A.P., and Shiel Jr., William C., M.D., F.A.A.P., co- editors, *Webster's New World Medical Dictionary*, Wiley Publishing Inc., New York, 2003, p. 340.

Chapter Two: Children with Down Syndrome
1. Kunz, Jeffrey R. M., M.D., and Finkel, Asher J., M.D., editors, *The American Medical Association Family Medical Guide,* Random House, New York, 1987, p. 668.
2. McKenna, M. A. J., *Down syndrome longevity seen linked to race, Atlanta Journal Constitution* newspaper, June 8, 2001.

Chapter Three: Children with Epilepsy, Seizures, and Strokes
1. *American Medical Association Family Medical Guide,* p. 289.
2. 2. Ibid, p. 269.
3. *Webster's New World Medical Dictionary, Second Addition,* Wiley Publishing, Inc, New York, 2003, p. 103.

Chapter Four: Children with Various Forms of Palsy
1. *American Medical Association Family Medical Guide, p. 684.*
2. *Webster's New World Medical Dictionary, Second Addition,* Wiley Publishing, Inc, New York, 2003, p. 33.

Chapter Five: Children with Meningitis
1. *American Medical Association Family Medical Guide, p. 274.*

Chapter Six: Children with Marfan Syndrome
1. *American Medical Association Family Medical Guide,* p. 671.

Chapter Eight: Children with Fragile X Syndrome
1. Batshaw, Mark L., M.D., editor, *Children with Disabilities,* Fourth Edition, Paul H. Brookes Publishing Co., Baltimore, 1977, p. 385.
2. Ibid, p. 378

Chapter Ten: Parents with Two Deve

Emma and Jessica

1. Maureen Barlow Pugh, Senior Dictionary, 27th Edition, Lippe Baltimore, p. 1121.

Chapter Eleven: Sib

1. Webster's New World Medical Dict

Epilogue

1. Buck, Pearl S., *The Child Who Never* Company, New York, 1950, p. 5.

2. 2. Ibid, p. 30.

References

Books, Newspapers, and Articles

1. Baptista, Robert and Martha, *Ric*, The Moody Bible Institute of Chicago, Chicago, 1981.
2. Barnard, Susan K. Article for the Atlanta Association for Retarded Citizen's *News and Views*, June, 1982.
3. Batshaw, Mark L. M.D., Editor, *Children with Disabilities*, Fourth Edition, Paul H. Brookes Publishing Co., Baltimore, 1977.
4. Boxhill, Edith Hillman, *Music Therapy for the Developmentally Disabled*, John R. Marozsan Publishers, an Aspen Publication, Rockville, MD, 1985.
5. Buck, Pearl S., *The Child Who Never Grew Up*, The John Day Company, 1950.
6. Doman, Glenn, *What To Do About Your Brain-Injured Child*, Paragon Press, Honesdale, PA, 1994.
7. Kingsley, Emily Pearl, *Raising A Child with A Disability, Parenting Tips*, Fall 1992.
8. Klein, Stanley D., Ph.D, and Kim Schive, *You Will Dream New Dreams*, Kensington Publishing Corp, New York, 2001.
9. Lobato, Debra J., *Brothers, Sisters, and Special Needs*, Paul H. Brookes Publishing Co., Baltimore, 1990.
10. Meyer, Donald, editor, *Views from Our Shoes, Growing Up with a Brother or Sister with Special Needs*, Woodbine House, 1997.
11. McKenna, M. A. J., *Down syndrome longevity seen linked to race, Atlanta Journal Constitution* newspaper, June 8, 2001.

12. Neal, Patricia, *As I Am*, Simon and Schuster, New York, 1988.
13. Nesmith, Jeff, *Surgeon General assails discrimination*, *Atlanta Journal Constitution* newspaper, Atlanta, December 17, 2001, p. D20.
14. Pueschel, Sigfried M., M.D., Bernier, James C., M.W.W., Weidenman, Leslie E., Ph.D., *The Special Child*, Paul H. Brookes Publishing Co., Baltimore, 1988.
15. Roberts, Alice Calvert, ScD., Thomas, Charles C., *The Aphasic Child*, Springfield, IL, 1970.

Organization Material

1. Atlanta Alliance on Developmental Disabilities, *Introduction to mental Retardation,* Atlanta, May 2001.
2. Governor's Council on Developmental Disabilities, *Georgia County Population Estimates for People with Developmental Disabilities and Prevalence Rates*, August 2001.
3. Little Friends, Inc., various newsletters, Naperville, IL.

Dictionaries

1. Stedman's Medical Dictionary, 27th Edition, Pugh, Maureen Barlow, senior editor, Lippencott Williams & Wilkins, Baltimore, 1999.
2. Webster's New World Medical Dictionary, Second Edition, co-edited by Hecht, Frederick, M.D., F.A.A.P., and Shiel Jr, William C. M.D., F.A.A.P., Wiley Publishing Inc., New York, 2003.

Glossary

The definitions to the terms below come from *Webster's New World Medical Dictionary*, Second Edition, Co-Edited by Frederick Hecht, M.D., F.A.A.P. and William C. Shiel Jr., M.D., F.A.C.P., Wiley Publishing, Inc., New York, 2003.

Alzheimer's disease: "A progressive degenerative disease of the brain that leads to dementia." (p. 15)

Anemia: "The condition of having a lower-than-normal number of red blood cells or quality of hemoglobin which diminishes the capacity of the blood to carry oxygen. Patients with anemia may feel tired, fatigue easily, appear pale, develop palpitations, and become short of breath. Children with chronic anemia are prone to infections and learning problems." (18)

Anoxia: "A deficiency of oxygen." (p. 23)

Antidepressant: "A medication that prevents or reduces the symptoms of clinical depression." (p. 24)

Aortic valve: "One of the four valves in the heart. The aortic valve is positioned at the beginning of the aorta. It permits blood from the left ventricle to flow to the aorta, and it prevents blood in the aorta from returning to the heart." (26)

Apgar score: "An objective score of the condition of a baby after birth. This score is determined by scoring the heart rate, respiratory effort, muscle tone, skin color and response to a catheter in the nostril. Each of these objective signs receives 0, 1, or 2 points. An Apgar score of 10 means an infant is in the best possible condition. The Apgar score is done routinely 60 seconds after the birth of the infant." (26)

Aphasia: "Literally, no speech. Aphasia may also be used to describe defects in spoken expression or comprehension of speech." (26)

Ataxia: "Poor coordination and unsteadiness due to the brain's failure to regulate the body's posture and regulate the strength and direction of limb movements." (33)

Attention deficit hyperactivity disorder (ADHD): "A disorder in which a person is unable to control behavior due to difficulty in processing neural stimuli, accompanied by an extremely high level of motor activity." (35)

Carpal tunnel syndrome: "A type of compression neuropathy caused by compression and irritation of the median nerve in the wrist. The nerve is compressed and irritated within the carpal tunnel, due to pressure from the transverse carpal ligament." (70)

Cerebral palsy: "An abnormality of motor function (the ability) to move and control movements) that is acquired at an early age, usually less than 1 year, and is due to a brain lesion that is nonprogressive. CP is frequently the result of abnormalities that occur while a fetus is developing inside the womb." (75)

Chemotherapy: "Treatment with drugs to kill cancer cells." (77)

Chromosome: "A carrier of genetic information that is visible under an ordinary light microscope...Generally the nucleus of a human cell contains two sets of chromosome-one set given by each parent. Each set has 23 single chromosome." (83)

Clubfoot: "A common malformation of the foot that is evident at birth. The foot is turned in sharply so that the person seems to be walking on his or her ankle." (88)

Coma: "A state of deep, unarousable unconsciousness. A coma may occur as a result of head trauma, disease, poisoning, or numerous other causes." (93)

Congenital defect: "A birth defect." (94)

Cyanosis: "A bluish color of the skin and the mucous membranes due to insufficient oxygen in the blood." (103)

Cyanosis: "A bluish color of the skin and the mucous membranes due to insufficient oxygen in the blood…Cyanosis can be present at birth, as in a 'blue baby', an infant with a malformation of the heart that permits into the arterial system blood that is not fully oxygenated." (103)

Cystic fibrosis: "A common grave genetic disease that affects the exocrine glands and is characterized by the production of abnormal secretions, leading to musus buildup that impairs the pancreas and, secondarily, the intestines. Mucus buildup in lungs can impair respiration." (104)

Developmental Disability: "Basically, a developmental disability is any physical or mental condition that can impair or limit a child's skills or causes a child to develop language, thinking, personal, social, and movement skills more slowly than other children." (Siegfried M. Pueschel, M.D, James, C. Bernier, M.S.W., and Leslie E. Weidenman, Ph.D., *The Special Child,* Paul H. Brookes Publishing Co., Baltimore, 1988, p. 3)

DNA: "Deoxyribonucleic acid, one of the two molecules (along with RNA) that encode genetic information." (122)

Down syndrome: "A common birth defect that is usually due to an extra chromosome 21. Down syndrome causes mental retardation, a characteristic facial appearance, and multiple malformations. It occurs most frequently in children born to mothers over age 35. It is associated with a major risk for heart problems, a lesser risk of duodenal atresia (partially undeveloped intestines0, and a minor but significant risk of acute leukemia…Unfortunately, most adults with Down syndrome eventually develop Alzheimer's disease as they grow older. Down syndrome was also once called mongolism." (124)

Encephalitis: "Inflammation of the brain, which may be caused by a bacterium, a virus...or an allergic reaction." (139)

Epilepsy: "A seizure disorder. When nerve cells in the brain fire electrical impulses at a rate up to four times higher than normal, a sort of electrical storm, called a seizure, occurs in the brain. Epilepsy is characterized by a pattern of repeated seizures." (144)

Epilepsy, grand mal: "Epilepsy that includes tonic-clonic (grand mal) seizures, which are the most obvious type of seizure. In the tonic phase, the body becomes rigid, and in the clonic phase, there is uncontrolled jerking. Tonic-clonic seizure may or may not be preceded by an aura, and these seizures are often followed by headache, confusion and sleep. They may last for mere seconds or continue for several minutes." (144)

Epilepsy, petit mal: "A form of epilepsy in which only absence (petit mal) seizures occur, with very brief, unannounced lapses in consciousness." (145)

Fever/pyrexia: "Technically any body temperature above the normal oral measurement of 98.6 degrees F. or the normal rectal temperature of 99 degrees F. (158)

Fragile X chromosome: "An X chromosome that has a fragile site and is associated with a common form of mental retardation. Fragile X chromosome is due to a trinucleotide repeat (a recurring motif of three bases) in the DNA at that spot." (167)

Fragile X syndrome: "The most common heritable form of mental retardation, which occurs in about 1 in 2,000 males and a smaller percentage of females. Characteristics of fragile X syndrome in boys include prominent or long ears, a long face, delayed speech, large testes, hyperactivity, tactile defensiveness, gross motor delays, and autistic-like behaviors. Much less is known about girls with fragile X syndrome than about boys with it. Only about half of all females who carry the genetic mutation for fragile X syndrome have symptoms themselves." (167)

Gene: "In classical genetics, a unit of inheritance. In molecular genetics, a sequence of chromosomal DNA that is required to make a functional product." (172)

Genetic: "Having to do with genes and genetic information." (172)

Hemorrhage: "Abnormal bleeding." (190)

Homeopathy: "Founded in the 19th century, a practice that is based on the concept that disease can be treated with minute doses of drugs thought capable of producing in healthy people the same symptoms as those of the disease being treated." (197)

Hurler syndrome: "An inherited error of metabolism characterized by deficiency of the enzyme alpha-L-iduronidase, which normally breaks down molecules called muscopolysaccharides. Without the activity of this enzyme, mucopolysccharides accumulate abnormally in the tissues of the body... Hurler syndrome patients [exhibit features such as] progressive mental degeneration, gross facial features, enlarged and deformed skull, small stature..." (200)

Hyperactivity: "A higher-than-normal level of activity." (202)

Hypertonia: "Increased tightness of muscle tone. Untreated hypertonia can lead to loss of function and deformity." (204)

Hypotonia: "Decreased muscle tone and strength that results in floppiness. Hypotonia is a common finding with cerebral palsy and other neuromuscular disorders." (206)

ILP: Individual lesson plan.

ITP Idiopathic thrombocytopenic purpura: "A condition characterized by the sudden, abnormal lowering of the platelet count." (220)

Kazmier syndrome: (see ch.7)

Leukemia: "Cancer of the blood cells." (235)

Lumbar puncture: "A procedure in which cerebrospinal fluid is removed from the spinal canal for diagnostic testing or treatment." (241)

Marfan syndrome: "An inherited disorder of connective tissue that is characterized by abnormalities of the eyes, skeleton, and cardiovascular system. Nearsightedness is the most common eye feature in Marfan syndrome…The skeleton shows bone overgrowth and lax joints. The arms and legs are unusually long, as are the fingers and toes." (250)

Meningitis: "Inflammation of the meninges, the three membranes that envelop the brain and the spinal cord. (257)

Mental retardation: "The condition of having an IQ measured as below 70 to 75 and significant delays or lacks in at least two areas of adaptive skills. Mental retardation is present from childhood. Between 2 and 3 percent of the general population meet the criteria for mental retardation." (261)

Microcephaly: "An abnormally small head due to failure of brain growth…it is almost always associated with developmental delays and mental retardation." (262)

Mitochondria: "Structures located in the cell's cytoplasm outside the nucleus. Mitochondria are responsible for energy production. Each consists of two sets of membranes…The mitochondria are the principal energy source of the cell. They not only convert nutrients into energy but also perform many other specialized tasks." (265)

Mitral valve: "A valve in the heart that is situated between the left atrium and the left ventricle. The mitral valve permits the blood to flow from the left atrium into the left ventricle, but not in the reverse direction." (266)

Neurologist: "A physician who specializes in the diagnosis and treatment of disorders of the nervous system." (283)

Occupational therapy: "Therapy designed to help patients gain or relearn skills needed for activities of daily living, including self-care, handwriting and other school-related skills, and work-related skills." (291)

Psychiatrist: "A physician who specializes in the prevention, diagnosis, and treatment of mental illness." (338)

Psychomotrist: A person who tests people for aptitude, intelligence and emotional disturbance.

Psychologist: "A professional who specializes in the diagnosis and treatment of diseases of the brain, emotional disturbance, and behavior problems." They cannot prescribe medication. (338)

Pyrexia: (See fever)

Pyloric stenosis: "Narrowing (stenosis) of the outlet of the stomach so that food cannot pass easily from it into the duodenum [beginning of the small intestines]. Pyloric stenosis results in feeding problems and projectile vomiting." (340)

Salmonella: "A group of bacteria that cause typhoid fever and other illnesses, including food poisoning, gastroenteritis, and enteric fever from contaminated food products." (360)

Schizophrenia: "One of several brain diseases whose symptoms may include loss of personality, agitation, catatonia, confusion, psychosis, unusual behavior, and social withdrawal." (363)

Scoliosis: "Lateral (sideways) curving of the spine." (364)

Seizure disorder: "One of a great many medical conditions that are characterized by episodes of uncontrolled electrical activity in the brain (seizures)...In some cases, uncontrolled seizures can cause brain damage, lowered intelligence, and permanent mental and physical impairment." (366)

Spinal tap: (See lumbar puncture)

Stroke: "The sudden death of brain cells due to lack of oxygen, caused by blockage of blood flow or rupture of an artery to the brain. Sudden loss of speech, weakness, or paralysis of one side of the body can be symptoms." (384)

Subarachnoid hemorrhage: "A bleeding into the subarachnoid, the space between the arachnoid and the pia mater, the innermost membranes surrounding the central nervous system. Subarachnoid hemorrhage typically occurs when an artery breaks open in the brain, such as from a ruptured aneurysm [a bulge in a vein or artery]." (385)

Resources for the Handicapped

Every city, town and community is different, but most have services for developmentally disabled children and adults. Finding them can often be frustrating. I am listing a few suggestions to help parents get started on their quest to finding the right programs.

1. Local Alliance on Developmental Disabilities
2. Association for Retarded Citizens
3. Your state Learning Resources System
4. Easter Seal
5. Check and see if there is a brain injury program in your area
6. Local school special education programs
7. Check telephone Yellow Pages for private special education schools
8. Check churches and synagogues for special education classes
9. Respite services
10. Special Olympics
11. Horseback riding therapy programs
12. Governor's Council on Developmental Disabilities
13. United Way
14. The Roosevelt Institute in Warm Springs, Georgia
15. Sheltered workshops
16. Check into Social Security Income (SSI); Social Security Administration 1-800-772-1213, http:/www.ssa.gov. Take money out of your child's name so he or she will be eligible for SSI/Medicaid when he or she is 18 years old.
17. Check with your lawyer about a trust for your child.

A Letter to Christopher

After receiving a letter from the Atlanta Association for Retarded Citizens in 1983 advising me that I had been awarded the Mary Lee Brookshire Award, I wrote a letter to my son, Christopher:

"Dear Christopher,

Because of you, I have been selected as volunteer of the Year by the Atlanta Association for Retarded Citizens. I know this may be hard for you to understand. But because of my love for you, I have spent the last sixteen years putting together programs where you could have the best special education classes daily and in Sunday school, and where there would be an adult living situation when you needed it. This was all for you my love.

But all of this changed my life and made me grow. I got to know many handicapped children and their parents. I worked with professionals in their fields who were also trying to help and educate the handicapped. And I met some pretty terrific people who gave of themselves to make a better life for those less fortunate then themselves. Your mom, Joann, leads the list.

Everyone we meet touches our lives, many make more of an imprint than others. You, Chris, have made the biggest imprint on my life. You made me realize that sweetness and beauty come from such simple things as the first time you said, 'Ma Ma.'

I know that life at times is very hard and frustrating for you. But know that because of you Arbor Academy was established and continues to help educate many children in the Atlanta Community, the *Havanah* Sunday school program is successfully providing religious education, and The Atlanta Group Home will provide a home for many handicapped adults.

So thank you for my award."

CPSIA information can be obtained
at www.ICGtesting.com
Printed in the USA
LVOW12s2236130417
530804LV00001B/2/P